AF564511

ENV BOOKS SERIES

METALS DISTRIBUTION IN ENVIRONMENT

Editors

Dr. Deep Mala
Inorganic and Physical Chemistry
Indian Institute of Science, Bengaluru
(India)
&
Dr. Pawan Kumar 'Bharti'
Society for Environment, Health
Awareness of Nutrition & Toxicology (SEHAT)
B-225/5D, Top Floor, Subhash Gali, Road No. 7, Block B
Ashok Nagar, Shahdara
Delhi-110093
(India)

DISCOVERY PUBLISHING HOUSE PVT. LTD.
INDIA

Published by:
Namit Wasan
DISCOVERY PUBLISHING HOUSE PVT. LTD.
4383/4B, Ansari Road, Darya Ganj
New Delhi-110 002 (India)
Phone : +91-11-23279245; 23253475; 43596065
E-mail : discoverybooksindia@gmail.com
discoverypublishinghouse@gmail.com
namitwasan9@gmail.com
web : www.discoverypublishinggroup.com

***First Edition:* 2019**

ISBN: 978-93-86841-91-9

Metals Distribution in Environment

Printed at:
Infinity Imaging Systems
Delhi

Preface

Metals are natural components of the Earth's crust. They cannot be degraded or destroyed. To a small extent they enter our bodies via food, drinking water and air. As trace elements, some heavy metals (e.g. copper, selenium, zinc) are essential to maintain the metabolism of the human body. However, at higher concentrations they can lead to poisoning. Heavy metal poisoning could result, for instance, from drinking-water contamination (e.g. lead pipes), high ambient air concentrations near emission sources, or intake via the food chain.

Heavy metals are dangerous because they tend to bioaccumulate. Bioaccumulation means an increase in the concentration of a chemical in a biological organism over time, compared to the chemical's concentration in the environment. Compounds accumulate in living things any time they are taken up and stored faster than they are broken down (metabolized) or excreted.

Heavy metals can enter a water supply by industrial and consumer waste, or even from acidic rain breaking down soils and releasing heavy metals into streams, lakes, rivers, and groundwater.

The present book updates the subject content of heavy metal distribution in various environmental components, metal detection in milk, metal remediation, biological role of metals, lead and arsenic poisoning and metal removal efficiency of plants.

Thanks are due to publisher and contributors from various institutions and universities.

The book will be helpful for the researchers, academia working in the field of heavy metal distribution in various environmental components, metal detection in milk, metal remediation, biological role of metals, lead and arsenic poisoning and metal removal efficiency of plants.

–Editors

(envbooks@gmail.com)

Contents

Pages: 1-6

Metals Distribution in Environment

Edited by: **Dr. Deep Mala & Dr. Pawan Kumar 'Bharti'**

ISBN: 978-93-86841-91-9

Edition: **2019**

Published by: **Discovery Publishing House Pvt. Ltd., New Delhi (India)**

Introduction

Environmental Pollution an undesirable and unwanted change in physical, chemical and biological characteristics of air, water and soil which is harmful for living organisms both animal and plants Pollution can take the form of chemical substances or energy, such as noise, heat or light. Pollutants, the elements of pollution, can be either foreign substances/energies or naturally occurring contaminants.

Faced with more and more stringent environmental regulations, nowadays metals are the priority pollutants of surface and ground waters. Water contamination with these compounds is becoming one of the most serious environmental problems because of the toxic nature of the heavy metal ions, even at low trace levels. With the rapid development of industries such as metal plating facilities, mining operations, tanneries, fertilisers, and paper industries, heavy metals wastewaters are directly or indirectly discharged into the environment increasingly. Unlike organic contaminants, heavy metals are not biodegradable and tend to accumulate in living organisms. Many heavy metal ions, such as mercury, cadmium, lead, nickel, and chromium, are known to be very toxic or carcinogenic. Due to the noxious effects of heavy metals, there are growing public health concerns about environmental pollution with heavy metals. Thus, it is imperative to remove or reduce heavy metal contamination in water in order to prevent or reduce contaminating the environment and the possibility of uptake in the food web.

Toxic metals are metals that are harmful to people's health. In very small amounts, these metals may be necessary to support life. However, in larger amounts, they are toxic. They may build up in biological systems and become health hazards. Below is a list of toxic metals, found in living and occupational environments.

METAL

Metals comprise 25% of the Earth's crust and are present in many aspects of modern life. The strength and resilience of some metals has led to their frequent use in, for example, high-rise building and bridge construction, as well as most vehicles, many home appliances, tools, pipes, and railroad tracks. Precious metals were historically used as coinage, but in the modern era, coinage metals have extended to at least 23 of the chemical elements.

The history of metals is thought to begin with the use of copper about 11,000 years ago. Gold, silver, iron (as meteoric iron), lead, and brass were likewise in use before the first known appearance of bronze in the 5th millennium BCE. Subsequent developments include the production of early forms of steel; the discovery of sodium—the first light metal—in 1809; the rise of modern alloy steels; and, since the end of World War II, the development of more sophisticated alloys.

HEAVY METALS

Heavy metals are natural components of the Earth's crust. They cannot be degraded or destroyed. To a small extent they enter our bodies via food, drinking water and air. As trace elements, some heavy metals (e.g. copper, selenium, zinc) are essential to maintain the metabolism of the human body. However, at higher concentrations they can lead to poisoning. Heavy metal poisoning could result, for instance, from drinking-water contamination (e.g. lead pipes), high ambient air concentrations near emission sources, or intake via the food chain.

Heavy metals are dangerous because they tend to bioaccumulate. Bioaccumulation means an increase in the concentration of a chemical in a biological organism over time, compared to the chemical's concentration in the environment. Compounds accumulate in living things any time they are taken up and stored faster than they are broken down (metabolized) or excreted.

Heavy metals can enter a water supply by industrial and consumer waste, or even from acidic rain breaking down soils and releasing heavy metals into streams, lakes, rivers, and groundwater.

TOXIC METALS

A toxic heavy metal is any relatively dense metal or metalloid that is noted for its potential toxicity, especially in environmental contexts. The term has particular application to cadmium, mercury, lead and arsenic, all of which appear in the World Health Organisation's list of 10 chemicals of major public concern. Other examples include manganese, chromium, cobalt, nickel, copper, zinc, selenium, silver, antimony and thallium.

Heavy metals are found naturally in the earth. They become concentrated as a result of human caused activities and can enter plant, animal, and human tissues via inhalation, diet, and manual handling. Then, they can bind to and interfere with the functioning of vital cellular components. The toxic effects of arsenic, mercury, and lead were known to the ancients, but methodical studies of the toxicity of some heavy metals appear to date from only 1868. In humans, heavy metal poisoning is generally treated by the administration of chelating agents. Some elements otherwise regarded as toxic heavy metals are essential, in small quantities, for human health.

ENVIRONMENTAL AND HEALTH RISKS

Effects of Antimony on the Environment

Antimony is a metal used in the compound antimony trioxide, a flame retardant. It can also be found in batteries, pigments, and ceramics and glass. Exposure to high levels of antimony for short periods of time causes nausea, vomiting, and diarrhea. There is little information on the effects of long-term antimony exposure, but it is a suspected human carcinogen. Most antimony compounds do not bioaccumulate in aquatic life.

Effects of Cadmium on the Environment

Cadmium derives its toxicological properties from its chemical similarity to zinc an essential micronutrient for plants, animals and humans. Cadmium is biopersistent and, once absorbed by an organism, remains resident for many years (over decades for humans) although it is eventually excreted.

In humans, long-term exposure is associated with renal disfunction. High exposure can lead to obstructive lung disease and has been linked to lung cancer, although data concerning the latter are difficult to interpret due to compounding factors. Cadmium may also produce bone defects (osteomalacia, osteoporosis) in humans and animals. In addition, the metal can be linked to increased blood pressure and effects on the myocardium in animals, although most human data do not support these findings.

The average daily intake for humans is estimated as 0.15μg from air and 1μg from water. Smoking a packet of 20 cigarettes can lead to the inhalation of around 2-4μg of cadmium, but levels may vary widely.

Effects of Chromium on the Environment

Chromium is used in metal alloys and pigments for paints, cement, paper, rubber, and other materials. Low-level exposure can irritate the skin and cause ulceration. Long-term exposure can cause kidney and liver damage, and damage too circulatory and nerve tissue. Chromium often accumulates in aquatic life, adding to the danger of eating fish that may have been exposed to high levels of chromium.

Effects of Copper on the Environment

Copper is an essential substance to human life, but in high doses it can cause anemia, liver and kidney damage, and stomach and intestinal irritation. People with Wilson's disease are at greater risk for health effects from overexposure to copper. Copper normally occurs in drinking water from copper pipes, as well as from additives designed to control algal growth.

Effects of Lead on the environment

In humans exposure to lead can result in a wide range of biological effects depending on the level and duration of exposure. Various effects occur over a broad range of doses, with the developing foetus and infant being more sensitive than the adult. High levels of exposure may result in toxic biochemical effects in humans which in turn cause problems in the synthesis of haemoglobin, effects on the kidneys, gastrointestinal tract, joints and reproductive system, and acute or chronic damage to the nervous system.

Lead poisoning, which is so severe as to cause evident illness, is now very rare indeed. At intermediate concentrations, however, there is persuasive evidence that lead can have small, subtle, subclinical effects, particularly on neuropsychological developments in children. Some studies suggest that there may be a loss of up to 2 IQ points for a rise in blood leadlevels from 10 to 20μg/dl in young children.

Average daily lead intake for adults in the UK is estimated at 1.6μg from air, 20μg from drinking water and 28μg from food. Although most people receive the bulk of their lead intake from food, in specific populations other sources may be more important, such as water in areas with lead piping and plumbosolvent water, air near point of source emissions, soil, dust, paint flakes in old houses or contaminated land. Lead in the air contributes to lead levels in food through deposition of dust and rain containing the metal, on crops and the soil. For the majority of people in the UK, however, dietary lead exposure is well below the provisional tolerable weekly intake recommended by the UN Food and Agriculture Organisation and the World Health Organisation.

Effects of Mercury on the Environment

Mercury is a toxic substance which has no known function in human biochemistry or physiology and does not occur naturally in living organisms. Inorganic mercury poisoning is associated with tremors, gingivitis and/or minor psychological changes, together with spontaneous abortion and congenital malformation.

Monomethylmercury causes damage to the brain and the central nervous system, while foetal and postnatal exposure have given rise to abortion, congenital malformation and development changes in young children.

Effects of Nickel on the Environment

Small amounts of Nickel are needed by the human body to produce red blood cells, however, in excessive amounts, can become mildly toxic. Short-term overexposure to nickel is not known to cause any health problems, but long-term exposure can cause decreased body weight, heart and liver damage, and skin irritation. The EPA does not currently regulate nickel levels in drinking water. Nickel can accumulate in aquatic life, but its presence is not magnified along food chains.

Effects of Selenium on the Environment

Selenium is needed by humans and other animals in small amounts, but in larger amounts can cause damage to the nervous system, fatigue, and irritability. Selenium accumulates in living tissue, causing high selenium content in fish and other organisms, and causing greater health problems in human over a lifetime of overexposure. These health problems include hair and fingernail loss, damage to kidney and liver tissue, damage to circulatory tissue, and more severe damage to the nervous system.

THE MOST IMPORTANTS DISASTERS WITH HEAVY METALS:

Minamata (1932)

Sewage containing mercury is released by Chisso's chemicals works into Minimata Bay in Japan. The mercury accumulates in sea creatures, leading eventually to mercury poisoning in the population.

Minamata Syndrome (1952)

In 1952, the first incidents of mercury poisoning appear in the population of Minimata Bay in Japan, caused by consumption of fish polluted with mercury, bringing over 500 fatalities. Since then, Japan has had the strictest environmental laws in the industrialised world.

Sandoz (1986-11-01)

Water used to extinguish a major fire carries c. 30 t fungicide containing mercury into the Upper Rhine. Fish are killed over a stretch of 100 km. The shock drives many FEA projects forwards. See also "Pollution of the Rhine at Basel/Sandoz".

Spanish Nature Reserve Contaminated after Environmental Disaster (1998-04)

Toxic chemicals in water from a burst dam belonging to a mine contaminate the Coto de Donana nature reserve in southern Spain. C. 5 million m_ of mud containing sulphur, lead, copper, zinc and cadmium flow down the Rio Guadimar. Experts estimate that Europe's largest bird sanctuary, as well as Spain's agriculture and fisheries, will suffer permanent damage from the pollution.

REFERENCES

https://www.hindawi.com/journals/bca/2017/4309198/

https://www.lenntech.com/processes/heavy/heavy-metals/heavy-metals.htm

Pawan Kumar Bharti (2012): Heavy Metals in Environment, Publisher: Lambert Academic Publishing GmbH & Co. KG, Saarbrucken, Germany ISBN 978-3-659-15133-0

https://www.wikilectures.eu/w/Toxic_Metals_in_Environment

VLADIMIR, Bencko. Hygiene and Epidemiology : Selected Chapters. First edition. 2011. ISBN 978-80-246-0793-1.

KUMAR, Vinay. Pathological basis of Disease. Eigth Edition. 2010. ISBN 978-80-246-0793-1.

LANDRIGAN, Philip J. Occupational and Community Exposures to Toxic Metals: Lead, Cadmium, Mercury and Arsenic. Western journal of Medicine [online]. 1982, y. 1982, vol. 137, p. 531-539

https://en.wikipedia.org/wiki/Toxic_heavy_metal

https://en.wikipedia.org/wiki/Metal

Pages: 7-45

Metals Distribution in Environment
Edited by: **Dr. Deep Mala & Dr. Pawan Kumar 'Bharti'**
ISBN: 978-93-86841-91-9
Edition: **2019**
Published by: **Discovery Publishing House Pvt. Ltd., New Delhi (India)**

Detection of Toxic Heavy Metals in Milk Powder by ICP-MS

L.N. Ranathunga[1]; B.C. Jayawardana[2]
Esakkimuthu M[3] and Liyanage R[4]

ABSTRACT

Milk powder as a nutritious dairy product occupies a significant portion in a healthy diet. Heavy metal contaminated milk is a huge worldwide concern as it affects on the safety of consumers. Intake of contaminated milk powder can cause direct and indirect adverse health hazards to humans due to long-term exposure to toxic heavy metals. Thus, the safety, quality and the consumers' acceptability of milk powder decreases when it is contaminated with toxic heavy metals. The aim of this study was to determine the concentrations of potentially toxic heavy metals including arsenic (As), cadmium (Cd), chromium (Cr), mercury (Hg) and lead (Pb) in milk powder (Full Cream Milk Powder and Non-fat Milk Powder), available in major supermarket chains in *Kurunegala* district. Total 54 samples (18 different brands as triplicates) were evaluated. *Inductively coupled plasma mass spectrometer (ICP-MS)* was used for the quantitative determination of heavy metals performed after the microwave digestion of the samples with HNO_3 (70% v/v) acid. All the brands had lower values for As, Cr and Hg while four brands had significantly higher values ($P<0.0001$) for Pb (0.14575 ± 0.01 mg/kg, 0.15538 ± 0.03 mg/kg, 0.12063 ± 0.03 mg/kg, and 0.09913 ± 0.03 mg/kg) and one brand had significantly higher value for Cd (0.3163 ± 0.43 mg/kg) than the maximum standards (0.025 mg/kg for Pb and 0.007 mg/kg for Cd) established by the World Health Organization in terms of heavy metal contents.

Keywords: Milk Powder; Heavy metals; *Kurunegala*; *ICP-MS*.

[1] **Faculty of Agriculture, Aquinas College of Higher Studies, Colombo, Sri Lanka**
[2] **Faculty of Agriculture, University of Peradeniya, Sri Lanka**
[3] **Kerala Agricultural University, RARS, Pilicode, India**
[4] **National Institute of Fundamental Studies, Hanthana, Kandy, Sri Lanka**

INTRODUCTION

The natural resources are being destroyed by humans for acquiring their necessities with the beginning of the civilization. However, the exploitation has been increasing at a higher rate and in non-judicious manner during past few decades especially with the advent of industrial revolution. Industrialization has brought many unwanted substances and social problems; one of these problems is the pollution of the environment (Rai *et al.*, 2011). Environment pollution is a global issue which negatively affects on human health. In recent decades, human activities have made troubles on the Earth living systems severely. The human population has doubled in the past 40 years and it will be continued for next 40 years also. The expansion of infrastructure and agriculture necessitated by this population growth has increased the pace of land transformation and pollution of the environment (Hooke, 2012). The environmental pollution occurs in the perspective of air pollution, water and land/soil pollution allowing humans to suffer from diseases and with other associated problems. The environmental pollution is not only seriously affecting on the human but also the whole ecosystems including animals and plants (Khan, 2013).

The presence of inorganic pollutants such as metal ions in the ecosystem causes a major environmental problem worldwide. Toxic metals and their corresponding compounds coming to the earth's surface contaminate earth's water but can also contaminate underground water, land resources and air as well. There are numerous metals and metallic compounds which are significantly toxic to human beings and ecological environments. Out of those, heavy metals constitute an important part of environmental pollutants and as a source of poisoning for humans and animals. They are present in various forms in the soil, natural water, air and may become contaminants in food and drinking water (Ojedokun & Bello, 2016). Heavy metal contamination refers to the excessive deposition of toxic heavy metals in the ecosystems caused by basically human activities. Heavy metals in the ecosystems induce biological toxicities for living organisms on the earth directly and indirectly through food chains and food webs (Su *et al.*, 2014). Heavy metals are the natural elements with a higher atomic weight and a density than that of water. Their multiple industrial, domestic, agricultural, medical and technological applications have led to their wide distribution in the environment; rising concerns over their potential effects on human health and the environment (Rusyniak *et al*, 2010). Among various elementary categories of heavy metals, Pb, Cr, As, Zn, Cd, Cu, Hg, and Ni are classified as priority heavy metals since they are commonly abundant and contaminate the ecosystems constantly (Wuana & Okieimen, 2011).

Livestock production plays a vital role in the life of farmers in developing countries (Sugiyama *et al*, 2003). Milk is a whitish liquid food generally produced by the mammary secretory cells of female cow in the process called lactation (Guetouache *et al.*, 2014). The dairy industry which is constituted with raw milk and milk based products is an important integral part of the livestock sector since it provides food, nutritional requirements, income, employment and many other contributions to rural economy as well as to the development of the country (Qian *et al*, 2011). Bovine milk and dairy products have long traditions in human nutrition as bovine milk contains bulk of nutrients such as lipids, proteins, carbohydrates, amino acids, vitamins and minerals needed for growth and development. It also contains immunoglobulins, hormones, growth factors, cytokines, nucleotides, peptides, polyamines, enzymes and other bioactive peptides as well (Haug *et al.*, 2007).

Contamination of food commodities from heavy metal residues is a serious problem encountered especially in third world countries and it is a matter of great concern for food safety and human health regulatory bodies. Although the dairy industry provides an integral part of the human food requirement, food symbolizes a drastic risk since their long time exposure can lead to toxicological effects for humans. Farm animals are important indicators of the environmental pollution from heavy metals. Exposure of farm animals to heavy metals Cause one of the major public health concerns worldwide especially with the milking animals. Many dairy products were detectedwith heavy metal residues to an extent that surpassed the maximum residue limits established by international regulatory agencies (Javed *et al.*, 2013).

Intake of contaminated milk containing even low levels of heavy metals such as Cd and Pb can cause various clinical abnormalities or may pass without clinical signs. Grazing land can be contaminated with heavy metals from their parent materials, atmospheric deposits, continuous application of large amounts of fertilizer, disposal of industrial waste sludge and vehicle emissions. In addition to that, packaging and technological processes used to bring foods to the consumer can significantly increase the total concentration of heavy metals (de Castro *et al.*, 2010). Heavy metals can contaminate milk through exposure of lactating cow to pollution or consumption of feeding stuffs and water with toxicants. Moreover, contamination can also be attributed to the manner of manufacturing dairy products where toxicants have the possibility to be included during the production process. Animals reared on contaminated fodder become continuous source of heavy metal residues in edible tissues and milk (History, 2010).

Although milk and milk products provide good quality nutrients necessary for a strong physical and mental health, the presence of toxic elements such as heavy metals in milk and milk products may create health problems especially for infants, school age children, and old people who consume large quantity of those products (Siddiki *et al.*, 2012). This is the problem in cow's milk that is being consumed by humans in liquid or powder form. Powdered milk is an essential and popular dairy product for nutritional food requirements. It contains both the basic and additional nutritional requirements needed by different age categories (Solidum *et al.*, 2012).

Consumption of dairy products in Sri Lanka, particularly powdered milk has experienced a substantial growth over last few decades. Household expenditures on powdered milk are led by both imported brands and local brands (Madushani & Gunaratne, 2010). By the time of 2013, the local production, imports and per capita availability of milk powder has significantly increased compared with previous data. The local production and total imports involve 11610 metric tons and 89910 metric tons while the per capita availability occupies 4.92 kg per year (Department of Census and Statistics; Sri Lanka, 2013). The recent data demonstrates that the livestock sector of Sri Lanka contributes to 0.7% of GDP at present. According to the available data Powdered milk and milk products imports have been increased by 3.3% compared to 2013 growth rate which may resulted as a consequence of low growth rate of the dairy sector (Department of Animal Production and Health, 2014).

Analytical measurements are essential to maintain and control processes, making and adjusting precautions, establishing products' quality and to guarantee quality of the product to the end users. This study was carried out to determine the heavy metal concentrations in both full cream and non fat milk powder available in Sri Lankan markets. The well-established validated method was followed as the analytical protocol which includes microwave digestion for samples preparation and the inductively coupled plasma mass spectrometry (ICP-MS) for elementary analysis (Khan *et al.*, 2013).

ENVIRONMENTAL POLLUTION

Pollution is defined as accumulation of unsuitable material and energy in the environment as a result of basically human activities. The contributors which are responsible for environmental pollution are called environmental pollutants. A pollutant can be a physical, chemical or biological material which is released into the environment that can directly or indirectly damage to humans and other living organisms on earth. In recent decades, changes happened due to human activities have doubled causing many people to suffer on their lives. The human population has doubled in the past 40 years and is projected to increase by the same amount again in the next 40. Environment pollution now has become a worldwide problem and its potential to influence on the health of human populations as well as other living organisms is great. Pollution reaches its most significant proportions in places where the densely settled urban-industrial centers of the more developed countries. In developing and most poor countries of the world more than 80% polluted water is being used for irrigation activities in industrial, urban and semi urban areas. Industries which settled as clusters in urban and semi urban areas with densely population lead to pollute the environment without stopping (Hooke, 2012; Khan, 2013; Rai *et al*, 2011).

Since last few decades there is an increasing global concern on the public health influences caused by the environmental pollution, Human exposure to environment pollution now has significantly increased than the past. Pollution occurs as a result of anthropogenic and natural activities. Industrial based anthropogenic activities and natural disasters play a vital contribution on the environment pollution nowadays. At present, the application of environmental auditing procedures in any economic sector is voluntary but effective and practicable future legislation protocols could well make it mandatory. It is considered that environmental pollution control programs should arise as nationwide effort relying upon voluntary participation. Tourism industry is another source of potential harm to the environment. Extensive levels of pollution can cause creating a lot of damage to human & animal health, plants & trees including tropical rainforests, as well as other aquatic and terrestrial habitats. Environmental pollution occurs as air pollution, water pollution and soil/land pollution causing significant non beneficial health related burdens for humans (Khan, 2013).

AIR POLLUTION

Air pollution has become an extremely serious problem for the modern industrialized world. The air we breathe is an essential ingredient for a healthy life. Unfortunately polluted air is common throughout the world specially in developed countries. Air pollution may be defined as any atmospheric condition in which certain substances are present in such concentrations that may produce undesirable effects on man and ecosystem. These substances include gases, particulate matters, radioactive materials and many others (Rai *et al*, 2011).

Rapid growth in urban population, increasing industrialization, and rising demands for energy and motor vehicles, poor environmental regulation, less efficient technology of production, congested roads, age and poor maintenance of vehicles are the worsening air pollution levels. Not only that but also air pollution is caused of ill health and death by natural and man-made sources, major man-made sources of ambient air pollution include tobacco smoke, combustion of solid fuels for cooking, heating, home cleaning agents, insecticides industries, automobiles, power generation and poor environmental regulation. The natural sources include incinerators and waste disposals, forest and agricultural fires. In the recent past, air pollution has also been associated with diseases of the central nervous system (CNS), including stroke, Alzheimer's disease, Parkinson's disease, and neuro-developmental disorders. It has been demonstrated that various components of air pollution, such as nanosized particles, can easily translocate to the CNS where they can activate innate immune responses. Furthermore, systemic inflammation arising from the pulmonary or cardiovascular system can affect CNS health (Genc *et al.*, 2012).

The recent discovery of genes linked to susceptibility to inflammatory bowel diseases (IBD) explains only a fraction of the hereditary variance for these diseases. This, together with evidence of increases in incidence of IBD in the past few decades of enhanced industrialization, suggests that environmental factors could contribute to disease pathogenesis. Gaseous pollutants may also induce systemic negative effects in the living bodies (Beamish *et al.*, 2011).

WATER POLLUTION

Water resources and water quality affect the economic, social and political development of the society. Water becomes contaminated by unexpected substances, it is considered as harmful for human and aquatic lives. This water is termed as polluted water. Various causes are responsible for polluting water. Some natural causes are mixture of biodegraded portion of animal and plants to pure water, siltation by erosion of river banks etc. Domestic wastes, industrial wastes, fertilizers etc. are manmade pollutants of water. Necessity of water for each and every living being needs no description. If the intaking water is polluted, it will do harm that is for sure. The worst part is, this transports to others through food chain. At present, the water pollution cannot be completely prevented but minimization is very much needed. (Bagul *et al.*, 2015)

The pesticides belong to a category of chemicals used worldwide as herbicides, insecticides, fungicides, rodenticides, molluscicides, nematicides, and plant growth regulators in order to control weeds, pests and diseases in crops as well as for health care of humans and animals. The positive aspect of application of pesticides renders enhanced crop/food productivity and drastic reduction of vector-borne diseases. However, their unregulated and indiscriminate applications have raised serious concerns about the entire environment in general. Pesticides cause serious health hazards to living systems because of their rapid fat solubility and bioaccumulation in non-target organisms. Even at low concentration, pesticides may exert several adverse effects, which could be monitored at biochemical, molecular or behavioral levels. The factors affecting water pollution with pesticides and their residues include drainage, rainfall, microbial activity, soil temperature, treatment surface, application rate as well as the solubility, mobility and half life of pesticides (Agrawal *et al.*, 2010).

Due to the discharge of large amounts of metal-contaminated wastewater, industries bearing heavy metals are the most hazardous among the chemical-intensive industries. Because of their high solubility in the aquatic environments, heavy metals can be absorbed by living organisms.

Once they enter the food chain, large concentrations of heavy metals may accumulate in the human body. If the metals are ingested beyond the permitted concentration, they can cause serious health disorders. (Barakat, 2011).The presence of inorganic pollutants such as metal ions in the ecosystem causes a major environmental problem. Toxic metal compounds coming to the earth's surface not only contaminate earth's water (seas, lakes, ponds and reservoirs),but can also contaminate underground water in trace amounts by leaking from the soil after rain and snow. There are numerous metals which are significantly toxic to human beings and ecological environments, they include arsenic (As), chromium (Cr), copper (Cu), lead (Pb), cadmium (Cd), mercury (Hg), zinc (Zn), manganese(Mn) nickel (Ni), etc. Heavy metals constitute an important part of environmental pollutants and source of poisoning. They are present (in various forms) in the soil, natural water and air and may become contaminants in food and drinking water. Some of them are constituents of pesticides, paints and fertilizers application. Concentration of metal beyond the tolerance level may be regarded as toxic if it affects the growth or metabolism of cells. The lethal toxicity mechanism of a high concentration of heavy metal during a short term exposure disrupts the respiratory surface while during long term exposure; the metal gets accumulated in the internal organs. Due to various advancements in industrial activities, the levels of discharge of these heavy metals have increased. Since the numerous threats posed by heavy metals in the environment, it is very important to reduce the presence of these toxic metals in environment. (Ojedokun *et al.*, 2016).

The volume of sewage water generated by domestic, industrial and commercial sources has increased along with the increasing population, urbanization, improved living conditions, and economic development. In the urban areas of many (developing) countries, urban and peri-urban agriculture depends, at least to a certain extent, on sewage water as a source of irrigation water. The quality of water and the conditions under which this water is used vary significantly. In poor countries, this water may, in extreme cases, take the form of diluted raw sewage, even if this practice is considered illegal. However, the quality of the wastewater used and the nature of its use vary enormously, both between and within countries. In many low income countries in Africa, Asia and Latin America, the wastewater tends to be untreated (Balkhair *et al.*, 2015).

LAND/SOLID WASTE POLLUTION

Improper management of solid waste is one of the main causes of environmental pollution. Land pollution is one of the major forms of environmental catastrophe our world is facing today. Heavy metal industries have produced wastes that are deposited into landfills without special precautions posit that approximately half of the population lives in the Vicinity of waste sites that do not conform to contemporary standards.

Coal and uranium mines have produced serious pollution problems, and much of the solid industrial waste containing heavy metals is disposed without pretreatment (Khan, 2013). Evidence has accumulated that exposure to widespread environmental toxicants make the world to suffer (Cao *et al.*, 2016). Environmental regulations and standards are important as they maintain balance among competing resources and help protect human health and the environment (Liu *et al.*, 2015)

HEAVY METAL TOXICITY

Metals which have high density or high atomic weight compared with water are known as heavy metals (Farag, 2000). Some metalloids are also classified as heavy metals since they can induce toxicity even at low level of their concentrations (Duffus, 2002). In recent years, the environmental and global public health concerns on heavy metals have been increased as they play a vital role associated with the environmental pollution worldwide. Human and animal exposure has increased adversely as a result of a considerable increase of their uses in various applications such as agricultural development involvements, industrial activities, domestic uses and number of various technological advances (Bradl *et al.*, 2005).

Heavy metals are naturally present throughout the earth's crust. But most of environmental pollution and human exposure is directly resulted from anthropogenic activities as people use excessively metals and metal-containing compounds for various operations such as industrial, mining and smelting activities, domestic and agricultural productions (Shallari *et al.*, 1998).The environmental pollution due to heavy metals can also occur by natural phenomena such as metal corrosions, leaching of heavy metals along with soil erosion of metallic ions, atmospheric depositions, metallic evaporation occurs from water resources to soil and ground water while weathering and volcanic eruptions have also been significantly contribute to heavy metal pollution as well (Nriagu, 1989). Industrial sources include metal processing in refineries, coal burning in power plants, petroleum combustion, nuclear power generating stations, textiles, plastics, microelectronics, wood preservation and paper processing operations (Baldauf *et al.*, 2001).

Soils can be contaminated by heavy metals and metalloids along with their accumulation through emissions from the rapidly developing industrial areas, disposal of high metal wastes, mine tailings, land application of fertilizers, spillage of petrochemicals, mine tailings, pesticides, sewage sludge, animal manures, wastewater irrigation, coal combustion residues and atmospheric deposition (Khan *et al.*, 2008). Heavy metals are included into a group of inorganic chemical hazards. Most commonly found heavy metals at contaminated sites are chromium (Cr), zinc (Zn), arsenic (As), lead (Pb), cadmium (Cd), copper (Cu), nickel (Ni) and mercury (Hg), and so on (Mulligan *et al.*, 2001).

Soils are the main basins for heavy metals released into the environment by aforementioned anthropogenic activities and unlike organic contaminants which are oxidized to carbon (IV) oxide by microbial action, most heavy metals do not tend to undergo microbial or chemical degradation although changes in their chemical forms (speciation) and bioavailability somehow possible (Kirpichtchikova *et al.*, 2006), and their total level of concentration in soils persists for a long time after their introduction (Adriano, 2001). The presence of toxic metals in soil can negatively affect on the biodegradation of organic contaminants. Heavy metal contamination of soil may create risks and hazardous incidences to humans and the ecosystem through the food chain (soil-plant-human or soil-plant-animal-human), direct ingestion or contact with contaminated soil, drinking of contaminated ground water, in land usability for agricultural production causing food insecurity, reduction in food quality (safety and marketability) via phytotoxicity, reduction and land tenure problems (Farag, 2000).

The demand for excessive food production and the increase in land fragmentation and exploitation of marginal land for agricultural food production practices lead to strong dependence on inorganic fertilizer in the agricultural farming systems. The uncontrolled applications of inorganic fertilizer have caused a serious destruction of the soil and water resources at a significant rate. On the other hand, large amounts of sewage sludge are being generated which require careful handling and disposal procedures to minimize its impact on the environment. Land application is the most popular disposal method but it may entail environmental hazards and decrease plant growth (Pathak *et al.*, 2009) which is also the main disposal outlet in industrialized countries (Bruun, *et al.*, 2006). In agriculture, crop yield decrease following sewage sludge application has been attributed to high concentration of heavy metals (Singh & Agrawal, 2010) and to phytotoxic substances in the sludge (Su *et al.*, 2014).

Heavy metal-induced toxicity and carcinogenicity involves many mechanistic aspects, some of which are not clearly elucidated or understood. However, each metal is known to have unique features and physic-chemical properties that confer to its specific toxicological mechanisms of action. Out of heavy metals, Arsenic (As), Cadmium (Cd), Chromium (Cr), Lead (Pb) and Mercury (Hg) are known as most abundant and priority heavy metals that pollute the environment frequently (Rusyniak *et al.*, 2010).

ARSENIC

Environmental Occurrence, Industrial Production and Use

Arsenic is a ubiquitous element that is detected at low concentrations in virtually all environmental matrices. The major inorganic forms of arsenic include the trivalent arsenite and the pentavalent arsenate. The organic forms are the methylated metabolites – monomethylarsonic acid (MMA), dimethylarsinic acid (DMA) and trimethylarsine oxide. Environmental pollution by arsenic occurs as a result of natural phenomena such as volcanic eruptions and soil erosion, and anthropogenic activities (ATSDR, 2007). Several arsenic-containing compounds are produced industrially, and have been used to manufacture products with agricultural applications such as insecticides, herbicides, fungicides, algicides, sheep dips, wood preservatives, and dye-stuffs. They have also been used in veterinary medicine for the eradication of tapeworms in sheep and cattle. Arsenic compounds have also been used in the medical field for at least a century in the treatment of syphilis, yaws, amoebic dysentery, and trypanosomaiasis (Smith *et al.*, 2000).

Arsenic-based drugs are still used in treating certain tropical diseases such as African sleeping sickness and amoebic dysentery, and in veterinary medicine to treat parasitic diseases, including filariasis in dogs and black head in turkeys and chickens. Recently, arsenic trioxide has been approved by the Food and Drug Administration as an anticancer agent in the treatment of acute promeylocytic leukemia. Its therapeutic action has been attributed to the induction of programmed cell death (apoptosis) in leukemia cells (Wang *et al.*, 1998).

POTENTIAL FOR HUMAN EXPOSURE

It is estimated that several million people are exposed to arsenic chronically throughout the world, especially in countries like Chile, Uruguay, Mexico and south Asia where the ground water is contaminated with high concentrations of arsenic. Exposure to arsenic occurs via the oral route (ingestion), inhalation, dermal contact, and the parenteral route to some extent. Arsenic concentrations in air range from 1 to 3 ng/m^3 in remote locations (away from human releases), and from 20 to 100 ng/m^3 in cities. Its water concentration is usually less than 10μg/L, although higher levels can occur near natural mineral deposits or mining sites. Its concentration in various foods ranges from 20 to 140 ng/kg. Natural levels of arsenic in soil usually range from 1 to 40 mg/kg, but pesticide application or waste disposal can produce much higher values ((Mandal & Suzuki, 2002).

Contamination with high levels of arsenic is a wide concern because arsenic can cause a number of human health effects. Several epidemiological studies have reported a strong association between arsenic exposure and increased risks of both carcinogenic and systemic health effects (Tchounwou *et al.*, 2003). Interest in the toxicity of arsenic has been heightened by recent reports of large populations in West Bengal, Bangladesh, Thailand, Inner Mongolia, Taiwan, China, Mexico, Argentina, Chile, Finland and Hungary that have been exposed to high concentrations of arsenic in their drinking water and are displaying various clinicopathological conditions including cardiovascular and peripheral vascular disease, developmental anomalies, neurologic and neurobehavioural disorders, diabetes, hearing loss, portal fibrosis, hematologic disorders (anemia, leukopenia and eosinophilia) and carcinoma (Committee On Toxicology, 2001).

Arsenic exposure affects virtually all organ systems including the cardiovascular, dermatologic, nervous, hepatobilliary, renal, gastro-intestinal, and respiratory systems (Tchounwou *et al.*, 2003). Research has also pointed to significantly higher standardized mortality rates for cancers of the bladder, kidney, skin, and liver in many areas of arsenic pollution. The severity of adverse health effects is related to the chemical form of arsenic, and is also time- and dose-dependent (Tian *et al.*, 2008).

CADMIUM

Environmental Occurrence, Industrial Production and Use

Cadmium is a heavy metal of considerable environmental and occupational concern. It is widely distributed in the earth's crust at an average concentration of about 0.1 mg/kg. The highest level of cadmium compounds in the environment is accumulated in sedimentary rocks, and marine phosphates contain about 15 mg cadmium/kg (Wells *et al.*, 2002). Cadmium is frequently used in various industrial activities. The major industrial applications of cadmium include the production of alloys, pigments, and batteries. Although the use of cadmium in batteries has shown considerable growth in recent years, its commercial use has declined in developed countries in response to environmental concerns. This decline has been linked to the introduction of stringent effluent limits from plating works and, more recently, to the introduction of general restrictions on cadmium consumption in certain countries (United States Environmental Protection Agency, 2014).

Potential for Human Exposure

The main routes of exposure to cadmium are via inhalation or cigarette smoke, and ingestion of food. Skin absorption is rare. Human exposure to cadmium is possible through a number of several sources including employment in primary metal industries, eating contaminated food, smoking cigarettes, and working in cadmium-contaminated work places, with smoking being a major contributor (Paschal *et al.*, 2000). Other sources of cadmium include emissions from industrial activities, including mining, smelting, and manufacturing of batteries, pigments, stabilizers, and alloys (Services, 2008). Cadmium is also present in trace amounts in certain foods such as leafy vegetables, potatoes, grains and seeds, liver and kidney, and crustaceans and mollusks (Satarug *et al.*, 2003). In addition, foodstuffs that are rich in cadmium can greatly increase the cadmium concentration in human bodies. Examples are liver, mushrooms, shellfish, mussels, cocoa powder and dried seaweed. An important distribution route is the circulatory system whereas blood vessels are considered to be main stream organs of cadmium toxicity. Chronic inhalation exposure to cadmium particulates is generally associated with changes in pulmonary function and chest radiographs that are consistent with emphysema (Davison *et al.*, 1988). Workplace exposure to airborne cadmium particulates has been associated with decreases in olfactory function (Mascagni *et al.*, 2003). Several epidemiologic studies have documented an association of chronic low-level cadmium exposure with decreases in bone mineral density and osteoporosis (Akesson *et al.*, 2006).

Exposure to cadmium is commonly determined by measuring cadmium levels in blood or urine. Blood cadmium reflects recent cadmium exposure (from smoking, for example). Cadmium in urine (usually adjusted for dilution by calculating the cadmium/creatinine ratio) indicates accumulation, or kidney burden of cadmium (Jarup *et al.*, 1998). Blood and urine cadmium levels are typically higher in cigarette smokers, intermediate in former smokers and lower in nonsmokers (Becker *et al.*, 2002). Thus the continuing use of cadmium in industrial applications, the environmental contamination and human exposure to cadmium have dramatically increased during the past century (Satarug *et al.*, 2010).

CHROMIUM

Environmental Occurrence, Industrial Production and Use

Chromium (Cr) is a naturally occurring element present in the earth's crust, with oxidation states (or valence states) ranging from chromium (II) to chromium (VI) (Assem & Zhu, 2007). Chromium compounds are stable in the trivalent [Cr (III)] form and occur in nature in this state in ores, such as ferrochromite. The hexavalent [Cr (VI)] form is the second-most stable state. Elemental chromium [Cr (0)] does not occur naturally. Chromium enters into various environmental matrices (air, water, and soil) from a wide variety of natural and anthropogenic sources with the largest release coming from industrial establishments. Industries with the largest contribution to chromium release include metal processing, tannery facilities, chromate production, stainless steel welding, and ferrochrome and chrome pigment production. The increase in the environmental concentrations of chromium has been linked to air and wastewater release of chromium, mainly from metallurgical, refractory, and chemical industries. Chromium released into the environment from anthropogenic activity occurs mainly in the hexavalent form [Cr (VI)] (Wilburg *et al.*, 2000). Hexavalent chromium [Cr (VI)] is a toxic industrial pollutant that is classified as human carcinogen by several regulatory and non-regulatory agencies (U.S. Environmental Protection Agency, U.S.E., ORD & Assessment, N.C. for E, 2013).

The health hazard associated with exposure to chromium depends on its oxidation state, ranging from the low toxicity of the metal form to the high toxicity of the hexavalent form. All Cr (VI) containing compounds were once thought to be man-made, with only Cr (III) naturally ubiquitous in air, water, soil and biological materials. Recently, however, naturally occurring Cr(VI) has been found in ground and surface waters at values exceeding the World Health Organization limit for drinking water of 50 μg of Cr(VI) per liter (Velma *et al.*, 2010). Chromium is widely used in numerous industrial processes and as a result, is a contaminant of many environmental systems (Cohen *et al.*, 1993). Commercially chromium compounds are used in industrial welding, chrome plating, dyes and pigments, leather tanning and wood preservation. Chromium is also used as anticorrosive in cooking systems and boilers (Wang *et al.*, 2006).

Potential for Human Exposure

It is estimated that more than 300,000 workers are exposed annually to chromium and chromium-containing compounds in the workplace. In humans and animals, [Cr (III)] is an essential nutrient that plays a role in glucose, fat and protein metabolism by potentiating the action of insulin. However, occupational exposure has been a major concern because of the high risk of Cr-induced diseases in industrial workers occupationally exposed to Cr (VI) (Saha *et al.*, 2011). Also, the general human population and some wildlife may also be at risk. It is estimated that 33 tons of total Cr are released annually into the environment (Wilburg *et al.*, 2000). The U.S. Occupational Safety and Health Administration (OSHA) recently set a "safe" level of 5μg/ m 3, for an 8-hr time-weighted average, even though this revised level may still pose a carcinogenic risk (Zhang *et al*, 2011). For the general human population, atmospheric levels range from 1 to 100 ng/cm ^{3}, but can exceed this range in areas that are close to Cr manufacturing. Non-occupational exposure occurs via ingestion of chromium containing food and water whereas occupational exposure occurs via inhalation. Chromium concentrations range between 1 and 3000 mg/kg in soil, 5 to 800 μg/L in sea water, and 26 μg/L to 5.2 mg/L in rivers and lakes (Assem & Zhu, 2007).

Chromium content in foods varies greatly and depends on the processing and preparation. In general, most fresh foods typically contain chromium levels ranging from <10 to 1,300 μg/kg. Present day workers in chromium-related industries can be exposed to chromium concentrations two orders of magnitude higher than the general population. Even though the principal route of human exposure to chromium is through inhalation, and the lung is the primary target organ, significant human exposure to chromium has also been reported to take place through the skin (Holmes *et al.*, 2008). For example, the widespread incidence of dermatitis noticed among construction workers is attributed to their exposure to chromium present in cement (Shelnutt *et al.*, 2007). Occupational and environmental exposure to Cr (VI) containing compounds is known to cause multiorgan toxicity such as renal damage, allergy and asthma, and cancer of the respiratory tract in humans (IPCS - International Programme on Chemical Safety, 1988).

Breathing high levels of chromium (VI) can cause irritation to the lining of the nose, and nose ulcers. The main health problems seen in animals following ingestion of chromium (VI) compounds are irritation and ulcers in the stomach and small intestine, anemia, sperm damage and male reproductive system damage. Chromium (III) compounds are much less toxic and do not appear to cause these problems. Some individuals are extremely sensitive to chromium (VI) or chromium(III), allergic reactions consisting of severe redness and swelling of the skin have been noted. An increase in stomach tumors was observed in humans and animals exposed to chromium (VI) in drinking water. Accidental or intentional ingestion of extremely high doses of chromium (VI) compounds by humans has resulted in severe respiratory, cardiovascular, gastrointestinal, hematological, hepatic, renal, and neurological effects as part of the sequelae leading to death or in patients who survived because of medical treatment (Wilburg *et al.*, 2000).

LEAD

Environmental Occurrence, Industrial Production and Use

Lead is a naturally occurring bluish-gray metal present in small amounts in the earth's crust. Although lead occurs naturally in the environment, anthropogenic activities such as fossil fuels burning, mining, and manufacturing contribute to the release of high concentrations. Lead has many different industrial, agricultural and domestic applications. It is currently used in the production of lead-acid batteries, ammunitions, metal products (solder and pipes), and devices to shield X-rays. An estimated 1.52 million metric tons of lead were used for various industrial applications. Out of all of that amounts, lead acid batteries production accounted for 83 percent, and the remaining usage covered a range of products such as ammunitions (3.5 percent), oxides for paint, glass, pigments and chemicals (2.6 percent), and sheet lead (1.7 percent) (McKenna *et al.*, 2013).

In recent years, the industrial use of lead has been significantly reduced from paints and ceramic products, caulking and pipe solder (The, 1992). Despite this progress, it has been reported that among 16.4 million with more than one child younger than 6 years per household, 25% of homes still had significant amounts of lead-contaminated deteriorated paint, dust, or adjacent bare soil (Jones, 2012). Lead in dust and soil often re-contaminates cleaned houses (Farfel & Chisolm, 1991) and contributes to elevating blood lead concentrations in children who play on bare, contaminated soil (CDC, 2012). Today, the largest source of lead poisoning in children comes from dust and chips from deteriorating lead paint on interior surfaces (Lanphear *et al.*, 1998). Children who live in homes with deteriorating lead paint can achieve blood lead concentrations of 20μg/dL or greater (Mielke, 1999).

Potential for Human Exposure

Exposure to lead occurs mainly via inhalation of lead-contaminated dust particles or aerosols, and ingestion of lead-contaminated food, water, and paints (Flora *et al.*, 2012). Adults absorb 35 to 50% of lead through drinking water and the absorption rate for children may be greater than 50%. Lead absorption is influenced by factors such as age and physiological status. In the human body, the greatest percentage of lead is taken into the kidney, followed by the liver and the other soft tissues such as heart and brain, however, the lead in the skeleton represents the major body fraction (Lanphear, 2005). The nervous system is the most vulnerable target of lead poisoning. Headache, poor attention spam, irritability, loss of memory and dullness are the early symptoms of the effects of lead exposure on the central nervous system (CDC, 2012). Since the late 1970's, lead exposure has decreased significantly as a result of multiple efforts including the elimination of lead in gasoline, and the reduction of lead levels in residential paints, food and drink cans, and plumbing systems (Flora *et al.*, 2012).

Several programs implemented by states have not only focused on banning lead in gasoline, paint and soldered cans, but have also supported screening programs for lead poisoning in children and lead abatement in housing (The, 1992). Despite the progress in these programs, human exposure to lead remains a serious health problem (Pirkle *et al.*, 1994). Lead is the most systemic toxicant that affects several organs in the body including the kidneys, liver, central nervous system, hematopoietic system, endocrine system, and reproductive system. Lead exposure usually results from lead in deteriorating household paints, lead in the work place, lead in crystals and ceramic containers that leaches into water and food, lead use in hobbies, and lead use in some traditional medicines and cosmetics (The, 1992).

Several studies concluded that blood lead levels have assessed the magnitude of lead exposure by age, gender, race, income and degree of urbanization (Pirkle *et al.*, 1994).Although the results of these surveys have demonstrated a general decline in blood lead levels since the 1970s, they have also shown that large populations of children continue to have elevated blood lead levels (> 10μg/dL). Hence, lead poisoning remains one of the most common pediatric health problems in the world today (Kaul *et al.*, 1999). Exposure to lead is of special concern among women particularly during pregnancy. Lead absorbed by the pregnant mother is readily transferred to the developing fetus (Ong *et al.*, 1985). Human evidence corroborates animal findings (Corpas *et al.*, 1995), linking prenatal exposure to lead with reduced birth weight and preterm delivery.

MERCURY

Environmental Occurrence, Industrial Production and Use

Mercury is a heavy metal belonging to the transition element series of the periodic table. It is unique in that it exists or is found in nature in three forms (elemental, inorganic, and organic), with each having its own profile of toxicity (Clarkson *et al.*, 2003). At room temperature elemental mercury exists as a liquid which has a high vapor pressure and is released into the environment as mercury vapor. Mercury also exists as a cation with oxidation states of +1 (mercurous) or +2 (mercuric) (Guzzi *et al.*, 2008). Methylmercury is the most frequently encountered compound of the organic form found in the environment, and is formed as a result of the methylation of inorganic (mercuric) forms of mercury by microorganisms found in soil and water (Dopp *et al.*, 2004). Mercury is a widespread environmental toxicant and pollutant which induces severe alterations in the body tissues and causes a wide range of adverse health effects (Bhan & Sarkar, 2005).

Both humans and animals are exposed to various chemical forms of mercury in the environment. These include elemental mercury vapor (Hg 0), inorganic mercurous (Hg +1), mercuric (Hg +2), and the organic mercury compounds (Zahir *et al.*, 2005). Because mercury is ubiquitous in the environment, humans, plants and animals are all unable to avoid exposure to some form of mercury (Holmes *et al.*, 2009). Mercury is utilized in the electrical industry (switches, thermostats, batteries), dentistry (dental amalgams), and numerous industrial processes including the production of caustic soda, in nuclear reactors, as antifungal agents for wood processing, as a solvent for reactive and precious metal, and as a preservative of pharmaceutical products (Tchounwou *et al.*, 2003). The industrial demand for mercury peaked in 1964 and began to sharply decline between 1980 and 1994 as a result of bans on mercury additives in paints, pesticides, and the reduction of its use in batteries (United States Environmental Protection Agency, 1997).

Potential for Human Exposure

Humans are exposed to all forms of mercury through accidents, environmental pollution, food contamination, dental care, preventive medical practices, industrial and agricultural operations, and occupational operations. The major sources of chronic, low level mercury exposure are dental amalgams and fish consumption. Mercury enters water as a natural process of off-gassing from the earth's crust and also through industrial pollution. Algae and bacteria methylate the mercury entering the waterways. Methyl mercury then makes its way through the food chain into fish, shellfish, and eventually into humans (Sanfeliu *et al.*, 2003). The two most highly absorbed species are elemental mercury (Hg 0) and methyl mercury (MeHg). Dental amalgams contain over 50% elemental mercury. The elemental vapor is highly lipophilic and is effectively absorbed through the lungs and tissues lining the mouth. After Hg 0 enters the blood, it rapidly passes through cell membranes, which include both the blood-brain barrier and the placental barrier (Hoffmeyer *et al.*, 2006). Once it gains entry into the cell, Hg 0 is oxidized and becomes highly reactive Hg 2+. Methyl mercury derived from eating fish is readily absorbed in the gastrointestinal tract and because of its lipid solubility, can easily cross both the placental and blood-brain barriers. Once mercury is absorbed it has a very low excretion rate. A major proportion of what is absorbed accumulates in the kidneys, neurological tissue and the liver. All forms of mercury are toxic and their effects include gastrointestinal toxicity, neurotoxicity, and nephrotoxicity (Tchounwou *et al.*, 2003).

MILK

Milk is secreted out by milking a dairy female animal who is under the good health condition. It must be collected efficiently without containing colostrum (MacLachlan & Bhula, 2009). Milk is a white color liquid food basically produced by the mammary secretory cells of females in the process called lactation; it is one of the defining characteristics of mammals. Milk secreted in the first days after parturition is called colostrums. The quality of milk is paramount; therefore, it must be properly stored and transported in optimal conditions (Guetouache *et al.*, 2014).

Bovine milk and dairy products have long traditions in human nutrition. The consumption of milk and milk products vary considerably among regions (Do Nascimento, 2004). In the western societies, the consumption of milk has decreased during the last decades. This trend may partly be explained by the claimed negative health effects that have been attributed to milk and milk products. This criticism has arisen especially because milk fat contains a high fraction of saturated fatty acids assumed to contribute to heart diseases, weight gain and obesity. The association between food and health is well established and recent studies have shown that modifiable risk factors seem to be of greater significance for health than previously anticipated (Yusuf *et al.*, 2004). Prevention of disease may in the future be just as important as treatment of diseases. Indeed, many consumers of today are highly aware of health-properties of food, and the market for healthy food and food with special health benefits is increasing. Milk is a complex food made up of components, which may have negative or positive health effects, respectively. Milk composition can be altered by the feeding regime thus giving improved nutritional consumption of the milk for human consumption (Haug *et al.*, 2007).

Milk Composition

Bovine milk contains the nutrients needed for growth and development and is a resource of lipids, proteins, amino acids, vitamins and minerals. It contains immunoglobulins, hormones, growth factors, cytokines, nucleotides, peptides, polyamines, enzymes and other bioactive peptides. The lipids in milk are emulsified in globules coated with membranes. The proteins are in colloidal dispersions as micelles. The casein micelles occur as colloidal complexes of protein and salts, primarily calcium (Dalgleish & Corredig, 2012). Lactose and most minerals are in solution. Milk composition has a dynamic nature, and the composition varies with stage of lactation, age, breed, nutrition, energy balance and health status of the udder. Colostrums differ considerably to milk; the most significant difference is the concentration of milk protein that may be about the double in colostrum compared to later in lactation (Ontsouka *et al.*, 2003). The change in milk composition during the whole lactation period seems to match the changing need of the growing infant, giving different amounts of components important for nutrient supply, specific and non-specific host defense, growth and development. Specific milk proteins are involved in the early development of immune response, whereas others take part in the non-immunological defence (e.g. lactoferrin). Milk contains many different types of fatty acids (Jensen, 2002). All these components make milk a nutrient rich food item. (Haug *et al.*, 2007)

Milk as a Food

Milk contains components that are essential to humans such as proteins, carbohydrates, fat, water, all the B-vitamins, vitamins A and D, calcium and phosphorus. It also provides energy. An important protein in milk is casein (in many cases 80% of the milk protein). This is the base for cheese making. Casein is linked to calcium phosphate, which is why milk contains a relatively large amount of this salt that is a very important nutrient for humans and animals. In addition to casein, milk contains whey proteins (20% of the milk protein). The whey proteins are in most cases not incorporated in the cheese; they remain in the whey. Whey proteins (globulins and albumins) have a very high nutritive value. Milk protein is of a high quality. This means that the human body can use a large part of the protein efficiently. Proteins in various other foodstuffs have a complementary effect. In combination with cereals, potatoes, meat, eggs or nuts in one meal, the body can use an even greater percentage of the milk protein. (Ebing, 2006)

Heavy Metals and Milk

Environmental pollution has been a major area of concern worldwide. Industrial and agricultural processes have caused an increased concentration of toxicants like heavy metals in the environment and as a result being taken up by plants or animals into their systems which cause further distribution of toxicants to the environment. This is the case in cow's milk that is being consumed by humans in liquid or powder form. Heavy metals can contaminate milk through exposure of lactating cow to pollution or consumption of feeding stuffs and water with toxicants. Moreover, contamination can also be attributed to the manner of manufacturing dairy products where toxicants have the possibility to be included during the production process (Fowler *et al.*, 2015). With the increasing number of toxicants being present in the environment the safety of people is at risk. Children are particularly vulnerable to environmental toxicants because of their possibly greater relative exposure and the effects on their growth and physiological development (Peabody *et al.*, 2006). Powdered milk is the essential food needed by growing children. It contains both the basic and additional requirement needed by children especially during their developmental years. This milk may be contaminated by heavy metals that at certain levels may cause toxicity to consumers.This toxicity is attributed to accumulation of heavy metals in the body which are not metabolized to excretable products. Knowing that toxic heavy metals may be present in powdered milk products, confirmation of their presence and corresponding quantities are necessary to assess if the commercial products being marketed are safe to use (Solidum *et al.*, 2012).

Although heavy metals are largely remaining in ground water and soil but in certain areas their level increase and they tend to accumulate to toxic levels in human and animal tissues deriving food from water and soils. Living organisms normally require some of these heavy metals up to certain limits and in case excess accumulation occurs it will lead to severe detrimental effects (Liang & Wong, 2003). Foodstuffs grown on contaminated soil or irrigated with impure water accumulate metal contents and are a big source of heavy metals exposure to the animals and humans. Along with these factors many occupations involve direct contact of workers to the heavy metals like dental surgeons, painters and welders etc (Mohammad *et al.*, 2008). Food animals reared on contaminated fodder become continuous source of heavy metal residues in edible tissues and milk. Heavy metal contamination in meat and other edible tissues is a matter of great concern for food safety and human health. These metals are toxic in nature and even at relatively low concentrations can cause adverse effects (Alturiqi & Albedair, 2012). The preceding lines reflect the sensitivity of threat being posed to general public health. This problem needs an immediate attention of health regulatory authorities and the researchers as well (History, 2010).

From a nutritional point of view, metal elements in the composition of milk products can be grouped in essential metals (Fe, Mn, Cu, Zn,Co, Cr, etc.) and in non-essential metals (represented mainly by Hg, Cd, Pb, etc.). The presence of the latter, even in low concentrations, leads to metabolic disorders with extremely serious consequences. It is very important to mention that for both heavy metal categories the increase of their concentration above admitted limits considered optimal has toxic effects on consumers of milk and milk products. This is why concentration levels for some heavy metals in milk and milk products are ruled by every country's sanitary regulations (Gogoa *et al.*, 2006).

Pollution from heavy metal residues is a global environmental threat as they are widely present in the earth's crust, in air, water and food (Matlock, Henke & Atwood, 2002). The increase in heavy metal pollution in the ecosystem is because of various human and natural activities (Klimmek *et al.*, 2001). These activities include dumping of wastes, unintentional and process spillages, use of agricultural pesticides and related chemicals, movement of contaminants into a fertile land as vapors, by mobilization of soil, or as dust, or dispersal of sewage mire. All these sources contribute towards contamination of the environment. Heavy metal residues in feed and food symbolize a drastic risk and their long time exposure can lead to toxicological effects. Excessive exposure to elements such as Cd, Pb, As, Cr and Hg is toxic for plants, animals and human beings (Llobet *et al.*, 2003). These metals have direct as well as indirect respective effects on the health of animals and human (Parkpain *et al.*, 2000).

In some rural areas, pollution from heavy metals has been attributed to disposal of industrial effluents and sewage sludge which cause s problems for grazing animals because they deposit heavy metals on pastures, grasses or forages (Juniper *et al.*, 2006). Farm animals are important indicators of the environmental pollution from heavy metals. Exposure of farm animals to heavy metals constitutes especially a major public health concern considering that these animals are often reared for their meat and milk products. These concerns were raised for some milk products from cattle and goats, which reportedly contained heavy metal residues to an extent that surpassed the maximum residue limits established by international regulatory agencies. Contamination from heavy metal residues is a serious problem encountered especially in third world countries and it is a matter of great concern for food safety and human health regulatory bodies. Metals in drinking water and food supply causes slow poisoning and risk of death in more than 100 million people worldwide (Ojedokun & Bello, 2016). These metals are toxic in nature and even at relatively low concentrations can cause adverse health effects. The preceding lines reflect the sensitivity of threat being posed to general public health from heavy metal contamination. This problem needs an immediate attention of health regulatory authorities and the researchers as well (Javed *et al.*, 2013).

Pollution of foods with environmental toxic metals even in trace quantities has attracted considerable attention in the global era with rapid transportation. The simple and inexpensive monitoring of food pollution needs to be developed for reducing or eliminating the amounts of toxic elements into the environment. Milk and milk products provide good quality nutrients necessary for a strong healthy body and mind, and act as a primary source of nutrients in diets all around the world. However, the presence of toxic elements in milk and milk products may create health problems especially for infants, school age children, and old people who consume large quantity of those products. Their presence in milk and its products is caused by different agricultural activities. Irrigation with toxic metal contaminated water and use of pesticides, parasiticides, drugs, and environmental disinfectants to cows may result in toxic metal contamination in feeds (Hristov *et al.*, 2007). As the mammary glands are the most physiologically sensitive part of dairy cows, the input and output of toxic metals in these organisms are clearly reflected in the milk. Heavy metals, specially cadmium, arsenic, zinc, and lead, are ubiquitously found in nature and, therefore, their contamination to milk and milk products must be considered. Among these toxic metals, zinc is the most abundant one and provided to humans. Although an adequate amount of zinc is physiologically important, exposure to the excess amount is harmful and toxic aspects of zinc arise. Therefore, it becomes consumers' benefits to monitor whether the zinc concentration in milk or milk products is adequate or not. Analytical methods towards hazardous chemical compounds in foods have attracted much attention. (Siddiki *et al.*, 2012).

Breastfeeding is necessary for optimal growth and development of infants. There are innumerable and unique health and neurodevelopment advantages to short and long-term breastfeeding. Nevertheless partial and non-breastfeeding take place worldwide. The occurrence of necessary essential nutrients and micronutrients in cow's milk has made it the alternative food of choice for the human infant. In such non-ideal circumstances infant feeding practices have relied on technical advances in the food industry to improve upon mainstream cow milk-based products. In this realistic scenario, it should be recognized that pasture and animal foodstuffs can be contaminated with pollutants and, as a consequence, increase the risk of the non-breastfed infant being exposed to hazardous substances. Grazing land can be contaminated with and from parent materials, atmospheric deposits, continuous application of large amounts of fertilizer, disposal of industrial waste sludge and vehicle emissions. In addition to that, packaging and technological processes used to bring foods to the consumer can significantly increase the total concentration of Pb and Cd. Therefore, potentially toxic elements deriving from environmental pollution or accidental contamination may be transferred to cow's milk and consumed by vulnerable infants. Intake of contaminated milk containing low levels of Cd and Pb can cause various clinical abnormalities or may pass without clinical signs. However, studies have shown that dietary intake of selected nutritional elements might help counteract the effects of cadmium and lead. Animal studies showed that the amount of calcium in food is related to tissue lead accumulation (de Castro *et al.*, 2010).

DAIRY SECTOR IN SRI LANKA

Sri Lanka is becoming increasingly dependent on the global dairy market to fulfill its growing needs for dairy products. The demand for dairy products in Sri Lanka is largely met through imports. Currently, dry milk powder is the format that is most consumed in Sri Lanka. The consumption of milk products has almost doubled and the consumption of fresh milk has already dropped drastically. The governments from the time of independence have recognized the importance of the dairy sector in the country and have taken various policy measures for its development. However, the availability of relatively cheap milk powders in the international market and the concerns about the large number of consumers, have prevented the governments in the past from providing the required price incentives for the dairy producers to expand dairy production in the country (Lanka, 2008). Inconsistent policies for the industry, low productivity of animals, low farm-gate price of milk, high cost of milk production, poor extension services and inadequate education on animal health among dairy farmers, absence of new investments in the livestock sector due primarily to a lack of state support and financial services, poor marketing options available and inadequate milk-processing facilities, failure to update the technologies, including the development of a proper collection and distribution network in the sector and absence of proper consumer education to appreciate the value of fresh milk are the key constraints on the local dairy development which cause to create a demand for the imported milk powder for consumption (Ranaweera, 2015).

Sri Lankan dairy industry has its validity in providing thousands of job opportunities and cheap animal protein to the nation. But trends in the industry could be mainly explained by imports of milk and milk products (Department of Animal Production and Health, 2010). The livestock sector of Sri Lanka contributes to 0.7% of GDP at present. Though, the livestock sector contribution to national GDP is reducing due to its marginal growth (0.3%), the consumption of livestock products has increased dramatically over the last two decades with the increase of per capita income and urbanization. Formal milk collection has increased only by 6.8 % in 2014, which unfortunately marked a 3.3% decrement in growth rate which may resulted as a consequence of low growth rate of the dairy sector. Powdered milk and milk products imports have been increased by 3.3% compared to 2013 and may attribute to the consumer preference (Department of Animal Production and Health, 2014). Consumers largely depend on imported brands and local brands of milk powder (Madushani & Gunaratne, 2010). By 2013, the local production, imports and per capita availability of milk powder has significantly increased compared with previous data. The local production and total imports involve 11610 metric tons and 89910 metric tons while the per capita availability occupies 4.92 kg per year (Department of Census and Statistics; Sri Lanka, 2013).

MATERIALS AND METHODS

Location of the Study

The study was conducted at the Department of Animal Science, Faculty of Agriculture, University of Peradeniya. Digestion of milk samples were carried out at the National Institute of Fundamental Studies, Hanthana road Kandy. The Inductive Couple Plasma Mass spectrometric (ICP-MS) analyses were conducted at the laboratories in the Department of Geology, Faculty of Science, University of Peradeniya.

MILK POWDER COLLECTION

Commercially available 18 brands of Full Cream Milk Powder and Non-Fat Milk Powder were purchased from local supermarkets in Kurunegala district. All the samples with their original packages were transferred to the laboratory and stored in well-cleaned cupboards. These were processed for analysis within one week after purchasing and before expired.

SAMPLING PROCEDURE

Each brand was named according to the alphabetical order from A to R. Samples were prepared as triplicates and 1g of each sample was used for the microwave digestion.

DIGESTION PROCESS

1. Preparation of Glassware

All glassware including volumetric flasks, funnels and beakers were thoroughly cleaned metal free water, and soaked overnight in an acid bath containing 20% HNO_3(v/v) solution. The glassware was rinsed several times with de-ionized metal free water and dried in drying oven (Khan *et al.*, 2013).

2. Preparation of Digestion Vessels

A 5 mL of concentratedHNO_3 (70% Analytical Grade, Sigma Aldrich, USA) was added to 16 digestion vessels then placed them in the rotator of the microwave digester (910905, Mars One Touch Technology Microwave Digestion System, CEM Corporation, USA). Then the vessels were cleaned at 121 °C, for 10 min ramp to temperature, at maximum power of 1000 W, for 15 min. After cooling (10 min), the well-cleaned vessels were washed several times with de-ionized metal free water and placed them upside down until the inside moisture gets evaporated completely.

3. Microwave Digestion

A 1 g of sample was accurately measured using analytical balance (PS 450/X, Radway Wagi Elektroniczne, Poland) and placed in digestion vessels. Then 8 ml of concentrated HNO_3 (70% Analytical Grade, Sigma Aldrich, USA) was added to each digestion vessel, placed in the microwave work station (910905, Mars One Touch Technology Microwave Digestion System,

CEM Corporation, USA) and digested at 210 ^{0}C, with 15 min ramp to temperature, at maximum power of 1000 W, for 30 min. After cooling (15 min), the digested samples were transferred to volumetric flask and diluted to 25 mL with de-ionized water, filtered through filter papers (Whatman NO. 42) into 15 ml Falcon tubes and finally labeled for analysis (Khan *et al.*, 2013). There were overall 56 samples including two blanks.

Fig. 2.1: Microwave Digester (910905, Mars One Touch Technology Microwave Digestion System, CEM Corporation, USA)

ICP-MS ANALYSIS

Samples were brought to the laboratory in the Department of Geology, Faculty of Science, University of Peradeniya in a properly sealed box without any external contaminations. 5 ml of each sample was then filtered into new properly labeled 15 ml Falcon tubes using micro-filters (0.1 micron). Finally, the stock solutions were added to each solution to detect heavy metals by ICP-MS. Throughout the sampling procedure, microwave digestion and ICP-MS analysis, a clean environment was maintained in order to reduce the external metal contaminations.

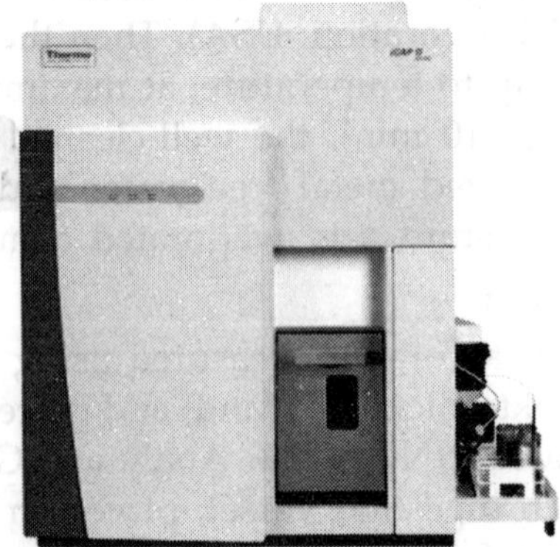

Fig. 2.2: Inductive Couple Plasma Mass Spectrometer (ICP-MS)

STATISTICAL ANALYSIS

The data was analyzed by SAS University Edition Software Package. The experimental design was Completely Randomized Design and the means were separated by Duncan's Multiple Range Test.

RESULTS AND DISCUSSION

Back Calculations of the Data Received from ICP-MS

Heavy metal content (As, Cd, Hg, Cr and Pb) were expressed as ppb (Past per Billion). Back calculations was done according to the below equation in order to convert the values into mg/kg,

Concentration = Value $\times 10^{-3} \times 25$ (Dilution Factor) mg/kg

Table 2.1: Maximum limits for As, Cd, Hg, Cr and Pb established by Codex Alimentarius

Heavy Metal	Maximum Limit (mg/kg)
As	0.015
Cd	0.007
Hg	0.005
Cr	2
Pb	0.025

The analyzed values were compared with the maximum standards (CODEX STAN 193-1995) established by the Codex Alimentarius.

Arsenic Content of Milk Powder

Table 2.2: Total Arsenic concentration of different milk powder brands

Brand	Concentration (mg/kg)
(1)	(2)
A	0.005 ± 0.0012^{b}
B	0.004625 ± 0.0009^{bc}
C	0.004125 ± 0.0019^{bc}
D	0.004125 ± 0.0041^{bc}
E	0.003125 ± 0.0002^{bc}
F	0.003125 ± 0.0019^{bc}
G	0.002875 ± 0.0026^{bc}
H	0.002625 ± 0.0037^{bc}
I	0.002375 ± 0.0009^{bc}
J	0.00225^{bc}
K	0.00125 ± 0.0014^{bc}
L	0.001125 ± 0.0012^{bc}
M	0.001125 ± 0.0009^{bc}

(Table Contd...)

(1)	(2)
N	0.001 ± 0.0007[bc]
O	0.000875 ± 0.0009[bc]
P	0.000875 ± 0.0002[bc]
Q	0.00075 ± 0.0004[bc]
R	0.000625 ± 0.0005[c]

Values are expressed as Mean ± SD (Standard Deviation)
Mean values within a column with different superscript letters were significantly different ($P<0.0001$)

Contamination with high levels of arsenic is a huge concern since arsenic can cause a number of negative human health effects (Tchounwou *et al.*, 2003). Analyzed data shows that there was a significant difference ($P<0.0001$) between the maximum limit and the mean values for As obtained from different brands. Brand A had relatively high As value compared with other brands. There was no significant difference among other brands while lowest value for the As content was represented by brand R (0.000625 ± 0.0005).

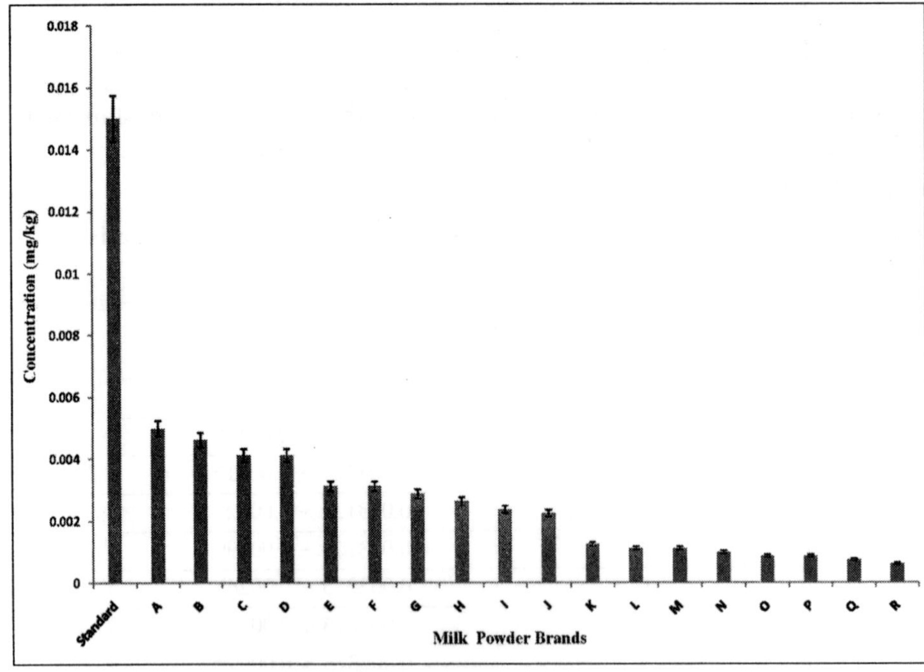

Fig. 2.3: Variations of Arsenic concentrations in different milk brands

Cadmium Content of Milk Powder

Table 2.3: Total Cadmium concentration of different milk powder brands

Brand	Concentration (mg/kg)
A	0.0039 ± 0.0005[b]
B	0.0115 ± 0.0078[b]
C	0.0231 ± 0.0094[b]
D	0.0108 ± 0.0103[b]
E	0.0113 ± 0.0046[b]
F	0.0224 ± 0.0048[b]
G	0.0123 ± 0.0095[b]
H	0.0099 ± 0.0055[b]
I	0.0284 ± 0.0267[b]
J	0.018 ± 0.0124[b]
K	0.009 ± 0.0055[b]
L	0.3163 ± 0.4398[a]
M	0.0069 ± 0.0005[b]
N	0.0109 ± 0.0009[b]
O	0.0185 ± 0.018[b]
P	0.008 ± 0.0046[b]
Q	0.0104 ± 0.0062[b]
R	0.0121 ± 0.0143[b]

Values are expressed as Mean ± SD (Standard Deviation)
Mean values within a column with different superscript letters were significantly different ($P<0.0001$)

Cadmium is a heavy metal with considerable environmental and occupational concern. It is widely distributed in the earth's crust at an average concentration of around 0.1 mg/kg (Wells, Duce & Huber, 2002). The analyzed data shows that the all the brand except brand L were not significantly different when compared with the maximum limit (0.007 mg/kg) for Cd established by the Codex Alimentarius. The brand L showed a significant higher value for Cd (0.3163± 0.4398) than the established maximum limit by Codex Alimentarius for heavy metal contamination in milk powder.

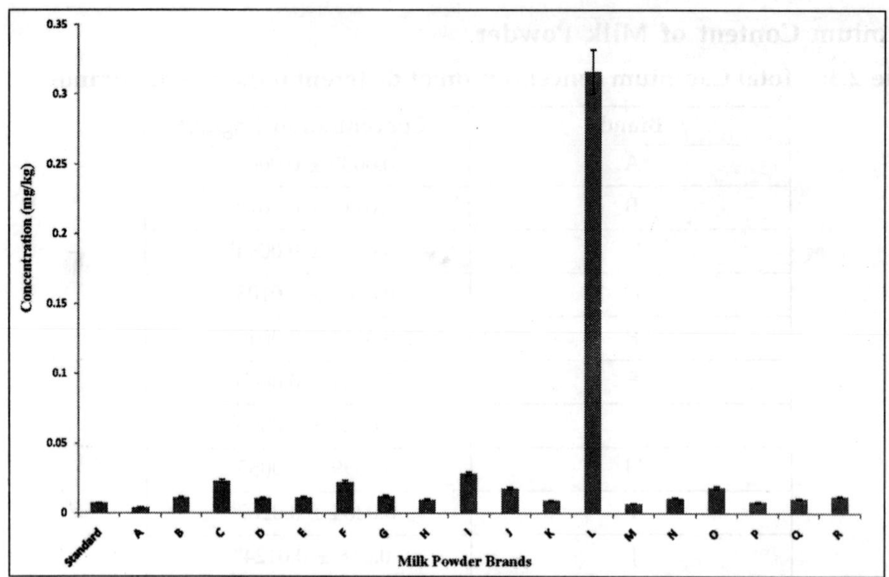

Fig. 2.4: Variations of Cadmium concentrations in different milk brands

Mercury Content of Milk Powder

Table 2.4: Total Mercury concentration of different milk powder brands

Brand	Concentration (mg/kg)
A	0.002625 ± 0.003[ab]
B	0.0025 ± 0.0028[ab]
C	0.004 ± 0.0004[ab]
D	0.0025 ± 0.0032[ab]
E	0.004[ab]
F	0.001375 ± 0.0016[ab]
G	0.000375 ± 0.0005[b]
H	0.004 ± 0.0021[ab]
I	0.0015 ± 0.0004[ab]
J	0.00025b[b]
K	0.002125 ± 0.0019[ab]
L	0.004 ± 0.0032[ab]
M	0.0005± 0004b[b]
N	0.001125 ± 0.0009[ab]
O	0.001± 0.0004[ab]
P	0.000875 ± 0.0002[ab]
Q	0.001375 ± 0.0016[ab]
R	0.001875 ± 0.0019[ab]

Values are expressed as Mean ± SD (Standard Deviation)

Mean values within a column with different superscript letters were significantly different ($P<0.0001$)

Mercury is a heavy metal which belong to the transition element series of the periodic table. It is found in nature in three forms (elemental, inorganic, and organic), each with its own profile of toxicity (Clarkson *et al* 2003). It is a widespread environmental toxicant and pollutant which induces severe alterations in the body tissues and causes a wide range of adverse health effects (Bhan & Sarkar, 2005). The data showed that there is no any significant difference (P<0.0001) among brands in terms of Hg compared except brand G, J and M since they represent a significant lower value (P<0.0001) compared with maximum limits for Hg (0.005 mg/kg) established by Codex Alimentarius in terms of heavy metal contamination.

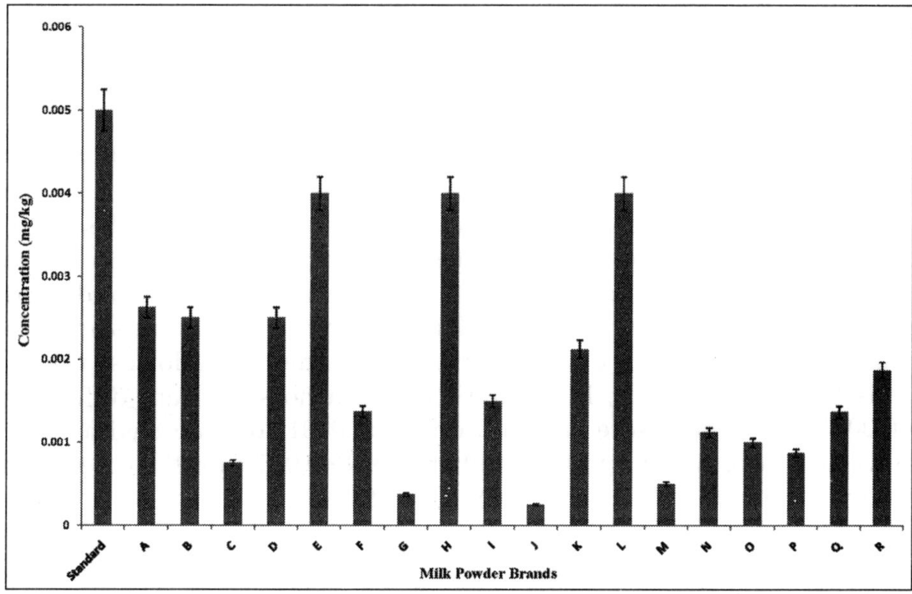

Fig. 2.5: Variations of Mercury concentrations in different milk brands

Table 2.5: Total Chromium concentration of different milk powder brands

Brand	Concentration (mg/kg)
(1)	(2)
A	0.1005 ± 0.0152^{gh}
B	0.12513 ± 0.009^{defg}
C	0.29163 ± 0.0083^{b}
D	0.206 ± 0.0134^{c}
E	0.148 ± 0.0163^{defg}
F	0.13263 ± 0.0053^{defg}
G	0.16125 ± 0.0131^{de}
H	0.1475 ± 0.0272^{defg}

(Table Contd...)

(1)	(2)
I	0.12425 ± 0.0173[defd]
J	0.12438 ± 0.0161[defg]
K	0.11263 ± 0.0214[defg]
L	0.09138 ± 0.0108[h]
M	0.12325 ± 0.0021[defg]
N	0.109 ± 0.0162[fgh]
O	0.12238 ± 0.003[defg]
P	0.121 ± 0.0063[defg]
Q	0.15688 ± 0.0602[def]
R	0.1685 ± 0.0194[dc]

Values are expressed as Mean ± SD (Standard Deviation)
Mean values within a column with different superscript letters were significantly different (P<0.0001)

Chromium (Cr) is a naturally occurring element in the earth's crust, with oxidation states (or valence states) ranging from chromium (II) to chromium (VI) (Assem & Zhu, 2007). All the milk powder brands had significantly lower values (P<0.0001) for Cr than the maximum standards (2 mg/kg) established by Codex Alimentarius. Among the lowest values, brands B, E, F, H, I, J, K, M, O and P showed no significant difference (P<0.0001) and They were significantly (P<0.0001) different with other brands, and there was a significant difference (P<0.0001) for the Cr content between the brands A, C, D, G, L, N, Q and R.

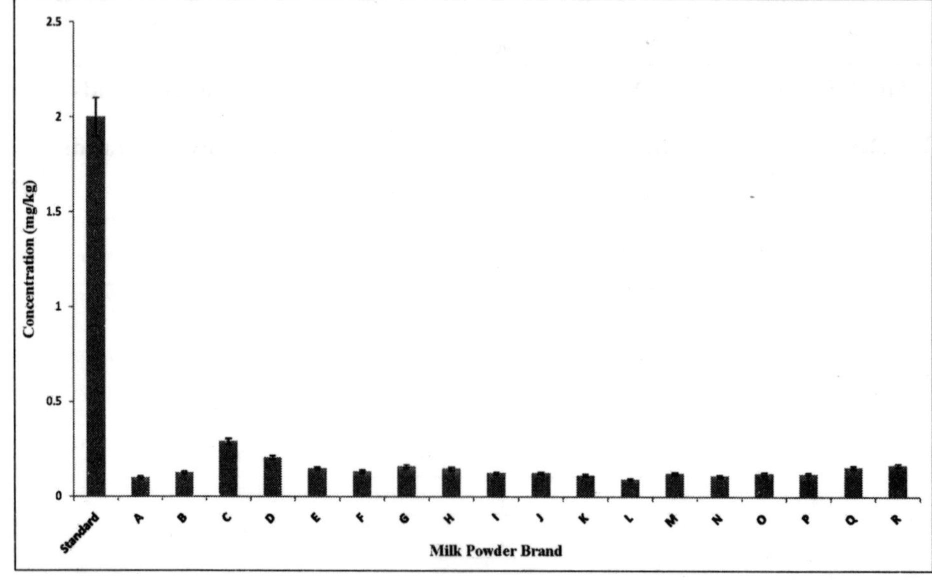

Fig. 2.6

Lead Content of Milk Powder

Table 2.6: Total lead concentration of different milk powder brands

Brand	Concentration (mg/kg)
A	0.09188 ± 0.0327^{bcd}
B	0.14575 ± 0.0124^{abc}
C	0.096 ± 0.0152^{bcd}
D	0.12063 ± 0.033^{abc}
E	0.09913 ± 0.027^{abc}
F	0.09225 ± 0.0099^{bcd}
G	0.09725 ± 0.001^{bcd}
H	0.09275 ± 0.0053^{bcd}
I	0.09063 ± 0.0083^{bcd}
J	0.09375 ± 0.0103^{bcd}
K	0.08688 ± 0.0348^{bcd}
L	0.08338 ± 0.0055^{bcd}
M	0.15538 ± 0.0313^{ab}
N	0.008 ± 0.0032^{dc}
O	0.08725 ± 0.0131^{bcd}
P	0.09713 ± 0.032^{bcd}
Q	0.09388 ± 0.0044^{bcd}
R	0.08663 ± 0.0154^{bcd}

Values are expressed as Mean ± SD (Standard Deviation)
Mean values within a column with different superscript letters were significantly different (P<0.0001)

Lead is a naturally occurring bluish-gray metal present in small amounts in the earth's crust(McKenna *et al*, 2013). Brand B, D and E were not significantly different (P<0.0001) in terms of Pb content. However, there were no significantly different (P<0.0001) withother brands. The brands M and N are also significantly different between them and among the other brands in terms of Pb content. Brand B, D, E and M had significantly higher values for Pb than the established maxium limit (0.025 mg/kg) by Codex alimentarius.

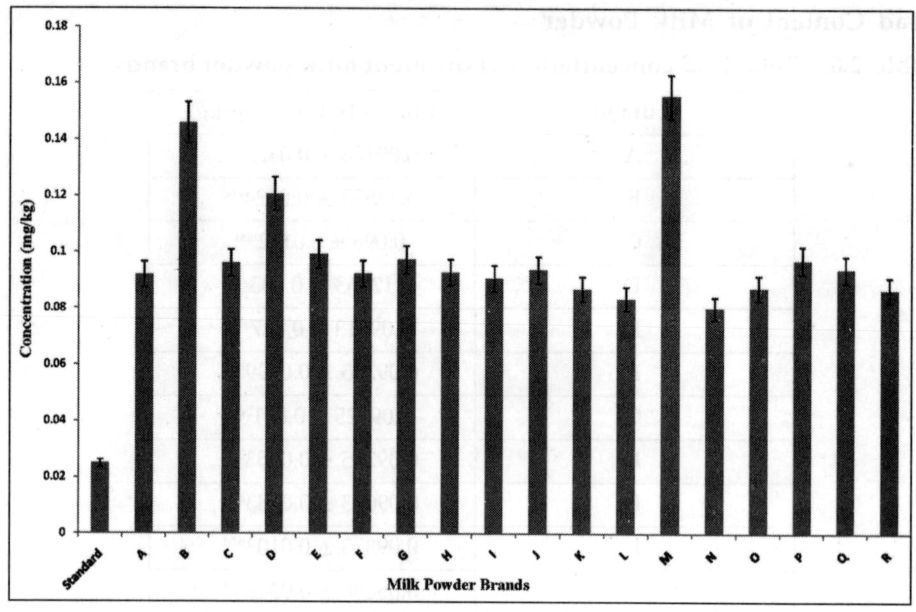

Fig. 2.7

RECOMMENDATIONS

Research findings are essential in order to ensure the safety of consumers. Since there is no available literature in Sri Lanka in terms of analyzing milk powder for heavy metals, researchers must pay their attention on to fill up the history for future researchers. Periodical analysis of milk powder is a must since it is largely consumed by local people as a nutritional supplement. Authorities and officials should implement strict rules and regulations in order toprohibit such contaminated milk powder brands from the markets. People should be made aware on the matters of findings to establish the wellbeing of consumers.

CONCLUSION

In conclusion, the study revealed that there is risk of heavy metal contamination especially for Pb and Cd in milk powder collected from Kurunegala area. Four milk powder brands including one of the most popular one (B, D, E and M) had significantly higher values ($P<0.0001$) for Pb while brand L contained a significantly higher value ($P<0.0001$) for Cd. All of the brands were not significant ($P<0.0001$) for As, Cr and Hg indicating no any health risk associated with them for consumers.

REFERENCES

Adriano, D.C., 2001. *Trace Elements in Terrestrial Environments. Biogeochemistry, Bioavailability, and Risks of Metals*, Available at: http://dx.doi.org/10.1071/EN06057\nhttp://link.springer.com/10.1007/978-0-387-21510-5.

Akesson, A. *et al.*, 2006. Cadmium-induced Effects on Bone in a Population-based Study of Women. *Environmental Health Perspectives*, 114(6), pp. 830-834.

Alturiqi, A.S. & Albedair, L.A., 2012. Evaluation of some Heavy Metals in Certain Fish, Meat and Meat Products in Saudi Arabian Markets. *Egyptian Journal of Aquatic Research*, 38(1), pp. 45-49.

Assem, L. & Zhu, H., 2007. Chromium Toxicological Overview. *Health Protection Agency*, (Iii), pp. 1-14. Available at: http://www.hpa.org.uk/webc/HPAwebFile/HPAweb_C/1194947362170.

ATSDR, 2007. *Toxicological Profile for Arsenic*, Available at: http://dx.doi.org/10.1155/2013/286524.

Baldauf, R.W., Lane, D.D. & Marote, G.A., 2001. Ambient Air Quality Monitoring Network Design for Assessing Human Health Impacts from Exposures to Airborne Contaminants. *Environmental Monitoring and Assessment*, 66(1), pp. 63-76.

Becker, K. *et al.*, 2002. German Environmental Survey 1998 (GerES III): Environmental Pollutants in Blood of the German Population. *International Journal of Hygiene and Environmental Health*, 205(4), pp. 297-308. Available at: http://www.ncbi.nlm.nih.gov/pubmed/12068749.

Bhan, A. & Sarkar, N.N., 2005. Mercury in the Environment: Effect on Health and Reproduction. *Reviews on Environmental Health*, 20(1), pp. 39-56.

Bruun, S. *et al.*, 2006. Application of Processed Organic Municipal Solid Waste on Agricultural Land - A Scenario Analysis. *Environmental Modeling and Assessment*, 11(3), pp. 251-265.

de Castro, C.S.P. *et al.*, 2010. Toxic Metals (Pb and Cd) and their Respective Antagonists (Ca and Zn) in Infant Formulas and Milk Marketed in Brasilia, Brazil. *International Journal of Environmental Research and Public Health*, 7(11), pp. 4062-4077.

CDC, 2012. Response to Advisory Committee on Childhood Lead Poisoning Prevention Recommendations in "Low Level Lead Exposure Harms Children: A Renewed Call of Primary Prevention." *Morbidity Mortality Weekly*, 61(20), p. 383. Available at: http://www.cdc.gov/nceh/lead/ACCLPP/CDC_Response_Lead_Exposure_Recs.pdf.

Clarkson, T.W., Magos, L. & Myers, G.J., 2003. The Toxicology of Mercury — Current Exposures and Clinical Manifestations. *N Engl J Med*, 34918349, pp. 1731-7.

Cohen, M.D. *et al.*, 1993. Mechanisms of Chromium Carcinogenicity and Toxicity. *Critical Reviews in Toxicology*, 23(3), pp. 255-281.

Committee On Toxicology, 2001. *Arsenic in Drinking Water 2001 Update*.

Corpas, I. *et al.*, 1995. Testicular Alterations in Rats due to Gestational and Early Lactational Administration of Lead. *Reproductive Toxicology*, 9(3), pp. 307-313.

Dalgleish, D.G. & Corredig, M., 2012. The Structure of the Casein Micelle of Milk and Its Changes During Processing. *Annual Review of Food Science and Technology*, 3(1), pp. 449-467.

Davison, A.G. *et al.*, 1988. Cadmium Fume Inhalation and Emphysema. *The Lancet*, 331(8587), pp. 663-667.

Department of Census and Statistics, S.L., 2013. Production, Imports and Availability of Milk & Milk Products. Available at: http://www.statistics.gov.lk/agriculture/Livestock/MilkProduction.html.

Dopp, E. *et al.*, 2004. *Environmental Distribution, Analysis, and Toxicity of Organometal(loid) Compounds*, Available at: <Go to ISI>://WOS:000221760300002.

Duffus, J.H., 2002. *"Heavy Metals " – A Meaningless Term?*

Farag, A., 2000. Heavy Metals in Drinking Water and their Environmental Impact on Human Health. *Icehm*, pp. 542-556.

Farfel, M.R. & Chisolm, J.J., 1991. An Evaluation of Experimental Practices for Abatement of Residential Lead-based Paint: Report on a Pilot Project. *Environmental Research*, 55(2), pp. 199-212.

Flora, G., Gupta, D. & Tiwari, A., 2012. Toxicity of Lead: A Review with Recent Updates. *Interdisciplinary Toxicology*, 5(2), pp. 47-58. Available at: http://www.pubmedcentral.nih.gov/article render. fcgi? artid= 3485653 &tool = pmcentrez & rendertype=abstract.

Fowler, B., Alexander, J. & Oskarsson, A., 2015. *Toxic metals in food. Chapter 6.*, Available at: http://www.sciencedirect.com/science/article/pii/B9780444594532000068.

G.L.W.E.N. Madushani and L.H.P. Gunaratne, 2010b. Consumer Preferences for Different Attributes of Powdered Milk: A Conjoint Analysis.

Gogoa, I. *et al.*, 2006. Aas Detection of Heavy Metal in Sheep Cheese (the Banat Area, Romania)., 2006, pp. 1-6.

Guetouache, Mourad, Guessas, Bettache, M. & Samir, 2014. Composition and Nutritional Value of Raw Milk., 2(December), pp. 115-122.

Guzzi, G. & La Porta, C.A.M., 2008. Molecular Mechanisms Triggered by Mercury. *Toxicology*, 244(1), pp.1-12.

Haug, A., Hostmark, A. & Harstad, O., 2007. Bovine Milk in Human Nutrition - a Review. *Lipids in Health and Disease*, 6(1), p. 25. Available at: http://www.lipidworld.com/content/6/1/25.

Health, D. of A.P., 2010. Livestock Statistical Bulletin., 3, pp. 1-4.

Health, D. of A.P., 2014. *Livestock Statistical Bulletin* M.G.D.N. S. Dr. D.L.N. Kumudinie, Mrs. M. Wickramsinghe, Mrs. M.I.S. Marasinghe, Mr. M.K.C. Nuwan Kumara, Mrs. R. Wijesinghe, Mr. M. Jayasinghe & M.S. Wickramasinghe, eds., Health, Department of Animal Production and Health.

History, A., 2010. Pakistan Veterinary Journal. *Animals*, 8318(2), pp. 85-92. Available at: http://www.pvj.com.pk/pdf-files/31{_}3/192-194.pdf.

Hoffmeyer, R.E. *et al.*, 2006. Molecular Mimicry in Mercury Toxicology. *Chemical Research in Toxicology*, 19(6), pp. 753-759.

Holmes, A.L., Wise, S.S. & Wise, J.P., 2008. Carcinogenicity of Hexavalent Chromium. *Indian Journal of Medical Research*, 128(4), pp. 353-372.

Holmes, P., James, K.A.F. & Levy, L.S., 2009. Is low-level Environmental Mercury Exposure of Concern to Human Health? *Science of the Total Environment*, 408(2), pp. 171-182.

Hooke, R., 2012. Land Transfomation by Humans: A Review. *GSA Today*, 22(12), pp. 4-10.

Hristov, A N., Hazen, W. & Ellsworth, J.W., 2007. Efficiency of use of Imported Magnesium, Sulfur, Copper, and Zinc on Idaho Dairy Farms. *Journal of Dairy Science*, 90(6), pp. 3034-3043.

IPCS - International Programme on Chemical Safety, 1988. *Environmental Health Criteria 61 - Chromium*, Available at: http://www.inchem.org/ documents/ehc/ehc/ ehc61.htm\nhttp: //scholar.google.com/scholar?hl=en&btnG=Search&q=intitle: ENVIRONMENTAL+HEALTH+CRITERIA+61+(Chromium)#5.

J.N. Solidum, S.G.B., dela Cruz, K.M. & Padilla, R., 2012. A Quantitative Analysis on Cadmium and Chromium Contamination in Powdered Children's Milk Available in Metro Manila, Philippines. *International Conference on Environment and BioScience*, 44.

Järup, L. *et al*., 1998. Health Effects of Cadmium Exposure— A Review of the Literature and a Risk Estimate. *Scandinavian Journal of Work, Environment & Health*, 24 Suppl 1, pp. 1-51. Available at: http://www.ncbi.nlm.nih.gov/pubmed/9569444\nhttp:// www.sjweh.fi/download.php?abstract_id=281&file_nro=1.

Javed, I. *et al*., 2013. Heavy Metal Residues in Goat Meat During Winter and Summer Seasons., 3(12).

Javed, I. *et al*., 2009. Heavy Metal Residues in the Milk of Cattle and Goats during Winter Season. *Bulletin of Environmental Contamination and Toxicology*, 82(5), pp. 616-620.

Jensen, R.G., 2002. The Composition of Bovine Milk Lipids: January 1995 to December 2000. *Journal of Dairy Science*, 85(2), pp. 295-350. Available at: http:// linkinghub.elsevier.com/retrieve/pii/S0022030202740794\nhttp://dx.doi.org/ 10.3168/jds.S0022-0302(02)74079-4.

Jones, D.J., 2012. Primary Prevention and Health Outcomes: Treatment of Residential Lead-based Paint Hazards and the Prevalence of Childhood Lead Poisoning. *Journal of Urban Economics*, 71(1), pp. 151-164.

Juniper, D.T. *et al*., 2006. Selenium Supplementation of Lactating Dairy Cows: Effect on Selenium Concentration in Blood, Milk, Urine, and Feces. *Journal of Dairy Science*, 89(9), pp. 3544-3551. Available at: http://dx.doi.org/10.3168/jds.S0022-0302(06)72394-3.

K.W., A., D.A., S. & I., H.-P., 1994. Prenatal Lead Exposure in Relation to Gestational Age and Birth Weight: A Review of Epidemiologic Studies. *American Journal of Industrial Medicine*, 26(1), pp. 13-32. Available at: http://www.embase.com/search/results? subaction=viewrecord & from =export & id = L24184416n http://sfx.library.uu.nl/ utrecht?sid = EMBASE & issn =02713586&id=doi: &atitle= Prenatal+lead+ exposure+ in+relation+to+ gestational+age+and+ birth+weight:+A+review+of+epidemiologic+.

Kaul, B. *et al*., 1999. Follow-up Screening of Lead-poisoned Children near an Auto Battery Recycling Plant, Haina, Dominican Republic. *Environmental Health Perspectives*, 107(11), pp. 917-920.

Khan, D.M.A., 2013. Environmental Pollution., 175(April 2011), pp. 1-15.

Khan, N. *et al*., 2013. Method Validation for Simultaneous Determination of Chromium, Molybdenum and Selenium in Infant Formulas by ICP-OES and ICP-MS. *Food Chemistry*, 141(4), pp. 3566-3570. Available at: http://dx.doi.org/10.1016/ j.foodchem.2013.06.034.

Kirpichtchikova, T.A. *et al*., 2006. Speciation and Solubility of Heavy Metals in Contaminated Soil using X-ray Microfluorescence, EXAFS Spectroscopy, Chemical Extraction, and Thermodynamic Modeling. *Geochimica et Cosmochimica Acta*, 70(9), pp. 2163-2190.

Klimmek, S. *et al*., 2001. Comparative Analysis of the Biosorption of Cadmium, Lead, Nickel, and Zinc by Algae. *Environmental Science and Technology*, 35(21), pp. 4283-4288.

Lanka, S., 2008. Global Dairy Markets: Implications for Sri Lanka., 2006, pp. 2004-2008.

Lanphear, B., 2005. Childhood Lead Poisoning Prevention. *JAMA: The Journal of the American Medical ...*, 89(7), pp. 1129-1130. Available at: http://www.boe.ca.gov/info/fact_sheets/childhood_lead.htm\nhttp://jama.ama-assn.org/content/293/18/2274.short.

Lanphear, B.P. *et al.*, 1998. The Contribution of Lead-contaminated House Dust and Residential Soil to Children's Blood Lead Levels. A Pooled Analysis of 12 Epidemiologic Studies. *Environmental Research*, 79(1), pp. 51-68.

Liang, Y. & Wong, M.H., 2003. Spatial and Temporal Organic and Heavy Metal Pollution at Mai Po Marshes Nature Reserve, Hong Kong. *Chemosphere*, 52(9), pp. 1647-1658.

Llobet, J.M. *et al.*, 2003. Concentrations of Arsenic, Cadmium, Mercury, and Lead in Common Foods and Estimated Daily Intake by Children, Adolescents, Adults, and Seniors of Catalonia, Spain. *Journal of Agricultural and Food Chemistry*, 51(3), pp. 838-842.

MacLachlan, D.J. & Bhula, R., 2009. Transfer of Lipid-soluble Pesticides from Contaminated Feed to Livestock, and Residue Management. *Animal Feed Science and Technology*, 149(3-4), pp. 307-321.

Mandal, B.K. & Suzuki, K.T., 2002. Arsenic Round the World: A Review. *Talanta*, 58(1), pp. 201-235.

Mascagni, P. *et al.*, 2003. Olfactory Function in Workers Exposed to Moderate Airborne Cadmium Levels. In *NeuroToxicology*. pp. 717-724.

Matlock, M.M., Henke, K.R. & Atwood, D. A, 2002. Effectiveness of Commercial Reagents for Heavy Metal Removal from Water with New Insights for Future Chelate Designs. *Journal of Hazardous Materials*, 92(2), pp. 129-142.

McKenna, E. *et al.*, 2013. Economic and Environmental Impact of Lead-acid Batteries in Grid-connected Domestic PV systems. *Applied Energy*, 104, pp. 239-249.

Mielke, H.W., 1999. Lead in the Inner Cities. *American Scientist*, 87(1), pp. 62-73.

Mohammad, I.K. *et al.*, 2008. Oxidative Stress in Painters Exposed to Low Lead Levels. *Arhiv za higijenu rada i toksikologiju*, 59(3), pp. 161-9. Available at: http://www.degruyter.com/view/j/aiht.2008.59.issue-3/10004-1254-59-2008-1883/10004-1254-59-2008-1883.xml?rskey=LBwUuM&result=3.

do Nascimento, J.R.O., 2004. Functional dairy products. *Revista Brasileira de Ci{ê}ncias Farmac{ê}uticas*, 40, p.441.

Nriagu, J.O., 1989. A Global Assessment of Natural Sources of Atmospheric Trace Metals. *Nature*, 338, pp. 47-49.

Ojedokun, A.T. & Bello, O.S., 2016. Sequestering Heavy Metals from Wastewater using Cow Dung. *Water Resources and Industry*, 13, pp. 7-13. Available at: http://dx.doi.org/10.1016/j.wri.2016.02.002.

Ong, C.N. *et al.*, 1985. Concentrations of Lead in Maternal Blood, Cord Blood, and Breast Milk. *Archives of Disease in Childhood*, 60(8), pp. 756-759. Available at: http://www.ncbi.nlm.nih.gov/pmc/articles/PMC1777426/\nhttp://www.ncbi.nlm.nih.gov/pmc/articles/PMC1777426/pdf/archdisch00719-0068.pdf.

Ontsouka, C.E., Bruckmaier, R.M. & Blum, J.W., 2003. Fractionized Milk Composition during Removal of Colostrum and Mature Milk. *Journal of Dairy Science*, 86(6), pp. 2005-2011. Available at: http://dx.doi.org/10.3168/jds.S0022-0302(03)73789-8.

Parkpain, P., Sreesai, S. & Delaune, R.D., 2000. Bioavailability of Heavy Metals in Sewage Sludge-Amended Thai Soils. *Water, Air & Soil Pollution*, 122(1/2), pp. 163-182. Available at: http://search.ebscohost.com/login.aspx? direct=true &db =eih& AN=16604237&site=ehost-live.

Paschal, D.C. *et al.*, 2000. Exposure of the U.S. Population Aged 6 Years and Older to Cadmium: 1988-1994. *Archives of Environmental Contamination and Toxicology*, 38(3), pp. 377-383.

Pathak, A., Dastidar, M.G. & Sreekrishnan, T.R., 2009. Bioleaching of Heavy Metals from Sewage Sludge: A Review. *Journal of Environmental Management*, 90(8), pp. 2343-2353.

Peabody, Taguiwalo, Robalino, F., 2006. Disease Control Priorities in Developing Countries 2nd Edition. *Disease Control Priorities in Developing Countries 2nd Edition*, pp. 1293-1307. Available at: http://www.worldbank.icebox.ingenta.com/content/wb/2302.

Pirkle, J.L. *et al.*, 1994. The Decline in Blood Lead Levels in the United States. The National Health and Nutrition Examination Surveys (NHANES). *JAMA*, 272(4), pp. 284-291. Available at: PM:8028141.

Qian, G. *et al.*, 2011. China's Dairy Crisis: Impacts, Causes and Policy Implications for a Sustainable Dairy Industry. *International Journal of Sustainable Development {&} World Ecology*, 18(5), pp. 434-441.

Rai, R. *et al.*, 2011. Gaseous Air Pollutants: A Review on Current and Future Trends of Emmission and Impact on Agriculture. *Scientic Research Banaras Hindu University, Varanasi*, 55, pp. 77-102.

Ranaweera, N.F.C., 2015. Sri Lanka/: Opportunities for Dairy Sector Growth Sector Review., 2003.

Rusyniak, D.E. *et al.*, 2010. Molecular, Clinical and Environmental Toxicology. *Nih*, 100, pp. 365-396. Available at: http://www.scopus.com/inward/record.url?eid=2-s2.0-77950880787{&}partnerID=tZOtx3y1.

Saha, R., Nandi, R. & Saha, B., 2011. Sources and Toxicity of Hexavalent Chromium. *Journal of Coordination Chemistry*, 64(10), pp. 1782-1806.

Sanfeliu, C. *et al.*, 2003. Neurotoxicity of Organomercurial Compounds. *Neurotoxicity Research*, 5(4), pp. 283-306.

Satarug, S. *et al.*, 2003. A Global Perspective on Cadmium Pollution and Toxicity in Non-occupationally Exposed Population. In *Toxicology Letters*. pp. 65-83.

Satarug, S. *et al.*, 2010. Cadmium, Environmental Exposure, and Health Outcomes. *Environmental Health Perspectives*, 118(2), pp. 182-190.

Services, H., 2008. *Draft Toxicological Profile for Cadmium*.

Shallari, S. *et al.*, 1998. Heavy Metals in Soils and Plants of Serpentine and Industrial Sites of Albania. *Science of the Total Environment*, 209(2-3), pp. 133-142.

Shelnutt, S.R., Goad, P. & Belsito, D.V, 2007. Dermatological Toxicity of Hexavalent Chromium. *Critical Reviews in Toxicology*, 37(5), pp. 375-87. Available at: http://eds.b.ebscohost.com.ezproxy.endeavour.edu.au/.

Siddiki, M.S., Ueda, S. & Maeda, I., 2012a. Fluorescent Bioassays for Toxic Metals in Milk and yoghurt. *BMC Biotechnology*, 12(1), p. 76. Available at: BMC.

Siddiki, M.S., Ueda, S. & Maeda, I., 2012b. Fluorescent Bioassays for Toxic Metals in Milk and Yoghurt. *BMC Biotechnology*, 12(1), p. 76. Available at: BMC.

Singh, R.P. & Agrawal, M., 2010. Variations in Heavy Metal Accumulation, Growth and yield of Rice Plants Grown at Different Sewage Sludge Amendment Rates. *Ecotoxicology and Environmental Safety*, 73(4), pp. 632-641.

Smith, A.H., Lingas, E.O. & Rahman, M., 2000. Contamination of Drinking-water by Arsenic in Bangladesh: A Public Health Emergency. *Bulletin of the World Health Organization*, 78(9), pp. 1093-1103.

Su, C., Jiang, L. & Zhang, W., 2014. A Review on Heavy Metal Contamination in the Soil Worldwide: Situation, Impact and Remediation Techniques. *Environmental Skeptics and Critics*, 3(2), pp. 24-38.

Sugiyama, M. *et al.*, 2003. Development of Livestock Sector in Asia/: An Analysis of Present Situation of Livestock Sector and its Importance for Future Development., pp. 1-9.

Tchounwou, P.B. *et al.*, 2003. Environmental Exposure to Mercury and its Toxicopathologic Implications for Public Health. *Environmental Toxicology*, 18(3), pp. 149-175.

Tchounwou, P.B. c, Patlolla, A.K. & Centeno, J.A., 2003. Carcinogenic and Systemic Health Effects Associated with Arsenic Exposure - A Critical Review. *Toxicologic Pathology*, 31(6), pp. 575-588. Available at: http://www.scopus.com/inward/record.url?eid=2-s2.0-0242468787&partnerID=40&md5=d985cf9e8d99f890e5af08b9b2b06602.

Tchounwou, P.B., Patlolla, A.K. & Centeno, J.A., 2003. Invited Reviews: Carcinogenic and Systemic Health Effects Associated with Arsenic Exposure—A Critical Review. *Toxicologic Pathology*, 31(6), pp. 575-588. Available at: http://tpx.sagepub.com/content/31/6/575.abstract.

The, A.S.B.Y., 1992. Preventing Lead Poisoning in young Children. *Kansas medicine/: the journal of the Kansas Medical Society*, 93(12), pp. 358-359.

Tian, C. *et al.*, 2008. Redox Status of thioredoxin-1 (TRX1) Determines the Sensitivity of Human Liver Carcinoma Cells (HepG2) to Arsenic Trioxide-induced Cell Death. *Cell Research*, 18(4), pp. 458-71. Available at: http://www.ncbi.nlm.nih.gov/pubmed/18157160.

U.S. Environmental Protection Agency, U.S.E., ORD & Assessment, N.C. for E., 2013. Integrated Risk Information System (IRIS). *U.S. Environmental Protection Agency, U.S. EPA*. Available at: http://www.epa.gov/iris/index.html.

United States Environmental Protection Agency, 2014. Cadmium (CASRN 7440-43-9) | IRIS | US EPA. *Integrated Risk Information System (IRIS)*. Available at: http://www.epa.gov/iris/subst/0141.htm.

United States Environmental Protection Agency, 1997. *Mercury Study Report to Congress: Health Effects of Mercury and Mercury Compounds.*

Velma, V., Vutukuru, S.S. & Tchounwou, P.B., 2010. Ecotoxicology of Hexavalent Chromium in Freshwater Fish: A Critical Review. *Reviews on Environmental Health*, 24(2), pp. 129-145.

Wang, X.-F. *et al.*, 2006. Oral Administration of Cr(VI) induced Oxidative Stress, DNA Damage and Apoptotic Cell Death in Mice. *Toxicology*, 228(1), pp. 16-23.

Wang, Z.G. *et al.*, 1998. Arsenic Trioxide and Melarsoprol Induce Programmed Cell Death in Myeloid Leukemia Cell Lines and Function in a PML and PML-RARalpha Independent Manner. *Blood*, 92, pp. 1497-1504.

Wells, P.G., Duce, R.A. & Huber, M.E., 2002. Caring for the Sea - Accomplishments, Activities and Future of the United Nations GESAMP (the Joint Group of Experts on the Scientific Aspects of Marine Environmental Protection). *Ocean and Coastal Management*, 45(1), pp. 77-89.

Wilburg, S., Ingerman, L., Citra, M. Osier, M., Wohlers, D., 2000. Toxicological Profile for Chromium. *Public Health*, (September), p. 421.

Wuana, R. A. & Okieimen, F.E., 2011. Heavy Metals in Contaminated Soils: A Review of Sources, Chemistry, Risks and Best Available Strategies for Remediation. *ISRN Ecology*, 2011, pp. 1-20.

Yusuf, S. *et al.*, 2004. Effect of Potentially Modifiable Risk Factors Associated with Myocardial Infarction in 52 Countries (the INTERHEART Study): Case Control Study. *The Lancet*, 364(9438), pp. 937-952.

Zahir, F. *et al.*, 2005. Low Dose Mercury Toxicity and Human Health. *Environmental Toxicology and Pharmacology*, 20(2), pp. 351-360.

Zhang, X.-H. *et al.*, 2011. Chronic Occupational Exposure to Hexavalent Chromium Causes DNA Damage in Electroplating Workers. *BMC Public Health*, 11(1), p. 224. Available at: http://www.biomedcentral.com/1471-2458/11/224.

Pages: 46-67

Metals Distribution in Environment

Edited by: **Dr. Deep Mala & Dr. Pawan Kumar 'Bharti'**

ISBN: 978-93-86841-91-9

Edition: **2019**

Published by: **Discovery Publishing House Pvt. Ltd., New Delhi (India)**

Metal Contamination and its Remediation
With Special Reference to Plant and its Mechanism

Shweta Pathak[1]; Prasann Kumar[2]
Prafull Kishor Patil[2]

ABSTRACT

Phytoremediation can be applied to both natural and inorganic contamination show in the dirt, water or air. Substantial metal is a normally happening component which has a colossal crumbling impact on the strength of the earth and it doesn't debase normally and overwhelming metals can't be demolished organically, they must be changed from one oxidation state or natural compound to another. Remediation of soil defiled with overwhelming metals is more troublesome than the remediation of different contaminants. Ecological contamination influences the nature of pedosphere, hydrosphere, climate, lithosphere and biosphere. Numerous endeavors have been made over the most recent two decades to decrease contamination sources and cure the dirtied soil and water assets. Phytoremediation, being more financially savvy and less symptoms than physical and compound methodologies, has increased expanding ubiquity in both scholastic and functional circle.

Keywords: Agriculture, Biotic, Cadmium, Density, Forage, High, Risk.

INTRODUCTION

Metal contamination of soils is ubiquitous around the globe. Metals enter the soil due to anthropogenic activities such as the use of sewage sludge, urban composts, fertilizers, pesticides, sewage irrigation, incineration

1 Department of Plant Physiology, I. Ag. Sci., BHU., Varanasi - 221 005, U.P., (India)

2 Department of Agronomy, School of Agriculture, Lovely Professional University, Jalandhar - 144 411 Punjab, (India)

of municipal waste, auto-vehicle exhausts, industrial emissions and metal mining and smelting (Hussain *et al.*, 2006; McGrath *et al.*, 2001; Murtaza *et al.*, 2010). These metals include iron (Fe), copper (Cu), manganese (Mn), zinc (Zn), cadmium (Cd), lead (Pb), chromium (Cr), mercury (Hg) and nickel (Ni) (McIntyre, 2003). Metals accumulate in the soil to toxic levels that may lead to accumulation of metals in plants to unacceptable levels. Metal accumulation is a subject of serious concern due to threat to plant growth, soil quality, animal and human health (McGrath *et al.*, 2001). Cleaning up soils to remove metals is a sign of the times, but it is a challenging task. Different technologies being used nowadays are ex situ which lead to destruction of soil structure, thus leaving it unusable with poor vegetative cover (He and Yang, 2007). Growing plants to clean up the soils is a cost-effective and environmentally friendly alternative (Yang *et al.*, 2005). Phytoremediation seems attractive due to non-invasive and non-destructive technologies which leave the soil intact and biologically productive (Wenzel, 2009). Plants respond differentially to metal contamination in soils and can be classified into different categories, depending upon their responses to metal contamination in their rooting medium. Plants can be classified into accumulators, indicators or excluders depending upon absorption and translocation of metals by the plants to above-ground parts (Baker, 1981). Accumulators can survive by maintaining high concentration of metals in their tissues. Indicator plants are reported to have mechanisms that control translocation of metals from roots to shoots and excluders restrict the entry of metals into plants at root level (Chaudhry *et al.*, 1998). Plants use different adaptive mechanisms to accumulate or exclude metals and thus maintain their growth. Accumulation and tolerance of metals by the plants is a complex phenomenon. Movement of metals across the root membrane, loading and translocation of metals through xylem and sequestration and detoxification of metals at the cellular and whole-plant levels are important mechanisms adopted by accumulator plants (Lombi *et al.*, 2002). Indicator plants absorb the metals from the soils and then restrict their movement to the shoots while excluders restrict the entry of metals into the plant roots. Understanding the mechanisms involved in phytoremediation is necessary to effectively use this technique on metal-contaminated soils. This chapter discusses different mechanisms adopted by plants for remediation of metal-contaminated soils.

PHYTOREMEDIATION AND MECHANISMS

Heavy metals degrade soil and water resources and thus pose a serious threat to human and animal health. This threat is further aggravated due to the persistent and non-biodegradable nature of metals (Gisbert *et al.*, 2003). Accumulation of metals in the bodies of animals and humans after entering the food chain has serious implications for health as some metals are known to damage DNA and cause cancer due to their mutagenic abilities

(Steinkellner *et al.*, 1998). Remediating the soils contaminated with metals is thus necessary for safe use of such soils and several in situ and ex situ technologies are used for this purpose. Phytoremediation is considered environmentally friendly, non-invasive and cost-effective technology to clean up the metal-contaminated soils. Plants adopt different mechanisms to grow in the metal-contaminated soils without adverse effects on their growth. Some plants exclude the metals from metabolically active sites by restricted uptake or root to shoot transfer of metals (Küpper *et al.*, 1999). Some other plants can tolerate high metal concentrations in their tissues through binding of metals with organic compounds, metal compartmentalization at cellular and sub-cellular levels and metabolic alterations (Küpper *et al.*, 1999; Peng *et al.*, 2006; Wei *et al.*, 2005). Heavy metals tolerance in plants may be defined as the ability of plants to survive in a soil that is toxic to other plants (Macnair *et al.*, 1999). Phytoremediation can be classified into phytoextraction, phytostabilization and phytovolatilization (Alkorta *et al.*, 2004; Raskin *et al.*, 1997), in addition to various other classes of phytoremediation which are beyond the scope of this chapter.

Phytoextraction

Removal of the metals from the soil by growing plants is known as phytoextraction. Metal-extracting plants absorb metals from the soils, transport and concentrate them in the above-ground parts of plants. The above-ground parts of the plants are harvested and can be safely processed for disposal or recycling of metals (Ali *et al.*, 2013; Garbisu and Alkorta, 2001). Plants used for phytoextraction must not only be metal tolerant but they must be fast growing with the potential to produce high biomass. However, most of the metal-accumulating plants are slow growing with low biomass production (Evangelou *et al.*, 2007). These characteristics of metal-accumulating plants have made the process of phytoextraction of metals very slow as phytoextraction is a function of tissue metals concentration and biomass produced (Chaney *et al.*, 2007). Such metal-accumulator plants having capacity to accumulate 100 mg kg"1 of cadmium (Cd), 1000 mg kg–1 of arsenic (As), cobalt (Co), copper (Cu), lead (Pb) or nickel (Ni) or > 10,000 mg kg–1 of manganese (Mn) and zinc (Zn), are classified as hyperaccumulator plants. Hyperaccumulation of heavy metals by plants depends upon several steps, including absorption and transportation of metals across the membranes of root cells, loading of metals into xylem and translocation to the shoots and sequestration and detoxification of metals within plant tissues (Yang *et al.*, 2005). Epidermis, trichomes and cuticle are the preferred sites of metal detoxification, and in many cases subsidiary and stomatal cells are protected against metal toxicity (Rascio and Navari-Izzo, 2011). Metal detoxification or sequestration traits are controlled by expression of genes encoding the protein responsible for exclusion of metals from cytoplasm and transfer across tonoplast and plasma membranes. Cation Diffusion Facilitator (CDF) family members like metal transporter proteins present in the tonoplast are overexpressed in Zn and Ni hyperaccumulators and these transporters are also reported to be involved in Ni accumulation by Ni hyperaccumulators (Gustin *et al.*, 2009; Hammond *et al.*, 2006; Persans *et al.*, 2001; Rascio and Navari-Izzo, 2011). About 400 plants have been identified as hyperaccumulators which constitute only < 0.2% of higher plants (McGrath and Zhao, 2003). Low biomass production of hyperaccumulators discourages their adoption on a commercial scale for phytoextraction. However, some high-biomass-producing plants capable of tolerating metals can be effectively used for phytoextraction on a commercial scale (Saifullah *et al.*, 2009). However, these species have an inherently low ability to absorb metals but can accumulate higher concentrations of metals if grown in the soils treated with chemical amendments to increase metal phytoavailability and plant uptake (Meers *et al.*, 2005).

Cellular Detoxification of Metals

Mechanisms of phytoextraction and hyperaccumulation have been studied considerably but still a lot more research is required to fully understand the mechanisms. Plants adopt different mechanisms to maintain their growth in metal-contaminated soil environments. Plants may immobilize, exclude, chelate compartmentalize metal ions or may release ethylene or stress proteins (Cobbett, 2000b). Phytoextraction of metals is a function of two factors; biomass and metal bioconcentration factor. Most plants have bioconcentration factors < 1 which make them unsuitable for use in phytoextraction, irrespective of biomass produced. However, most hyperaccumulators are known to have bioconcentration factors of > 1 (and in some cases the biocentration factors reach up to that of 50-100); the ratio of metal concentration between shoot and root is greater than one signifying efficient root to shoot translocation and having enhanced metal tolerance due to internal metal detoxification (McGrath and Zhao, 2003; Zhao *et al.*, 2003). A study focusing on the genetic basis of hyperaccumulation reveals that zinc (Zn) hyperaccumulation and tolerance are independent traits controlled by separate genes (Macnair *et al.*, 1999). Enhanced transfer of metals from roots to shoots (through decreased metal sequestration in roots or enhanced xylem loading) is an important component of metal hyperaccumulation and is evidenced by enhanced loading of histidine into xylem of *Alyssum lesbiacum* upon exposure to Ni (Krämer *et al.*, 1996; Lasat *et al.*, 1998). Hypertolerance is necessary for hyperaccumulation which is achieved through internal detoxification mediated by metal compartmentation and complexation. Metals are generally sequestered in leaf vacuoles and this is achieved through enhanced tonoplast transport of metals into vacuoles being controlled by a gene (Bert *et al.*, 2003; Küpper *et al.*, 2000; Macnair *et al.*, 1999; Vázquez *et al.*, 1994; Zhao *et al.*, 2000). The vacuole serves as the dumping site for most of the complexed metals in plants and yeast; but against the yeast, movement of Ni into vacuoles is not a pH-gradient-dependent phenomenon in plants (Ramsay and Gadd, 1997; Salt *et al.*, 1995). *Thlaspi goesingense* (Ni-hyperaccumulator) accumulates Ni by compartmentalizing intracellular Ni into leaf vacuoles (Krämer *et al.*, 2007). The Metal ion transporter gene TgMTP1 is found to be involved in transport and accumulation of Ni in shoot vacuoles (Freeman *et al.*, 2004). Vacuoles are the site of accumulation for large numbers of heavy metals including Cd and Zn (De, 2000), and Zn treatment was reported to enhance vacuolation in root meristematic cells of *Festuca rubra* L. (Davies *et al.*, 1991). Zinc, Al and Cu were found in the cell walls, vacuoles and mucilage vesicles and higher concentrations of oxygen were found in the areas where Zn, Al and Cu were localized, indicating sequestration of metals as oxides (Volland *et al.*, 2011). Among different mechanisms, metal chelation with ligands is an important mechanism adopted by plants to detoxify the metals within plant tissues (Cobbett, 2000b; Cobbett and Goldsbrough, 2002). As the metals enter the cytosol of plant cells, metal ions are bound with organic molecules, thus protecting the metabolically active sites from the toxic effects of metals (Zenk, 1996). These ligands include organic acids, amino acids, peptides and polypeptides. Phytochelatins (PCs) and metallothioneins (MTs) are the two best metal-binding polypeptide ligands in the plant cells and bind metals through thiolate coordination (Clemens *et al.*, 2002; Cobbett, 2000a; Gupta *et al.*, 1999). A mutant *Arabidopsis thaliana* is very sensitive to Cd because it does not have the enzyme 'phytochelatin synthase' but it grows well as the wild type plant at normal Zn and Cu concentrations, which are two essential metal ions, indicating that phytochelatin is only involved in resistance to metal poisoning (Cobbett *et al.*, 1998). Cadmium is complexed with citrate in the vacuole when the cell is exposed to high Cd levels (Wagner, 1993). Glutathione (GSH) is one source of non-protein thiols found in variety of cell components like cytosol, chloroplast, endoplasmic reticulum, vacuole and mitochondria (Yadav, 2010). The thiol group forms mercaptide bonds with metals, thus making them an important biochemical molecule in the protection of plants against stresses caused by metals, exogenous and endogenous organic chemicals and oxidative stress (Mullineaux and Rausch, 2005; Rausch *et al.*, 2007). Exposure of plants to metals triggers the formation of reactive oxygen species and free radicals in the plants which damage metabolic components of cells. Excess reactive oxygen species in the plant cells initiate oxidation of amino acids, proteins, membrane lipids and DNA resulting in decreased growth and development (Ogawa and Iwabuchi, 2001). GSH decreases the level of reactive species in the plants cells and thus prevents the damage caused thereby (Foyer and Noctor, 2005). GSH causes cellular detoxification of metals and xenobiotics by conjugating with such molecules through S-transferase and conjugates are transported to vacuoles (Dixon *et al.*, 2002; Edwards and Dixon, 2005; Klein *et al.*, 2006; Yazaki, 2006). In addition to its protective role, GSH is the precursor for biosynthesis of phytochelatins which are excellent heavy-metal-binding peptides (Grill *et al.*, 1988). Nickel hyperaccumulator *Thlaspi* contained higher concentrations of GSH which is strongly correlated with Ni hyperaccumulation (Freeman *et al.*, 2004). It was observed by Freeman *et al.* (2004) that elevated levels of GSH in hyperaccumulators is due to enhanced activity of Ser acetyltransferase which provides plants with the ability to detoxify non-sequestered Ni. It was reported that there was a significant increase in histidine concentration in Ni hyperaccumulator *Alyssum* when exposed to high Ni concentration. Moreover, the supply of histidine to non-accumulators caused hyperaccumulation of Ni and enhanced transport towards shoots (Krämer *et al.*, 1996). Metallothioneins (MT) are low-molecular-weight cysteine-rich metal-binding proteins and are synthesized from mRNA (Memon and Schröder, 2009). Metallothioneins are reported to be involved in metal homeostasis in different ecotypes of Arabidopsis evidenced by correlation between MT RNA and metal tolerance level of Arabidopsis (Guo *et al.*, 2003, 2008). Metal detoxifications, development of plants and resistance against abiotic stress are some of the functions listed for metallothioneins in plants (Domènech *et al.*, 2006; Roosens *et al.*, 2005; Zhou *et al.*, 2005).

Rhizosphere Changes and Root Adaptations

The rhizosphere represents the soil volume around the plant root which is directly influenced by root activity (Hinsinger *et al.*, 2005). Plants change the bioavailability of metals in the rhizosphere due to changes in elemental concentration, soil reaction (pH), partial pressure of carbon dioxide (*p*CO2) and oxygen (*p*O2), redox potential, organic ligand concentration and microbial biomass (Kidd *et al.*, 2009; Wenzel *et al.*, 1999). Plant species differ in their effects on the rhizosphere due to the nature of root exudates, nutrient absorption strategies, root architecture, soil type and properties (Hinsinger *et al.*, 2008). Plants release about 10-20% of photosynthetic carbon from roots into the rhizosphere in the form of different rhizodepositions (Singer *et al.*, 2003). Root exudates are involved in weathering of soil parent material, mobilization and enhancement of nutrient uptake and stress resistance to toxic metals. Plants can enhance metal bioavailability by altering the rhizosphere. Some plants can mobilize sparingly soluble nutrients like iron (Fe) and phosphorus (P) in soil by releasing chelators into the rhizosphere. However, evidences are very rare regarding alteration of rhizosphere by hyperaccumulators for absorption of less soluble fractions of metals in the soil. It has been reported that root exudates of *Thlaspi caerulescens* cannot mobilize heavy metals in soil; rather, roots proliferate in pursuance of Zn in the soils but the mechanism involved in sensing Zn in soil is still unknown. Others have reported the release of metal-solubilizing phytosiderophores and hydrogen ions which can chelate metals or acidify the rhizosphere and increasing metals in soil solution (Lone *et al.*, 2008; Thangavel and Subbhuraam, 2004). Additionally, rhizomicrobes like rhizobacteria and *Mycorrhizal fungi* can increase the bioavailability of heavy metals in soil (Vamerali *et al.*, 2011). Several researchers have reported that the roots of hyperaccumulators proliferate in response to metal contamination in the soil to accumulate more metals while non-hyperaccumulators restrict their root growth as a result of metal contamination in soils (Schwartz *et al.*, 1999; Whiting *et al.*, 2001). These results indicate the presence of some mechanism in the roots triggering its preferred growth towards metal-rich areas of soil which still needs to be uncovered. Hyperaccumulator plants absorb excessive metals due to high-affinity transport systems across the plasma membranes of root tissues (Lasat, 2002; Wenzel, 2009). Hyperaccumulators like *Thlaspi caerulescens* grow their roots efficiently into metal-enriched areas for excessive absorption of metals (Schwartz *et al.*, 1999), while some other researchers have reported the development of dense root systems with a large proportion of fine roots by hyperaccumulators in metal-contaminated soils which enhance metal uptake (Himmelbauer *et al.*, 2005; Keller *et al.*, 2003). Conversely, roots and root debris can adsorb cationic metals/metalloids and thus can decrease their bioavailability (Keller *et al.*, 2003). Plant root can avoid or actively fetch heavy metals from polluted soils (Keller *et al.*, 2003; Schwartz *et al.*, 2003). Plant roots can increase metal solubility by changing speciation including acidification/alkalinization, modification of the redox potential, exudation of metal chelants and organic ligands (in particular low molecular organic acids and phytosiderophores) that compete with anionic species for binding sites (Fitz and Wenzel, 2002; Puschenreiter *et al.*, 2005). Increased metal solubility is not necessarily related to increased absorption of metals by the plants (Shenker *et al.*, 2001). Hyperaccumulator plants represent the main model for phytoextraction of metals from the soils but the main question of metal mobilization by these plants through rhizosphere. changes still needs to be answered. Alternately, pH in the rhizosphere of these plants can be manipulated by using amendments. Plants can mobilize the soil-bound metals by adopting different strategies which are briefly explained below. Plants can secrete metal-chelating substances into rhizosphere such as phytosiderophores for solubilizing Fe. Largely phytosiderophores have been studied for Fe mobilization but these compounds can also mobilize other metals. Mugineic and deoxymugeneic acids from barley and corn and avenic acid from oats are considered the best studied plant phytosiderophores (Kinnersley, 1993). Histidine is reported to be used by Ni hyperaccumulator, *Alyssum lesbiacum*, for the acquisition and transport of Ni (Krämer *et al.*, 1996). Roots can release metal reductase for the reduction and solublization of soil-bound metals (Raskin *et al.*, 1997). Some plants deficient in Fe or Cu can reduce these metals by releasing certain organic compounds and thereby increase their availability and absorption by the plants (Marschner and Römheld, 1994; Mejáre and Bülow, 2001; Raskin *et al.*, 1994). Alternately, some plants solubilize metals by acidifying their rhizospheres by releasing protons (Crowley *et al.*, 1991). Mycorrhizal association with roots or root colonization by bacteria can enhance the availability of metals. Hyperaccumulator *Thlaspi* species depleted labile and EDTA extractable fractions of the metals at high concentrations, whereas labile metal pools increase at low metal concentration (Puschenreiter *et al.*, 2003). It was concluded that the rhizosphere of Ni hyperaccumulator *Thlaspi goesingense* contained higher levels of dissolved organic carbon and some sugars than that of bulk soils (Wenzel *et al.*, 2003b). This signifies the ligand-induced solublization of metals in rhizosphere which helps in hyperaccumulation of metals by this species. Efficiency of phytoextraction depends on the availability of metals in the root zone which is affected by soil factors like cation exchange capacity, pH or organic matter contents (Evangelou *et al.*, 2007; Felix, 1997; Schmidt, 2003). Growing high-biomass crops is a key factor for the success of phytoextraction; however, the problem of low mobility of metals in the soil can be overcome by enhancing the mobility through application of chelating agents (Evangelou *et al.*, 2007). The chelant-assisted mobilization of metals could be environmentally unsafe due to leaching of mobilized metals into the ground water as these overcome the absorption capacity of most of the plants.

Phytostabilization

Some soils are highly contaminated to the extent that phytoextraction of metals from such soils would take a considerably longer period of time which is neither economical nor suitable. If such soils are not remediated, these could be a major source of metal dispersion into the environment. The risk posed by such soils can be decreased by using plants to stabilize the metals in the soil (Marques *et al.*, 2009). Phytostabilizing plants can grow in metal-contaminated soils by keeping the metals in below-ground parts, immobilizing in the rhizosphere through various mechanisms. Plants provide litter, vegetative cover, v decrease the leaching losses from soil, control erosion and release organic matter to the soil and thus bind metals (Pulford and Watson, 2003; Robinson *et al.*, 2006). In phytostabilization, plants immobilize the metals in the rhizosphere thereby leaving them less bioavailable and less toxic to plants, animals and humans or retain the metals in the roots by restricting their translocation to above-ground parts (Mendez and Maier, 2008; Wong, 2003). Additionally, plants provide vegetative cover to reduce the aeolian dispersion of metals into the environment.

Mechanisms of Phytostabilization

Plants sequester the metals in the rhizosphere through adsorption and precipitation of metals into less soluble forms like carbonates and sulphides of metals, metal complexes with organic compounds, metal adsorption on root surfaces and metal accumulation in root tissues (Mendez and Maier, 2008; Wong, 2003). The presence of plants in metal-contaminated soils promotes heterotrophic microbial communities which may, in turn, promote plant growth and participate in metal stabilization. Metal-tolerant plants with the capacity to keep the metals out of metabolic sites (shoots) are the best candidates for phytostabilization. Although such plants have developed mechanisms to restrict the metals in the rhizosphere or roots, even then concentration of metals in shoots must be monitored (Mendez and Maier, 2008). The *Cynodon dactylon* was found to be the best accumulator of As in roots and thus a promising candidate for phytostabilization and have wide adaptations in Pb- and Zn-contaminated soils (Leung *et al.*, 2007). Mycorrhizae play an important role in stabilization by binding the metals with hyphae and some mycorrhizae like ericoid and *Ectomycorrhizal fungi* colonizing in *Cynodon dactylon* can modify the rhizosphere by excreting organic acids and thus stabilizing metals in the rhizosphere (Meharg, 2003). Hyphae of *Mycorrhizal fungi* contain polyphosphate which can bind heavy metals up to saturation and > 60% metals are reported to be retained in apoplast cell walls (Bücking and Heyser, 1999, 2000; Yang *et al.*, 2005). Some plants can detoxify the metals in the rhizosphere by releasing organic acids thus tendering the metals less available (Brunner *et al.*, 2008; Qin *et al.*, 2007). Another process of metal detoxification is immobilization of metals in fine roots through binding with pectins in the cell walls and to the negatively charged cytoplasm-membrane surfaces due to their strong electrochemical potential (Kochian *et al.*, 2005; Rengel and Zhang, 2003). Lupin (*Lupinus albus* L.) stabilized As and Cd in contaminated soil by increasing pH due to release of citrate and accumulation in root nodules (Vázquez *et al.*, 2006). Some plants have the ability to reduce the valence of metals by releasing redox enzymes and thus toxic metals are converted into less toxic forms (Ali *et al.*, 2013). Transformation of tetravalent chromium (more toxic) to trivalent chromium (less toxic) is the best-studied example of this strategy being adopted by the plants (Bluskov *et al.*, 2005). Some plants accumulate metals to high concentrations in their roots and restrict their translocation to shoots and thus become good candidates for phytostabilization (Pignattelli *et al.*, 2012). Phytostabilization has very promising results for stabilization of chromium and lead in soils. Hexavalent chromium (Cr6+) is highly toxic and is transformed into less soluble and less toxic trivalent chromium (Cr3+) by deep-rooted plants (Chaney *et al.*, 1997; James, 1996). Lead (Pb) is present in the soil in different species which are mostly bioavailable but the Pb-phosphate mineral, chloropyromorphite, is insoluble and non-bioavailable (Chaney *et al.*, 1997; Cotter-Howells, 1996).

Formation of chloropyromorphite is induced by roots of *Agrostis capillaris* growing in highly contaminated Pb/Zn mine waste soils (Cotter-Howells and Caporn, 1996). Norway spruce (*Picea abies*) and poplar (*Populus tremula*) accumulate 10 to 20 times more Cu and Zn in their roots compared to those plants grown in uncontaminated soils and accumulation was restricted to fine root, cell walls and epidermis (Brunner *et al.*, 2008). Plants which can survive in metal-contaminated soils without affecting growth and maintain low concentrations of metals in aerial parts, even though concentration of metals is very high in the roots, are known as metal excluder plants (Baker, 1981; Krämer, 2010; Wei *et al.*, 2005). Several plants with the potential to exclude metals from aerial parts have been identified. These include Ni-excluders such as *Silene vulgaris, Zea mays* L., Cu excluder *Hyparrhenia hirta* and Co excluder *Armeria maritima* (Brewin *et al.*, 2003; Poschenrieder *et al.*, 2001; Seregin *et al.*, 2003; Wenzel *et al.*, 2003a). Although, excluder plants can grow in metal-contaminated soils without affecting their growth and keeping metal concentration in aerial parts at minimum levels, it is most important that metal concentration should not exceed standards for agricultural products (Wei *et al.*, 2005). Plants use different strategies to exclude metals from the tissues and these may include the role of mycorrizae, cell walls and plasma membranes (Hall, 2002). Mycorrhizae can play an effective role in amelioration of metal toxicity in plants. Mycorrhizae generally adopt the same mechanisms as those are adopted by higher plants like binding to extracellular materials or sequestration in the vacuolar compartment (Hall, 2002; Tam, 1995). In relation to the role of ectomycorrhizae in metal tolerance by the host plant, most mechanisms that have been proposed involve various exclusion processes that restrict metal movement to the host roots (Jentschke and Godbold, 2000). These have been extensively reviewed and assessed and include absorption of metals by the hyphal sheath, reduced access to the apoplast due to the hydrophobicity of the fungal sheath, chelation by fungal exudates and adsorption onto the external mycelium (Jentschke and Godbold, 2000). Clearly, from the variation between species described above, these different exclusion mechanisms are likely to vary in significance between different plant-fungal interactions. Discovering the mechanisms of metal exclusion and genes responsible for metal exclusion and their ultimate induction in field crops is very important and thus can lead to the safe use of metal-contaminated soils (Wei *et al.*, 2005). Several hypotheses have been suggested regarding the mechanisms of metal exclusion. These include metal binding in cell walls, exudation of metal-chelating ligands and formation of redox and pH barriers at the plasma membrane (Taylor, 1987). There are contradictory reports about the role of the cell wall in metal tolerance of plants (Hall, 2002). Some researchers found that the cell wall plays a very minor role in metal tolerance, whereas others have found heavy metals accumulated in the cell wall as bound with protein or as silicates (Bringezu *et al.*, 1999). The cell membrane is the first living structure of the plant which is likely be damaged by metals. Metal toxicity causes leaky behaviour of the plasma membrane due to oxidation of protein thiols, inhibition of HATPase, alternation of composition and fluidity of membrane lipids (Astolfi *et al.*, 2005; Devi and Prasad, 1999; Hall, 2002). Thus protection of the plasma membrane against metal toxicity damage is the key to metal tolerance in plants. Metal-tolerant plants opt for homeostasis to sustain the high concentration of metals due to their inability to tolerate reactive oxygen species or free radicals (Dietz *et al.*, 1999; Sharma and Dietz, 2009; Panda *et al.*, 2003). Aluminium tolerance in wheat is initiated by extracellular chelation of Al with citrate and malate (Delhaize and Ryan, 1995) and release of organic acids from roots has also been reported in Al-resistant Arabidopsis (Larsen *et al.*, 1998). Phytostabilization is considered a very good alternative for those soils which cannot be immediately remediated through phytoextraction. Efficiency of phytostabilization can be enhanced by involving soil amendments like zeolites, beringite, steel shot and hydroxyapatite (Lothenbach *et al.*, 1998). *Vetiveria zizanioides, Sesbania rostrata,* herb legume and *Leucaena leucocephala* have been successfully grown in metal-contaminated soils for metal stabilization (Shu *et al.*, 2002; Zhang *et al.*, 2001).

Phytovolatilization

Transformation of toxic metals and metalloids like mercury (Hg), selenium (Se) and arsenic (As) into less toxic and volatile forms released through foliage by plants into the atmosphere is known as phytovolatilization (Malik and Biswas, 2012; Marques *et al.*, 2009). In phytostabilization metals are assimilated into organic compounds which are volatile in nature and ultimately released into atmosphere as biomolecules (Marques *et al.*, 2009). *Brassica Juncea* has been shown to volatilize Se into the atmosphere through assimilation of Se from the soil into organic seleno-amino acids, seleno-cysteine and seleno-methionine which later can be biomethylated to form the volatile compound dimethylselenide (Banuelos *et al.*, 1993; Banuelos and Meek, 1990; Terry *et al.*, 2000). A gene responsible for reducing mercuric ion into elemental mercury through enzyme mercury reductase has been introduced into *Arabidopsis thaliana* which ultimately volatilizes large amounts of Hg into the atmosphere (Rugh *et al.*, 1996). The practical application of phytovolatilization is questioned due to the release of toxic volatile compounds into the atmosphere and a risk assessment should be done. However, some researchers have reported that volatile compounds released into the atmosphere are dispersed and diluted in the atmosphere and pose no environmental risk (Lin *et al.*, 2000; Meagher *et al.*, 2000). Arsenic was successfully volatilized in a frond of *Pteris vittata* in the form of arsenic compounds, arsenite and arsenate (Sakakibara *et al.*, 2010).

PLANT USED FOR PHYTOREMEDIATION

Indian Mustard (*Brassica juncea L.*)

Brassicaceae species can accumulate certain metals while producing high quantities of biomass in the process and Indian mustard is the best among them as it is tolerant to heavy metals, grows fast and produces large amount of above ground biomass. Indian mustard can remove three times more cadmium than others, it also reduces 28% of lead and 48 % of selenium. It is also effective against Zinc, Mercury and Copper as well. *Brassica juncea* accumulate heavy metals like cadmium, chromium, copper, nickel, lead and zinc in the above ground parts, but some studies has shown that both *Brassica napus* and *Brassica juncea* accumulated more Copper in roots than in shoots under Copper stress for 7 and 14 days in hydroponic solution [Feigle *et al.*, 2013].

White Willows (*Salix species*)

Salix alba is a water loving plant and it has shown great response to heavy metals and diesels. It can accumulate heavy metals like cadmium, lead, nickel in their root. But the accumulation levels of heavy metals and diesel pollutants were higher in the case of the *Brassicaceae* family. Significant results were shown on the Cadmium, lead and zinc accumulation in and among plant parts of willow *Salix species*. Metals can be accumulated in all plant organs in different concentrations and the metal accumulates in the tissues would be increased with exposure time. Furthermore, the effect of soil pH on metal accumulation, and the correlation between metals were analysed. Cadmium, Lead and Zinc accumulation were found in root, stem, twig, and leaf of willow species. Results showed that all parts of willow species accumulated significantly more Cadmium, Lead and Zinc in contaminated soils than in uncontaminated soils. However, the metal accumulation was significantly different among plant parts. Willow species were proven to be prosperous accumulators of Cd (twigs and leaves), Pb (roots and twigs) and Zn (twigs). We found that Cadmium accumulation rates in stems are higher in soils with lower pH. A significant positive correlation was found between the accumulations of Cd and Zn in stems. Accumulation rates of Cd (both in leaves and twigs) and Zn (in twigs) were increased significantly with exposure time and the accumulation was successful for at least 3 years [Tozser de *et al.* 2017].

Poplar Tree (*Populus deltoids*)

Plants have several defense mechanisms against the harmful effects of heavy metals present in excess in soils and ground-waters. Poplars (*Populus spp.*) are widely cultivated because of their rapid growth and high biomass production and have naturally well-designed root system which take up large quantities of water, so they are used as an experimental model for phytoremediation purposes. According to the research from National Institute of Environmental Health Sciences, Chlorinated solvents such as trichloroethylene, or the well-known carcinogenic carbon tetrachloride (95% of substance removed) is the organic pollutants that hybrid poplars remediates.

Sunflower (*Helianthus annus*)

Helianthus annus is considered as the bioindicator of Lead. Helianthus annus is useful as a lead accumulator in the contaminated areas. They accumulate lead in all plant parts, highest lead accumulation in *Helianthus annus* was seen in roots and leaves followed by stem and seeds. This plant can also accumulate zinc. Studies found that translocation of zinc was higher than lead from root to shoot.

Rye Grass (*Lolium perenne L.*)

This plant has the capability to alter the metal distribution in the soil, indicating phytostabilization of the contaminants. Rye grass has the ability to phytostabilise Lead present in the contaminated site making the polluted area more sustainable for other varieties of vegetation to grow. They reduce the contaminant migration from the soil to the groundwater as rye grass can induce immobilization of the contaminants.

Eucalyptus (*Eucalyptus Globulus*)

Eucalyptus is an interesting plant for phytoremediation purposes due to its high transpiration activity. It has been employed mainly in hydraulic containment of landfill leachate and contaminated area drainage. Moreover the rapid growth and the potential use of the wood for energy and paper production has made Eucalyptus important for secondary wastewater treatment through tree irrigation. Eucalyptus is tolerant to heavy metals like cadmium, zinc, copper, lead and to arsenic, which tend to accumulate these heavy metal (King *et al.*, 2008; Arrigada *et al.*, 2010; Peng *et al.*, 2012; Gomes *et al.*, 2012; Fine *et al.*, 2013).

CONCLUSION

Metal contamination of soils is a widespread problem around the globe with varying intensities and magnitudes in different regions. Several remediation technologies have already been discussed in detail elsewhere with each one carrying a wide range of merits and demerits. Every technology is aimed at the safe use of metal-contaminated soils for environmental quality and safe food chains. Among all remediation methods, phytoremediation is considered to be environmentally friendly, non-disruptive and low in cost. At the same time, adoption of phytoremediation technology on a commercial scale warrants serious consideration of issues of being slow and time consuming and the fate of the plants being used. A variety of plants have been identified which are capable of accumulating high concentrations of metals in their aerial parts (phytoextraction), retaining the metals in roots or stabilizing the metals in soils and thus restricting their translocation to the shoots (phytostabilization) and removing the metals from the soil through synthesis of volatile compounds (phytovolatilization). Each of the aforementioned technologies involves distinct mechanisms which are already explained in detail. The choice of phytoremediation technology to be employed for remediation of metal-contaminated sites depends on soil type, metal type, degree and extent of contamination and environmental disturbance involved. An understanding of the different mechanisms involved would really improve the decision making in the adoption of a specific technology. Among different phytoremediation technologies, phytoextraction is being widely used and a wide range of hyperaccumulator plants capable of accumulating high concentrations of metals have been identified. However, most of hyperaccumulators are slow growing and low-biomass-producing plants which make this technology a slow process. Chelant-assisted phytoextraction through fast-growing and high-biomass-producing plants is an alternative option, but leaching or run-off of solubilized metals into surface and sub-surface water bodies is a serious issue. Identification and induction of genes responsible for hyperaccumulation in hyperaccumulator plants into those plants which are capable of accumulating metals and producing high biomass could revolutionize the phytoremediation technology.

REFERENCES

Ali, H., Khan, E., Sajad, M.A., 2013. Phytoremediation of Heavy Metals—Concepts and Applications. Chemosphere, 91, 869-881.

Alkorta, I., Hernández-Allica, J., Becerril, J., Amezaga, I., Albizu, I., Garbisu, C., 2004. Recent Findings on the Phytoremediation of Soils Contaminated with Environmentally Toxic Heavy Metals and Metalloids such as Zinc, Cadmium, Lead, and Arsenic. Rev. Environ. Sci. Biotechnol. 3, 71-90.

Anjum, N.A., Ahmad, I., Mohmood, I., Pacheco, M., Duarte, A.C., Pereira, E., Umar, S., Ahmad, A., Khan, N.A., Iqbal, M., 2012. Modulation of Glutathione and its Related Enzymes in Plants' Responses to Toxic Metals and Metalloids—A Review. Environ. Exp. Bot. 75, 307-324.

Astolfi, S., Zuchi, S., Passera, C., 2005. Effect of Cadmium on H+ATPase Activity of Plasma Membrane Vesicles Isolated from Roots of Different S-supplied Maize *Zea mays* L Plants. Plant Science 169, 361-368.

Baker, A.J., 1981. Accumulators and Excluders-strategies in the Response of Plants to Heavy Metals. J. Plant Nutr. 3, 643-654.

Banuelos, G., Cardon, G., Mackey, B., Ben-Asher, J., Wu, L., Beuselinck, P., Akohoue, S., Zambrzuski, S., 1993. Boron and Selenium Removal in Boron-laden Soils by Four Sprinkler Irrigated Plant Species. J. Environ. Qual. 22, 786-792.

Banuelos, G., Meek, D., 1990. Accumulation of Selenium in Plants Grown on Selenium-treated Soil. J. Environ. Qual. 19, 772-777.

Bert, V., Meerts, P., Saumitou-Laprade, P., Salis, P., Gruber, W., Verbruggen, N., 2003. Genetic basis of Cd Tolerance and Hyperaccumulation in *Arabidopsis halleri*. Plant and Soil 249, 9-18.

Bluskov, S., Arocena, J., Omotoso, O., Young, J., 2005. Uptake, Distribution, and Speciation of Chromium in *Brassica juncea*. Int. J. Phytoremediation 7, 153-165.

Brewin, L., Mehra, A., Lynch, P., Farago, M., 2003. Mechanisms of Copper Tolerance by *Armeria maritima* in Dolfrwynog Bog, North Wales-Initial Studies. Environmental Geochemistry and Health 25, 147-156.

Bringezu, K., Lichtenberger, O., Leopold, I., Neumann, D., 1999. Heavy Metal Tolerance of *Silene vulgaris*. J. Plant Physiol. 154, 536-546.

Brunner, I., Luster, J., Günthardt-Goerg, M.S., Frey, B., 2008. Heavy Metal Accumulation and Phytostabilisation Potential of Tree Fine Roots in a Contaminated Soil. Environ. Pollut. 152, 559-568.

Bücking, H., Heyser, W., 1999. Elemental Composition and Function of Polyphosphates in *Ectomycorrhizal fungi*—an X-ray Microanalytical Study. Mycol. Res. 103, 31-39.

Bücking, H., Heyser, W., 2000. Subcellular Compartmentation of Elements in Non-mycorrhizal and Mycorrhizal Roots of *Pinus sylvestris*: An X-ray Microanalytical Study. I. The Distribution of Phosphate. New Phytol. 145, 311-320.

Chaney, R.L., Angle, J.S., Broadhurst, C.L., Peters, C.A., Tappero, R.V., Sparks, D.L., 2007. Improved Understanding of Hyperaccumulation yields Commercial Phytoextraction and Phytomining Technologies. J. Environ. Qual. 36, 1429-1443.

Chaney, R.L., Malik, M., Li, Y.M., Brown, S.L., Brewer, E.P., Angle, J.S., Baker, A.J.M., 1997. Phytoremediation of Soil Metals. Curr. Opin. Biotechnol. 8, 279-284.

Chaudhry, T., Hayes, W., Khan, A., Khoo, C., 1998. Phytoremediation—focusing on Accumulator Plants that Remediate Metal-contaminated Soils. Australas. J. Ecotoxicol. 4, 37-51.

Clemens, S., Palmgren, M.G., Krämer, U., 2002. A Long way Ahead: Understanding and Engineering Plant Metal Accumulation. Trends Plant Sci. 7, 309-315.

Cobbett, C., Goldsbrough, P., 2002. Phytochelatins and Metallothioneins: Roles in Heavy Metal Detoxification and Homeostasis. Annu. Rev. Plant Biol. 53, 159-182.

Cobbett, C.S., 2000a. Phytochelatin Biosynthesis and Function in Heavy-metal Detoxification. Curr. Opin. Plant Biol. 3, 211-216.

Cobbett, C.S., 2000b. Phytochelatins and their Roles in Heavy Metal Detoxification. Plant Physiol. 123, 825-832.

Cobbett, C.S., May, M.J., Howden, R., Rolls, B., 1998. The Glutathione-deficient, Cadmium-sensitive Mutant, cad2-1, of Arabidopsis Thaliana is Deficient in γ-glutamylcysteine synthetase. Plant J. 16, 73–78.

Cotter-Howells, J., 1996. Lead Phosphate Formation in Soils. Environ. Pollut. 93, 9-16.

Cotter-Howells, J., Caporn, S., 1996. Remediation of Contaminated Land by Formation of Heavy Metal Phosphates. Appl. Geochem. 11, 335-342.

Crowley, D., Wang, Y., Reid, C., Szaniszlo, P., 1991. Mechanisms of Iron Acquisition from Siderophores by Microorganisms and Plants. Plant and Soil 130, 179-198.

Davies, K., Davies, M., Francis, D., 1991. The Influence of an Inhibitor of Phytochelatin Synthesis on Root Growth and Root Meristematic Activity in *Festuca rubra* L. in Response to zinc. New Phytol. 118, 565-570.

De, D., 2000. Plant Cell Vacuoles: An Introduction. Csiro Publishing.

Delhaize, E., Ryan, P.R., 1995. Aluminum Toxicity and Tolerance in Plants. Plant Physiology 107, 315.

Devi, S.R., Prasad, M., 1999. Membrane Lipid Alterations in Heavy Metal Exposed Plants, Heavy Metal Stress in Plants. Springer, 99-116.

Dietz, K.-J., Baier, M., Krämer, U., 1999. Free Radicals and Reactive Oxygen Species as Mediators of Heavy Metal Toxicity in Plants, Heavy Metal Stress in Plants. Springer, 73-97.

Dixon, D.P., Lapthorn, A., Edwards, R., 2002. Plant Glutathione Transferases. Genome Biol. 3, 3004. 3001-3004.3010.

Domènech, J., Mir, G., Huguet, G., Capdevila, M., Molinas, M., Atrian, S., 2006. Plant Metallothionein Domains: Functional Insight into Physiological Metal Binding and Protein Folding. Biochimie 88, 583-593.

Edwards, R., Dixon, D.P., 2005. Plant Glutathione Transferases. Methods Enzymol. 401, 169-186.

Evangelou, M.W., Ebel, M., Schaeffer, A., 2007. Chelate Assisted Phytoextraction of Heavy Metals from Soil. Effect, Mechanism, Toxicity, and Fate of Chelating Agents. Chemosphere 68, 989-1003.

Felix, H., 1997. Field Trials for *in situ* Decontamination of Heavy Metal Polluted Soils using Crops of Metal-accumulating Plants. Zeitschrift für Pflanzenernährung und Bodenkunde 160, 525-529.

Fitz, W.J., Wenzel, W.W., 2002. Arsenic Transformations in the Soil-rhizosphere-plant System: Fundamentals and Potential Application to Phytoremediation. J. Biotechnol. 99, 259-278.

Foyer, C.H., Noctor, G., 2005. Redox Homeostasis and Antioxidant Signaling: A Metabolic Interface between Stress Perception and Physiological Responses. The Plant Cell Online 17, 1866-1875.

Freeman, J.L., Persans, M.W., Nieman, K., Albrecht, C., Peer, W., Pickering, I.J., Salt, D.E., 2004. Increased Glutathione Biosynthesis Plays a Role in Nickel Tolerance in *Thlaspi nickel hyperaccumulators*. The Plant Cell Online 16, 2176-2191.

Garbisu, C., Alkorta, I., 2001. Phytoextraction: A Cost-effective Plant-based Technology for the Removal of Metals from the Environment. Bioresour. Technol. 77, 229-236.

Gisbert, C., Ros, R., De Haro, A., Walker, D.J., Pilar Bernal, M., Serrano, R., Navarro-Aviñó, J., 2003. A Plant Genetically Modified that Accumulates Pb is Especially Promising for Phytoremediation. Biochem. Biophys. Res. Commun. 303, 440-445.

Grill, E., Thumann, J., Winnacker, E., Zenk, M., 1988. Induction of Heavy-metal Binding Phytochelatins by Inoculation of Cell Cultures in Standard Media. Plant Cell Rep. 7, 375-378.

Guo, W.-J., Meetam, M., Goldsbrough, P.B., 2008. Examining the Specific Contributions of Individual *Arabidopsis metallothioneins* to Copper Distribution and Metal Tolerance. Plant Physiol. 146, 1697-1706.

Guo, W.J., Bundithya, W., Goldsbrough, P.B., 2003. Characterization of the *Arabidopsis metallothionein* Gene Family: Tissue-specific Expression and Induction during Senescence and in Response to Copper. New Phytol. 159, 369-381.

Gupta, D., Huang, H., Yang, X., Razafindrabe, B., Inouhe, M., 2010. The Detoxification of Lead in *Sedum alfredii* H. is not related to Phytochelatins but the Glutathione. J. Hazard. Mater. 177, 437-444.

Gupta, M., Tripathi, R., Rai, U., Haq, W., 1999. Lead induced Synthesis of Metal Binding Peptides (Phytochelatins) in Submerged Macrophyte *Vallisneria spiralis* L. Physiol. Mol. Biol. Plants 5, 173-180.

Gustin, J.L., Loureiro, M.E., Kim, D., Na, G., Tikhonova, M., Salt, D.E., 2009. MTP1-dependent Zn Sequestration into Shoot Vacuoles Suggests Dual Roles in Zn Tolerance and Accumulation in Zn-hyperaccumulating Plants. Plant J. 57, 1116-1127.

Hall, J., 2002. Cellular Mechanisms for Heavy Metal Detoxification and Tolerance. J. Exp. Bot. 53, 1-11.

Hammond, J.P., Bowen, H.C., White, P.J., Mills, V., Pyke, K.A., Baker, A.J., Whiting, S.N., May, S.T., Broadley, M.R., 2006. A Comparison of the *Thlaspi caerulescens* and *Thlaspi arvense* Shoot Transcriptomes. New Phytol. 170, 239-260.

He, Z.-l., Yang, X.-e., 2007. Role of Soil Rhizobacteria in Phytoremediation of Heavy Metal Contaminated Soils. J. Zhejiang Univ. Sci. B 8, 192-207.

Himmelbauer, M.L., Puschenreiter, M., Schnepf, A., Loiskandl, W., Wenzel, W.W., 2005. Root Morphology of *Thlaspi goesingense* Hálácsy Grown on a Serpentine Soil. J. Plant Nutr. Soil Sci. 168, 138-144.

Hinsinger, P., Courchesne, F., Violante, A., Huang, P., Gadd, G., 2008. Biogeochemistry of Metals and Metalloids at the Soil–root Interface. John Wiley & Sons, Hoboken, NJ.

Hinsinger, P., Gobran, G.R., Gregory, P.J., Wenzel, W.W., 2005. Rhizosphere Geometry and Heterogeneity Arising from Root-mediated Physical and Chemical Processes. New Phytol. 168, 293-303.

Hussain, S.I., Ghafoor, A., Ahmad, S., Murtaza, G., Sabir, M., 2006. Irrigation of Crops with Raw Sewage: Hazard Assessment of Effluent, Soil and Vegetables. Pak. J. Agric. Sci. 43, 97-102.

James, B.R., 1996. Peer Reviewed: The Challenge of Remediating Chromium-contaminated Soil. Environ. Sci. Technol. 30, 248A-251A.

Jentschke, G., Godbold, D., 2000. Metal Toxicity and Ectomycorrhizas. Physiologia Plantarum 109, 107-116.

Keller, C., Hammer, D., Kayser, A., Richner, W., Brodbeck, M., Sennhauser, M., 2003. Root Development and Heavy Metal Phytoextraction Efficiency: Comparison of different Plant Species in the Field. Plant and Soil 249, 67-81.

Kerkeb, L., Krämer, U., 2003. The Role of Free Histidine in Xylem Loading of Nickel in *Alyssum lesbiacum* and *Brassica juncea*. Plant Physiol. 131, 716-724.

Kidd, P., Barceló, J., Bernal, M.P., Navari-Izzo, F., Poschenrieder, C., Shilev, S., Clemente, R., Monterroso, C., 2009. Trace Element Behaviour at the Root–soil Interface: Implications in Phytoremediation. Environ. Exp. Bot. 67, 243-259.

Kinnersley, A.M., 1993. The Role of Phytochelates in Plant Growth and Productivity. Plant Growth Regul. 12, 207-218.

Klein, M., Burla, B., Martinoia, E., 2006. The Multidrug Resistance-associated Protein (MRP/ABCC) Subfamily of ATP-binding Cassette Transporters in Plants. FEBS Lett. 580, 1112-1122.

Kochian, L.V., Pineros, M.A., Hoekenga, O.A., 2005. The Physiology, Genetics and Molecular Biology of Plant Aluminum Resistance and Toxicity. Plant and Soil 274, 175-195.

Krämer, U., 2010. Metal Hyperaccumulation in Plants. Annu. Rev. Plant Biol. 61, 517-534.

Krämer, U., Cotter-Howells, J.D., Charnock, J.M., Baker, A.J., Smith, J.A.C., 1996. Free Histidine as a Metal Chelator in Plants that Accumulate Nickel. Nature, 379, 635-638.

Krämer, U., Talke, I.N., Hanikenne, M., 2007. Transition Metal Transport. FEBS Lett. 581, 2263-2272.

Küpper, H., Zhao, F.J., McGrath, S.P., 1999. Cellular Compartmentation of Zinc in Leaves of the Hyperaccumulator *Thlaspi caerulescens*. Plant Physiol. 119, 305-312. Küpper, H., Lombi, E., Zhao, F.-J., McGrath, S.P., 2000. Cellular Compartmentation of Cadmium and Zinc in Relation to other Elements in the Hyperaccumulator *Arabidopsis halleri*. Planta 212, 75-84.

Larsen, P.B., Degenhardt, J., Tai, C.-Y., Stenzler, L.M., Howell, S.H., Kochian, L.V., 1998. Aluminum-resistant Arabidopsis Mutants that Exhibit Altered Patterns of Aluminum Accumulation and Organic Acid Release from Roots. Plant Physiology 117, 9-17.

Lasat, M.M., 2002. Phytoextraction of Toxic Metals. J. Environ. Qual. 31, 109-120.

Lasat, M.M., Baker, A.J., Kochian, L.V., 1998. Altered Zn Compartmentation in the Root Symplasm and Stimulated Zn Absorption into the Leaf as Mechanisms Involved in Zn Hyperaccumulation in *Thlaspi caerulescens*. Plant Physiol. 118, 875-883.

Leung, H., Ye, Z., Wong, M., 2007. Survival Strategies of Plants Associated with Arbuscular *Mycorrhizal fungi* on Toxic Mine Tailings. Chemosphere 66, 905-915.

Lin, Z.-Q., Schemenauer, R., Cervinka, V., Zayed, A., Lee, A., Terry, N., 2000. Selenium Volatilization from a Soil–Plant System for the Remediation of Contaminated Water and Soil in the San Joaquin Valley. J. Environ. Qual. 29, 1048-1056.

Lombi, E., Tearall, K.L., Howarth, J.R., Zhao, F.-J., Hawkesford, M.J., McGrath, S.P., 2002. Influence of Iron Status on Cadmium and Zinc uptake by Different Ecotypes of the Hyperaccumulator *Thlaspi caerulescens*. Plant Physiol. 128, 1359-1367.

Lone, M.I., He, Z.-l., Stoffella, P.J., Yang, X.-e, 2008. Phytoremediation of Heavy Metal Polluted Soils and Water: Progresses and Perspectives. J. Zhejiang Univ. Sci. B 9, 210-220.

Lothenbach, B., Krebs, R., Furrer, G., Gupta, S., Schulin, R., 1998. Immobilization of Cadmium and Zinc in Soil by Al-montmorillonite and Gravel Sludge. Eur. J. Soil Sci. 49, 141-148.

Macnair, M.R., Bert, V., Huitson, S.B., Saumitou-Laprade, P., Petit, D., 1999. Zinc Tolerance and Hyperaccumulation are Genetically Independent Characters. Proceedings of the Royal Society of London. Series B: Biological Sciences 266, 2175-2179.

Malik, N., Biswas, A., 2012. Role of Higher Plants in Remediation of Metal Contaminated Sites. Sci. Rev. Chem. Commun. 2, 141-146.

Marques, A.P., Rangel, A.O., Castro, P.M., 2009. Remediation of Heavy Metal Contaminated Soils: Phytoremediation as a Potentially Promising Clean-up Technology. Crit. Rev. Environ. Sci. Technol. 39, 622-654.

Marschner, H., Römheld, V., 1994. Strategies of Plants for Acquisition of Iron. Plant and Soil 165, 261-274.

McGrath, S., Shen, Z., Zhao, F., 1997. Heavy Metal uptake and Chemical Changes in the Rhizosphere of *Thlaspi caerulescens* and *Thlaspi ochroleucum* Grown in Contaminated Soils. Plant and Soil 188, 153-159.

McGrath, S., Zhao, F., Lombi, E., 2001. Plant and Rhizosphere Processes Involved in Phytoremediation of Metal-contaminated Soils. Plant and Soil 232, 207-214.

McGrath, S.P., Zhao, F.-J., 2003. Phytoextraction of Metals and Metalloids from Contaminated Soils. Curr. Opin. Biotechnol. 14, 277-282.

McIntyre, T., 2003. Phytoremediation of Heavy Metals from Soils, Phytoremediation. Springer. pp. 97-123.

Meagher, R., Rugh, C., Kandasamy, M., Gragson, G., Wang, N., 2000. Engineered Phytoremediation of Mercury Pollution in Soil and Water using Bacterial Genes. Phytoremediation of Contaminated Soil and Water. Lewis Publishers, Boca Raton, FL. 201-219.

Meers, E., Ruttens, A., Hopgood, M., Samson, D., Tack, F., 2005. Comparison of EDTA and EDDS as Potential Soil Amendments for Enhanced Phytoextraction of Heavy Metals. Chemosphere 58, 1011-1022.

Meharg, A.A., 2003. The Mechanistic basis of Interactions between Mycorrhizal Associations and Toxic Metal cations. Mycol. Res. 107, 1253-1265.

Mejáre, M., Bülow, L., 2001. Metal-binding Proteins and Peptides in Bioremediation and Phytoremediation of Heavy Metals. Trends. Biotechnol. 19, 67-73.

Memon, A.R., Schröder, P., 2009. Implications of Metal Accumulation Mechanisms to Phytoremediation. Environ. Sci. Pollut. Res. 16, 162-175.

Mendez, M.O., Maier, R.M., 2008. Phytostabilization of Mine Tailings in Arid and Semiarid Environments—an Emerging Remediation Technology. Environ. Health Perspect. 116, 278.

Mishra, S., Tripathi, R., Srivastava, S., Dwivedi, S., Trivedi, P.K., Dhankher, O., Khare, A., 2009. Thiol Metabolism Play Significant Role during Cadmium Detoxification by *Ceratophyllum demersum* L. Bioresour. Technol. 100, 2155-2161.

Mullineaux, P.M., Rausch, T., 2005. Glutathione, Photosynthesis and the Redox Regulation of Stress-responsive Gene Expression. Photosynth. Res. 86, 459-474.

Murtaza, G., Ghafoor, A., Qadir, M., Owens, G., Aziz, M., Zia, M., 2010. Disposal and use of Sewage on Agricultural Lands in Pakistan: A Review. Pedosphere 20, 23-34.

Ogawa, K.I., Iwabuchi, M., 2001. A Mechanism for Promoting the Germination of *Zinnia elegans* Seeds by Hydrogen Peroxide. Plant and Cell Physiol. 42, 286-291.

Panda, S., Chaudhury, I., Khan, M., 2003. Heavy Metals Induce Lipid Peroxidation and Affect Antioxidants in Wheat Leaves. Biologia Plantarum 46, 289-294.

Peng, K., Li, X., Luo, C., Shen, Z., 2006. Vegetation Composition and Heavy metal uptake by Wild Plants at Three Contaminated sites in Xiangxi Area, China. J. Environ. Sci. Health. A 41, 65-76.

Persans, M.W., Nieman, K., Salt, D.E., 2001. Functional Activity and Role of Cation-efflux Family Members in Ni hyperaccumulation in *Thlaspi goesingense*. Proc. Natl. Acad. Sci. 98, 9995-10,000.

Pignattelli, S., Colzi, I., Buccianti, A., Cecchi, L., Arnetoli, M., Monnanni, R., Gabbrielli, R., Gonnelli, C., 2012. Exploring Element Accumulation Patterns of a Metal Excluder Plant Naturally Colonizing a Highly Contaminated Soil. J. Hazard. Mater. 227, 362-369.

Poschenrieder, C., Bech, J., Llugany, M., Pace, A., Fenés, E., Barceló, J., 2001. Copper in Plant Species in a Copper Gradient in Catalonia (North East Spain) and their Potential for Phytoremediation. Plant and Soil 230, 247-256.

Pulford, I., Watson, C., 2003. Phytoremediation of Heavy Metal-contaminated Land by Trees—A Review. Environ. Int. 29, 529-540.

Puschenreiter, M., Schnepf, A., Millan, I.M., Fitz, W.J., Horak, O., Klepp, J., Schrefl, T., Lombi, E., Wenzel, W.W., 2005. Changes of Ni Biogeochemistry in the Rhizosphere of the Hyperaccumulator *Thlaspi goesingense*. Plant and Soil 271, 205-218.

Puschenreiter, M., Wieczorek, S., Horak, O., Wenzel, W.W., 2003. Chemical Changes in the Rhizosphere of Metal Hyperaccumulator and Excluder Thlaspi species. J. Plant Nutr. Soil Sci. 166, 579-584.

Qin, R., Hirano, Y., Brunner, I., 2007. Exudation of Organic Acid Anions from Poplar Roots after Exposure to Al, Cu and Zn. Tree Physiol. 27, 313-320.

Ramsay, L.M., Gadd, G.M., 1997. Mutants of *Saccharomyces cerevisiae* Defective in Vacuolar Function Confirm a Role for the Vacuole in Toxic Metal ion Detoxification. FEMS Microbiol. Lett. 152, 293-298.

Rascio, N., Navari-Izzo, F., 2011. Heavy Metal Hyperaccumulating Plants: How and why do they do it? And what makes them so Interesting? Plant Sci. 180, 169-181.

Raskin, I., Kumar, P., Dushenkov, S., Salt, D.E., 1994. Bioconcentration of Heavy Metals by Plants. Curr. Opin. Biotechnol. 5, 285-290.

Raskin, I., Smith, R.D., Salt, D.E., 1997. Phytoremediation of Metals: Using Plants to Remove Pollutants from the Environment. Curr. Opin. Biotechnol. 8, 221-226.

Rausch, T., Gromes, R., Liedschulte, V., Müller, I., Bogs, J., Galovic, V., Wachter, A., 2007. Novel insight into the Regulation of GSH Biosynthesis in Higher Plants. Plant Biol. 9, 565-572.

Rengel, Z., Zhang, W.H., 2003. Role of Dynamics of Intracellular Calcium in Aluminium-toxicity Syndrome. New Phytol. 159, 295-314.

Robinson, B., Schulin, R., Nowack, B., Roulier, S., Menon, M., Clothier, B., Green, S., Mills, T., 2006. Phytoremediation for the Management of Metal Flux in Contaminated Sites. Forest Snow and Landscape Res. 80, 221-224.

Roosens, N.H., Leplae, R., Bernard, C., Verbruggen, N., 2005. Variations in Plant Metallothioneins: The Heavy Metal Hyperaccumulator *Thlaspi caerulescens* as a Study Case. Planta 222, 716-729.

Rugh, C.L., Wilde, H.D., Stack, N.M., Thompson, D.M., Summers, A.O., Meagher, R.B., 1996. Mercuric Ion Reduction and Resistance in Transgenic *Arabidopsis thaliana* Plants Expressing a Modified Bacterial merA gene. Proc. Natl. Acad. Sci. 93, 3182-3187.

Saifullah, Meers, E., Qadir, M., de Caritat, P., Tack, F.M.G., Du Laing, G., Zia, M.H., 2009. EDTA-assisted Pb Phytoextraction. Chemosphere 74, 1279-1291.

Sakakibara, M., Watanabe, A., Inoue, M., Sano, S., Kaise, T., 2010. Phytoextraction and Phytovolatilization of Arsenic from As-contaminated Soils by *Pteris vittata*. Proceedings of the Annual International Conference on Soils, 26. Sediments, Water and Energy.

Salt, D.E., Blaylock, M., Kumar, N.P., Dushenkov, V., Ensley, B.D., Chet, I., Raskin, I., 1995. Phytoremediation: A Novel Strategy for the Removal of Toxic Metals from the Environment using Plants. Nat. Biotechnol. 13, 468-474.

Schmidt, U., 2003. Enhancing Phytoextraction. J. Environ. Qual. 32, 1939-1954.

Schwartz, C., Echevarria, G., Morel, J.L., 2003. Phytoextraction of Cadmium with *Thlaspi caerulescens*. Plant and Soil 249, 27-35.

Schwartz, C., Morel, J.L., Saumier, S., Whiting, S.N., Baker, A.J., 1999. Root Development of the Zinc-hyperaccumulator Plant *Thlaspi caerulescens* as Affected by Metal Origin, Content and Localization in Soil. Plant and Soil 208, 103-115.

Seregin, I., Kozhevnikova, A., Kazyumina, E., Ivanov, V., 2003. Nickel Toxicity and Distribution in Maize Roots. Russian Journal of Plant Physiology 50, 711-717.

Seth, C.S., Kumar Chaturvedi, P., Misra, V., 2008. The Role of Phytochelatins and Antioxidants in Tolerance to Cd Accumulation in *Brassica juncea* L. Ecotoxicol. environ. saf. 71, 76-85.

Sharma, S.S., Dietz, K.-J., 2009. The Relationship between Metal Toxicity and Cellular Redox Imbalance. Trends in Plant Science 14, 43-50.

Shenker, M., Fan, T.-M., Crowley, D., 2001. Phytosiderophores Influence on Cadmium Mobilization and uptake by Wheat and Barley Plants. J. Environ. Qual. 30, 2091-2098.

Shu, W., Xia, H., Zhang, Z., Lan, C., Wong, M., 2002. Use of Vetiver and Three other Grasses for Revegetation of Pb/Zn Mine Tailings: Field Experiment. Int. J. Phytoremediation 4, 47-57.

Singer, A.C., Crowley, D.E., Thompson, I.P., 2003. Secondary Plant Metabolites in Phytoremediation and Biotransformation. Trends. Biotechnol. 21, 123-130.

Steinkellner, H., Mun-Sik, K., Helma, C., Ecker, S., Ma, T.H., Horak, O., Kundi, M., Knasmüller, S., 1998. Genotoxic Effects of Heavy Metals: Comparative Investigation with Plant Bioassays. Environ. Mol. Mutagen. 31, 183-191.

Sun, Q., Ye, Z.H., Wang, X.R., Wong, M.H., 2007. Cadmium Hyperaccumulation Leads to an Increase of Glutathione rather than Phytochelatins in the Cadmium Hyperaccumulator *Sedum alfredii*. J. Plant Physiol. 164, 1489-1498.

Tam, P.C., 1995. Heavy Metal Tolerance by Ectomycorrhizal Fungi and Metal Amelioration by *Pisolithus tinctorius*. Mycorrhiza 5, 181-187.

Taylor, G.J., 1987. Exclusion of Metals from the Symplasm: A Possible Mechanism of Metal Tolerance in Higher Plants. J. Plant Nutr. 10, 1213-1222.

Terry, N., Zayed, A., De Souza, M., Tarun, A., 2000. Selenium in Higher Plants. Annu. rev. Plant Biol. 51, 401-432.

Thangavel, P., Subbhuraam, C., 2004. Phytoextraction: Role of Hyperaccumulators in Metal Contaminated Soils. Proc. Indian Natl. Sci. Acad. B 70, 109-130.

Vamerali, T., Bandiera, M., Mosca, G., 2011. *In situ* Phytoremediation of Arsenic- and Metal-polluted Pyrite Waste with Field Crops: Effects of Soil Management. Chemosphere 83, 1241-1248.

Vázquez, M., Poschenrieder, C., Barcelo, J., Baker, A., Hatton, P., Cope, G., 1994. Compartmentation of Zinc in Roots and Leaves of the Zinc Hyperaccumulator *Thlaspi caerulescens* J. & C. Presl. Bot. Acta 107, 243-250.

Vázquez, S., Agha, R., Granado, A., Sarro, M., Esteban, E., Peñalosa, J., Carpena, R., 2006. Use of White Lupin Plant for Phytostabilization of Cd and As Polluted Acid Soil. Water, Air, and Soil Pollut. 177, 349-365.

Volland, S., Andosch, A., Milla, M., Stöger, B., Lütz, C., Lütz-Meindl, U., 2011. Intracellular Metal Compartmentalization in the Green Algal Model System *Micrasterias denticulata* (streptophyta) measured by Transmission Electron Microscopy–coupled Electron Energy Loss Spectroscopy1. J. Phycol. 47, 565-579.

Wagner, G.J., 1993. Accumulation of Cadmium in Crop Plants and its Consequences to Human Health. Adv. Agronomy 51, 173-212.

Wei, S., Zhou, Q., Wang, X., 2005. Identification of Weed Plants Excluding the uptake of Heavy Metals. Environment International 31, 829-834.

Wenzel, W., Bunkowski, M., Puschenreiter, M., Horak, O., 2003a. Rhizosphere Characteristics of Indigenously Growing Nickel Hyperaccumulator and Excluder Plants on Serpentine Soil. Environ. Pollut. 123, 131-138.

Wenzel, W., Lombi, E., Adriano, D., 1999. Biogeochemical Processes in the Rhizosphere: Role in Phytoremediation of Metal-polluted Soils, Heavy Metal Stress in Plants. Springer. 273-303.

Wenzel, W.W., 2009. Rhizosphere Processes and Management in Plant-assisted Bioremediation (Phytoremediation) of Soils. Plant and Soil 321, 385-408.

Wenzel, W.W., Bunkowski, M., Puschenreiter, M., Horak, O., 2003b. Rhizosphere Characteristics of Indigenously Growing Nickel Hyperaccumulator and Excluder Plants on Serpentine Soil. Environ. Pollut. 123, 131-138.

Whiting, S.N., Leake, J.R., McGrath, S.P., Baker, A.J., 2001. Assessment of Zn Mobilization in the Rhizosphere of *Thlaspi caerulescens* by Bioassay with Non-accumulator Plants and Soil Extraction. Plant and Soil 237, 147-156.

Wong, M.H., 2003. Ecological Restoration of Mine Degraded Soils, with Emphasis on Metal Contaminated Soils. Chemosphere 50, 775-780.

Yadav, S.K., 2010. Heavy Metals Toxicity in Plants: An Overview on the Role of Glutathione and Phytochelatins in Heavy Metal Stress Tolerance of Plants. S. Afr. J. Bot. 76, 167-179.

Yang, X., Feng, Y., He, Z., Stoffella, P.J., 2005. Molecular Mechanisms of Heavy Metal Hyperaccumulation and Phytoremediation. J. Trace Elem. Med. Biol. 18, 339-353.

Yang, X., Li, T., Yang, J., He, Z., Lu, L., Meng, F., 2006. Zinc Compartmentation in Root, Transport into Xylem, and Absorption into Leaf Cells in the Hyperaccumulating Species of Sedum Alfredii Hance. Planta 224, 185-195.

Yazaki, K., 2006. ABC Transporters involved in the Transport of Plant Secondary Metabolites. FEBS Lett. 580, 1183-1191.

Zenk, M.H., 1996. Heavy Metal Detoxification in Higher Plants—A Review. Gene 179, 21-30.

Zhang, S., Li, T., Huang, H., Zou, T., Zhang, X., Yu, H., Zheng, Z., Wang, Y., 2012. Cd Accumulation and Phytostabilization Potential of Dominant Plants Surrounding Mining Tailings. Environ. Sci. Pollut. Res. 19, 3879-3888.

Zhang, Z., Gao, X., Qiu, B., 2008. Detection of Phytochelatins in the Hyperaccumulator *Sedum alfredii* Exposed to Cadmium and Lead. Phytochemistry 69, 911-918. Zhang, Z., Shu, W., Lan, C., Wong, M., 2001. Soil Seed Bank as an Input of Seed Source in Revegetation of Lead/Zinc Mine Tailings. Restoration Ecol. 9, 378-385.

Zhao, F., Lombi, E., Breedon, T., 2000. Zinc Hyperaccumulation and Cellular Distribution in *Arabidopsis halleri*. Plant. Cell Environ. 23, 507-514.

Zhao, F., Lombi, E., McGrath, S., 2003. Assessing the Potential for Zinc and Cadmium Phytoremediation with the Hyperaccumulator *Thlaspi caerulescens*. Plant and Soil 249, 37-43.

Zhou, G.-K., Xu, Y.-F., Liu, J.-Y., 2005. Characterization of a Rice Class II Metallothionein Gene: Tissue Expression Patterns and Induction in Response to Abiotic Factors. J. Plant Physiol. 162, 686-696.

Zou, T., Li, T., Zhang, X., Yu, H., Luo, H., 2011. Lead Accumulation and Tolerance Characteristics of *Athyrium wardii* (Hook.) as a Potential Phytostabilizer. J. Hazard. Mater. 186, 683-689.

Pages: 68-73

Metals Distribution in Environment
Edited by: **Dr. Deep Mala & Dr. Pawan Kumar 'Bharti'**
ISBN: 978-93-86841-91-9
Edition: **2019**
Published by: **Discovery Publishing House Pvt. Ltd., New Delhi (India)**

Lead and Arsenic Poisoning through Fish and Chicken

Mona S. Zaki; Refat A. Youssef
Sami Shalby and Nagwa S. Rabie

ABSTRACT

General population exposure to arsenic and lead is mainly *via* intake of food and drinking water. Food is the most important source as fish meat, chicken meat and hens eggs but in some areas, arsenic in drinking water is a significant source of exposure to inorganic. Lead poisoning and arsenic exposure have become serious health risks in the past few decades. Lead poisoning or plubism is called toxicological condition, in which its exposure can cause either acute or chronic poisoning. Interferes with a number of body functions primarily affecting the central nervous, brain damage hematopoietic, hepatic and renal system producing serious disorders, high blood pressure, miscarriages, and behavioral problems in children. Contaminated soils such as mine-tailings are also a potential source of arsenic exposure. Absorption of arsenic in inhaled airborne particles is highly dependent on the solubility and the size of particles. Soluble arsenic compounds are easily absorbed from the gastrointestinal tract. However, inorganic arsenic is extensively methylated in humans and the metabolites are excreted in the urine. Arsenic (or metabolites) concentrations in blood, hair, nails and urine have been used as biomarkers of exposure. Speciated metabolites in urine expressed as either inorganic arsenic or the sum of metabolites (inorganic arsenic + MMA + DMA) is generally the best estimate of recent arsenic dose. Fish may accumulate toxinswhich can pass to human through its meat consumption. Accumulation of metals in fishdepends on

[1] **Hydrobiology Department, National Research Centre, Cairo, Egypt**
[2] **Soils and Water Uses Department, National Research Centre, Cairo, Egypt**
[3] **Animal Reproduction Department, National Research Center, Cairo, Egypt**
[3] **Poulatry Diseases Department, National Research Center, Cairo, Egypt**

concentrations of metals in water and food organism, on physiochemicalfactors and exposure duration. Heavy metals pollution in chickens is a problemdue to the health risk to human as a result toconsumptionits meat and eggs where inorganic arsenic is accumulated in the chicken breast meat and lead is deposited into the hen's eggs. It causes economic loses in poultry industry. It was found that arsenic toxicity results in many adverse conditions specially in broilers and broiler breeders chickens in form of increase mortalities and decrease in egg production.

Keywords: Lead, Arsenic, Poisin, Fish, Chicken

INTRODUCTION

Lead

The symptoms of acute lead poisoning are headache, irritability, abdominal pain and various symptoms related to the nervous system. Lead encephalopathyis characterized by sleeplessness and restlessness. Children may be affected by behavioural disturbances, learning and concentration difficulties. In severe cases of lead encephalopathy, the affected person may suffer from acute psychosis, confusion and reduced consciousness[1-2].

People who have been exposed to lead for a long time may suffer from memory deterioration, prolonged reaction time and reduced ability to understand. Individuals with average blood lead levels under 3 mol/l may show signs of peripheral nerve symptoms with reduced nerve conduction velocity and reduced dermal sensibility. If the neuropathy is severe the lesion may be permanent. The classical picture includes a dark blue lead sulphide line at the gingival margin. In less serious cases, the most obvious sign of lead poisoning is disturbance of haemoglobin synthesis, and long-term lead exposure may lead to anaemia[3-6].

Recent research has shown that long-term low-level lead exposure in children may also lead to diminished intellectual capacity[7-9].

Arsenic

It is a widely distributed metalloid, occurring in rock, soil, water and air. Inorganic arsenic is present in groundwater used for drinking in several countries all over the world (*e.g.* Bangladesh, Chile and China), whereas organic arsenic compounds (such as arsenobetaine) are primarily found in fish, which thus may give rise to human exposure[10-12].

Smelting of non-ferrous metals and the production of energy from fossil fuel are the two major industrial processes that lead to arsenic contamination of air, water and soil, smelting activities being the largest single anthropogenic source of atmospheric pollution. Other sources of contamination are the manufacture and use of arsenical pesticides and wood preservatives[13-16].

The working group of the EU DG Environment concluded that there were large reductions in the emissions of arsenic to air in several member countries of the European Union in the 1980s. In 1990, the total emissions of arsenic to the air in the member states were estimated to be 575 tonnes[17].

In 1996, the estimated total releases of arsenic to the air in the UK were50 tonnes[18].

Concentrations in air in rural areas range from 1 to 4 ng/m^3, where as concentrations in cities may be as high as 200 ng/m^3. Much higher concentrations (1000 ng/m3) have been measured near industrial sources[19].

Water concentrations are usually 10 g/l, although higher concentrations may occur near anthropogenic sources. Levels in soils usually range from 1 to 40 mg/kg, but pesticide application and waste disposal can result in much higher concentrations[21-22].

General population exposure to arsenic is mainly *via* intake of food and drinking water. Food is the most important source, but in some areas, arsenic in drinking water is a significant source of exposure to inorganic arsenic. Contaminated soils such as mine-tailings are also a potential source of arsenic exposure.

Absorption of arsenic in inhaled airborne particles is highly dependent on the solubility and the size of particles[23-24].

Soluble arsenic compounds are easily absorbed from the gastrointestinal tract. However, inorganic arsenic is extensively methylated in humans and the metabolites are excreted in the urine.

Arsenic (or metabolites) concentrations in blood, hair, nails and urine have been used as biomarkers of exposure.

Arsenic in hair and nails can be useful indicators of past arsenic exposure, if care is taken to avoid external arsenic contamination of the samples. Speciated metabolites in urine expressed as either inorganic arsenic or the sum of metabolites (inorganic arsenic + MMA + DMA) is generally the best estimate of recent arsenic dose. However, consumption of certain seafood may confound estimation of inorganic arsenic exposure, and should thus be avoided before urine sampling[25-27].

In Fish

The distribution of metals varies between fish species, depending on age, season, development status and other physiological factors[28]. Metals accumulate mainly in kidney, liver and intestine epithelium. Fish muscles contain low levels of metals, but are often examined for metal content due to their use for human consumption[29]. Analytical results were recorded for concentrations of arsenic, cadmium, copper, lead, mercury, selenium and zinc in freshwater fish collected in 1984 and temporal and geographic trends were evaluated by comparison with earlier finding[30].

Lead can cause deficits or decreases in survival, growth rates, development and metabolism[31].

In Chickens

The toxicity of these metals has two main aspects, the fact they have no known metabolic function but when present in the body disrupt normal cellular processes. Arsenic leading to toxicity and the potential of these heavy metals to accumulate in biological tissues, a process known as bio accumulation(32). This occurs because the metals are stored in particular organs, for example the liver and the kidney(33). Arsenic-based drugs were approved to prevent parasites in the chicken's gut. Poultry producers would routinely add roxarsone (inorganic arsenic, a known carcinogen), to their chickens feed, because arsenic is believed to speed the growth of chickens, and to give chicken meat a pink color that's pleasing to the shopper's eye. Inorganic arsenic accumulated in the chicken breast meat(34-35).

It was found that experimental exposure to heavy metal such as arsenic and lead in concentration of 0-30 ppm results in decrease broiler chickens feed intake and body weight after 56 days period of exposures(36).

Chickens that develop acute lead toxicity or poisoning will often present with sudden onset of muscle weakness, loss of appetite, marked weight loss, ataxia, drop in egg production and severe anemia. Chronic toxicity: Chronic lead toxicity may eventually result in degeneration of motor nerves in the chicken's spinal cord and axonal loss in the peripheral nerves. Muscle atrophy and myodegeneration are often also present.

Moreover experimental exposure of broiler breeder to arsenic (0.8 ppm) and lead (6.7 ppm) results in decrease egg production, egg weight and increase percentage of embryonic mortalities(37).

REFERENCES

1. *Department of Epidemiology*, Lars Järup, Hazards of Heavy Metal Contamination 2017.
2. Staessen JA, Roels HA, Emelianov D, Kuznetsova T, Thijs L, Vangronsveld J *et al.* Environmental Exposure to Cadmium, Forearm Bone Density, and Risk of Fractures: Prospective Population Study. Public Health and Environmental Exposure to Cadmium (PheeCad) Study Group. *Lancet* 1999; 353: 1140-4.
3. Alfven T, Elinder CG, Carlsson MD, Grubb A, Hellstrom L, Persson B *et al.* Low-level Cadmium Exposure and Osteoporosis. *J Bone Miner Res* 2000; 15: 1579-86.
4. Nordberg G, Jin T, Bernard A, Fierens S, Buchet JP, Ye T, Kong Q, Wang H. Low Bone Density and Renal Dysfunction following Environmental Cadmium Exposure in China. *Ambio* 2002; 6: 478-81.
5. Nishijo M, Nakagawa H, Morikawa Y, Tabata M, Senma M, Miura K *et al.* Mortality of Inhabitants in an Area Polluted by Cadmium: 15 Year Follow up. *Occup Environ Med* 1995; 52: 181-4.
6. IARC. Cadmium and Cadmium Compounds. In: *Beryllium, Cadmium, Mercury and Exposure in the Glass Manufacturing Industry*. IARC Monographs on the Evaluation of Carcinogenic Risks to Humans, Vol. 58. Lyon: International Agency for Research on Cancer, 1993; 119-237.

7. Kolonel LN. Association of Cadmium with Renal Cancer. *Cancer* 1976; 37: 1782-7.
8. Mandel JS, McLaughlin JK, Schlehofer B, Mellemgaard A, Helmert U, Lindblad P, McCredie M, Adami HO. International Renal-cell Cancer Study. IV. Occupation. *Int J Cancer* 1995; 61: 601-5.
9. Pesch B, Haerting J, Ranft U, Klimpel A, Oelschlagel B, Schill W. Occupational Risk Factors for Renal Cell Carcinoma: Agent-specific Results from a Case-control Study in Germany. MURC Study Group. Multicentre Urothelial and Renal Cancer Study. *Int J Epidemiol* 2000; 29: 1014-24.
10. WHO. *Inorganic Mercury.* Environmental Health Criteria, Vol. 118. Geneva: World Health Organization, 1991.
11. WHO. *Methyl Mercury.* Environmental Health Criteria, Vol. 101. Geneva: World Health Organization, 1990.
12. Sallsten G, Thoren J, Barregard L, Schutz A, Skarping G. Long-term use of Nicotine Chewinggum and Mercury Exposure from Dental Amalgam Fillings. *J Dent Res* 1996; 75: 594-8.
13. Lindh U, Hudecek R, Danersund A, Eriksson S, Lindvall A. Removal of Dental Amalgam and other Metal Alloys Supported by Antioxidant Therapy Alleviates Symptoms and Improves Quality of Life in Patients with Amalgam-associated Ill Health. *Neuroendocrinol Lett* 2002; 23: 459-82.
14. Langworth S, Bjorkman L, Elinder CG, Jarup L, Savlin P. Multidisciplinary Examination of Patients with Illness Attributed to Dental Fillings. *J Oral Rehabil* 2002; 29: 705-13.
15. Weiss B, Clarkson TW, Simon W. Silent Latency Periods in Methylmercury Poisoning and in Neurodegenerative Disease. *Environ Health Perspect* 2002; 110 (Suppl 5): 851-4.
16. Salonen JT, Seppanen K, Nyyssonen K, Korpela H, Kauhanen J, Kantola M, Tuomilehto J, Esterbauer H, Tatzber F, Salonen R. Intake of Mercury from Fish, Lipid Peroxidation, and the Risk of Myocardial Infarction and Coronary, Cardiovascular, and any Death in Eastern Finnishmen. *Circulation* 1995; 91: 645-55.
17. Guallar E, Sanz-Gallardo MI, van't Veer P, Bode P, Aro A, Gomez-Aracena J, Kark JD, Riemersma RA, Martin-Moreno JM, Kok FJ; Heavy Metals and Myocardial Infarction Study Group. Mercury, Fish Oils, and the Risk of Myocardial Infarction. *N Engl J Med* 2002; 347: 1747-54.
18. Yoshizawa K, Rimm EB, Morris JS, Spate VL, Hsieh CC, Spiegelman D, Stampfer MJ, Willett WC. Mercury and the Risk of Coronary Heart Disease in Men. *N Engl J Med* 2002; 347: 1755-60.
19. Mortada WI, Sobh MA, El-Defrawy MM, Farahat SE. Study of Lead Exposure from Automobile Exhaust as a Risk for Nephrotoxicity Among Traffic Policemen. *Am J Nephrol* 2001; 21: 274-9.
20. Elliott P, Arnold R, Barltrop D, Thornton I, House IM, Henry JA. Clinical Lead Poisoning in England: An Analysis of Routine Sources of Data. *Occup Environ Med* 1999; 56: 820-4.
21. Lidsky TI, Schneider JS. Lead Neurotoxicity in Children: Basic Mechanisms and Clinical Correlates. *Brain* 2003; 126: 5-19.
22. Steenland K, Boffetta P. Lead and Cancer in Humans: Where are we now? *Am J Ind Med* 2000; 38: 295-9.
23. WHO. *Arsenic and Arsenic Compounds*. Environmental Health Criteria, Vol. 224. Geneva: World Health Organization, 2001.

24. Chilvers DC, Peterson PJ. Global Cycling of Arsenic. In: Hutchinson TC, Meema KM (eds) *Lead, Mercury, Cadmium and Arsenic in the Environment*. Chichester: John Wiley & Sons 1987; 279-303.
25. DG Environment. Ambient air Pollution by As, Cd and Ni Compounds. Position Paper, Final Version, October 2000. Brussels: European Commission DG Environment.
26. Nriagu JO. History of Global Metal Pollution. *Science* 1996; 272: 223-4.
27. Annest JL. Trends in the Blood Level Leads of the US Population: The Second National Healthand Nutrition Examination Survey (NHANES II) 1976-1980. In: R.
28. Mendil, D., Demirci, Z., Tuzen, M., Soylak, M., (2010) Seasonal Investigation of Trace Element Contents in Commercially Valuable Fish Species from the Black Sea, Turkey. Food and Chemical Toxicology, 48, 865-870.
29. Lidwin-Ka□mierkiwicz, M., Pokorska, K., Protasowicki, M., Rajkowska, M., Wechterowicz, Z., (2009) Content of Selected Essentials and Toxic Metals in Meat of Freshwater Fish from West Pomeranian, Poland. Polish Journal of Food Nutrition and Science, 59(3), 219-224.
30. Schmitt C.J. and W. G. Brumbaugh (1990): National Contaminant Biomonitoring Program: Concentrations of Arsenic, Cadmium, Copper, Lead, Mercury, Selenium, and Zinc in U.S. Freshwater Fish, 197 & -1984. Arch. Environ. CO (lt~. Toxico!. 19,731-747 (1990).
31. Yilmaz, A.B., Sangün, M.K., Yağlioğllu, D., Turan C., (2010) Metals (Major, Essential to Non-essential) Composition of the Different Tissues of Three Demersal Fish from Iskenderun Bay, Turkey. Food Chemistry, 123, 410-415.
32. Mariam, I.S. and Nagre, S., (2004). Distribution of some Trace and Macro Minerals in Beef, Mutton and Poultry. International Journal of Agric and Biology, 6: 816-82.
33. Demirezen, O. and Uruc, K., (2006). Comparative Study of Trace Elements in Certain Fish, Meat and Meat Products. Food Chemistry, 32: 215-222.
34. Schmidt, C.W. (2013): Arsenical Association: Inorgang Arsenic may Accumulate in the Meat of the Treated Chicken *Environmental Health Perspectives.*
35. Nachman Keeve E., Patrick A. Baron, Georg Raber, Kevin A. Francesconi, Ana Navas-Acien and David C. Love (2013) *Arsenic in Chicken Meat, Environmental Health Perspectives May 2013.*
36. Okeke O.R., I.I. Ujah, P.A. C.Okoye., V.I.E Ajiwe and C.P. Eze (2015): Effect of Different Levels of Cadmium, Lead and Arsenic on the Growth Performance of Broiler and Layer Chickens. *IOSR Journal of Applied Chemistry (IOSR-JAC 8, 1 Ver. II. (Jan. 2015), PP* 57-59.
37. Vodela, J.K., J.A. Renden, S.D. Lenz, W.H. McElhenney, and B.W. Kemppainen, 1997. Drinking Water Contaminants (Arsenic, Cadmium, Lead, Benzene, and Trichloroethylene). 1. Interaction of Contaminants with Nutritional Status on General Performance and Immune Function in Broiler Chickens. Poultry Sci. 76: 1474-1492.

Pages: 74-98

Metals Distribution in Environment
Edited by: **Dr. Deep Mala & Dr. Pawan Kumar 'Bharti'**
ISBN: 978-93-86841-91-9
Edition: **2019**
Published by: **Discovery Publishing House Pvt. Ltd., New Delhi (India)**

Thermal Degradation of Biologically Active Surfactants Containing Transition Metal with Nitrogen and Sulphur Atoms for Sustainable Development of Society

Pragya Tank[1]
Rashmi Sharma[1]
Arun Kumar Sharma[2]

ABSTRACT

Surfactant derived from different fatty acids and edible oils with transition metal like copper (II) and exact information about their thermal degradation will play a vital role in its selection in specific applications in various fields of agro chemistry and pharmacology and in their selection as herbicides, fungicides, pesticides and insecticides.

Copper Soap have a tendency of complex formation with compounds containing donor atoms like N, S, O, Br etc. benzothiazole and other related compounds play significant role in biological activities due to the presence of nitrogen and sulphur atoms, which are responsible for their pharmacological activities.Coherence of biological activities of Copper soaps and other N and S containing compounds stimulated our interest to extend the studies in their cumulative form as complexes. It is anticipated that it will generate new hopes in various industrial, analytical and pharmacological applications.

Departmentof Chemistry
1 S.P.C. Govt. College Ajmer - 305 001 Rajasthan (India)
2 Govt. P.G. College Jhalawar - 326 001 Rajasthan (India)

The present work highlights:

1. Synthesis of Copper soaps derived from edible oils (Mustard, Soyabean) and their complexes with Urea, and 2 – amino – 6 – chloro Benzothiazole for comparative studies.
2. Kinetics of solid state was studied using thermal analysis (TGA).

INTRODUCTION

Of late, fascination for *Surface active agents*, or *surfactants*, is overwhelming on account of their interesting behavior at surfaces and interfaces. Surfactants are materials that tend not only to accumulate at the surface, but also, by their presence, change the properties of surfaces. They are capable of making a transition from a state of molecular disintegration to a colloidal state. Generally they are active at interfaces between solid–liquid, liquid-iquid or liquid-gas pairs of phases.

Due of their ability to lower interfacial tension, surfactants are used as emulsifiers, detergents, dispersing agents, foaming agents, wetting agents, penetrating agents and so forth. The use of surfactants as wood preservatives, water proofing & repellency agents, and in various industries of rubber, paints and varnishes etc. are relatively newer applications[1-4].

Many types of substances act as surfactants, but all share the property of amphipathy; the molecule is composed of a non-polar hydrophobic portion and a polar hydrophilic portion[5], which is therefore partly hydrophilic and partly hydrophobic. Often the hydrophilic part of the molecule is simply called the 'head' and the hydrophobic part – usually including an elongated alkyl substituent – is called the 'tail'

Surfactants are classified on the basis of the charge carried by the polar head group as anionic, cationic, nonionic or amphoteric[6]. Anionic surfactants bearing Copper ion are gaining popularity on account of their utilitarian effect such as foaming, herbicide, fungicide etc.[7-8]. These Copper containing surfactants play a vital role in various fields such as rubber industries, paints, varnishes, crop protection, stabilization of nylon threads, lubrication etc.[9-10]

All these properties led us to undertake the investigation pertaining to thermal behaviour, micellar features and fungicidal activities of Copper soaps and their corresponding complexes derived from edible oils available in the market, for their possible uses and applications in agriculture and industries.

CHEMISTRY OF COPPER

Copper (Cu) is a metal in I-B group of the periodic table with atomic number 29. Its natural isotopes are ^{63}Cu (69.1%) and ^{65}Cu (30.9%). Copper is highly ductile and malleable, and is an excellent conductor of heat and electricity, being second only to silver in the latter respect.

Copper has a single s-electron outside the filled 4d shell but cannot be grouped with alkalis in Group – I, since it has little in common with the alkalis except formal stoichiometries in the +1 oxidation state because ten d-electrons are rather ineffective in shielding the outer s-electron from the coulomb field of the nucleus. The first ionization potential of Cu is higher than that of alkalis. Since the electrons of the d-shell are also involved in metallic binding, the heat of sublimation and the melting point of Copper are also higher than those of alkalis. These factors are responsible for the more noble character of Copper and the effect is to make the compounds more covalent and to give them higher lattice energies.

The charge +2 is common in Copper. The d^9 arrangement of Cu^{+2} gives rise to square arrangements in which two ligands are attached by some what longer bonds, above and below the plane of the other four. Copper metal is known to form numerous complex compounds. The enthalpy of hydration of Cu^{+2} suggests that the di-positive ion is much more stable in aqueous solution.

Copper has a wide diversity of uses in electrical refrigeration, heavy industries, powder metallurgy and communications. Much of the Copper produced is utilized in various alloys.

Many Copper compounds are employed as pesticides, either alone [as Cu (I) oxide and Cu (II) sulphate] or in mixtures. Some examples of the latter are the pesticide Cupronil containing 35% Cu (II) carbonate hydroxide and 15% Zinc N,N-dimethyl dithiocarbamate. The fungicide Cuprozen which contains 37.5% Cu (II) chloride hydroxide and 15% Zineb (zinc ethylene–bis–dithiocarbamate), Bordeaux mixture –a fungicide prepared by reacting Cu (II) sulphate with hydrated lime and Burgundy mixture – a fungicide similar to Bordeaux mixture, but containing sodium carbonate instead of lime[11]. Copper compounds have catalytic properties in many reactions and can activate formation of chlorinated dioxins and dibenzofurans during incineration processes [Scheinberg]. Reed[12] reviewed the methods of the preparation of Copper soaps, described by several workers.[13-14].

APPLICATIONS OF NITROGEN AND SULPHUR CONTAINING COMPOUNDS

Benzothiazoles and other nitrogen and sulphur containing compounds have been serving as the basis of a variety of drugs for over five decades. They constitute an important and interesting class of heterocyclics not only for synthetic investigations but also for their usefulness.

Copper soaps have a tendency of complex formation with the compounds containing donor atoms like N, O, Br and S etc.[25-28] Urea, thiourea and benzothiazole possess nitrogen and sulphur atoms which are responsible for their pharmacological activities.

Coherence of biological activities of Copper soaps and Benzothiazoles and other N and S containing compounds stimulated our interest to extend the studies to their cumulative form as complexes. It is anticipated that it will generate new hopes in the pharmacological field.

Many nitrogen and sulphur containing compounds were synthesized and investigated for a wide range of pharmacological[29-30] and biological activities[31-32]. They have been used as tranquilizers[33], anti-heliminthics[34], anti-inflammatory[35], neuroleptics[36], anti-histamines[37], sedatives[38], antipsychotics[39], anti-viral[40], diuretics[41],fungicides[42-43], anesthetics[44], bacteriocides[45], antimalarials[46] etc. along with their activities.

One of the structural specificities considered responsible for such a wide spectrum of pharmacological activity in benzothiazole, is a fold along the nitrogen – sulphur axis. Structural resemblance applications have stimulated our interest to extend the synthetic and structural studies of benzothiazole complexes with a hope to obtain new compounds for therapeutic testing and better medicinal agents[47-54].

Recently work on poly-metallic complexes and transition metal complexes of heterocyclic ligands has been done; and their structure and biological characteristics have also been discussed[55-59]. All these references show that Copper soaps have a tendency for complex formation with compounds containing atoms like N, O, Cl, S, Br etc.[25, 60-63].

Medved and Filliporic[64] confirmed the formation of Copper butyro complex polarographically. Fisel[65] explained the formation of complex in electo-chromatographic analysis of soaps in the presence of bases. Kaufman and Lissling[66] prepared the solid green complex of one mole of Copper and four moles of oleic acid. Fisel[67] described the formation of complexes of Copper distearate and dipalmitate with amines.

Various scientists synthesized the Copper (II) complexes with benzothiazole and its derivatives, which show moderate antimicrobial activity against gram positive bacteria and fungi[68-71]. These complexes were found to possess fungicidal, herbicidal, anti-helminthic, insecticidal, pesticidal and nematocidal activity [27,29,30,43,72].Number of scientists investigated and reported the solubilization phenomenon and physical properties of several transition metal containing surfactants in aqueous andnon aqueous organic solvents[73-128.]

STRUCTRAL ASPECTS AND APPLICATIONS OF COPPER SURFACTANTS

Schulman and Riely[129], with the help of X-Ray diffraction propounded the concept that the structure of Copper (II) soaps consists of closely packed uniform water sphere in oil or oil in water. It has been pointed out by Anacker[130] that the molecular weight obtained for soap solutions is incompatible with the assumption of a spherical micelle. And according to Mc-Bain and Johnson[131], the spherical micelle concept is totally inadequate to account for the solubilization of hydrocarbons. In conformity with X-Ray diffraction data, Mc-Bain has postulated the existence of lamellar micelles. Shinoda[132] has supported this on the basis of the results obtained from the effects of alcohols on cmc. Ooshika[133] suggested that the change in cmc on addition of alcohol is due to lamellar micellar structure.

However, later Mc-Bain pointed out that it is not possible to account for all the properties of the soap solutions with only one kind of micelle; and he thus suggested the existence of both spherical ionic micelles and lamellar micelles[134].

Mc Bain and co-workers[135-136] suggested that soap solutions contain different proportions of the various micelles at different concentrations. It has been pointed out by Kolthoff and Stricks[137] that different type of micelles with different solubilising power are formed, and that with increase in soap concentration greater number of micelles with greater solubilising power are formed.

Matuura[138] investigated the IR spectra and X-Ray diffraction patterns of Copper oleate. Barclay and Kennard [139] studied the crystal structure of Copper formate by X-Ray technique. The IR spectra of Copper soaps, and Copper soaps with benzidine were also studied [94,140]. Grant[141] studied the NMR spectra of Copper stearate[142].

Various other workers have studied different spectral techniques like IR, ESR, NMR and magnetic moment studies of various complexes containing Copper so as to determine their geometrical and structural aspects[143-150].

Souza *et al.*[151] have investigated various edible vegetable oils and established their thermal stability and other kinetic parameters. It was established from the TGA curves that the thermal decomposition of edible oils takes place in three steps corresponding to the thermal degradation of polyunsaturated, monounsaturated and saturated fatty acids respectively. The various kinetic parameters evaluated included energy of activation, order of reaction and pre-exponential factor. The TGA/DTA analysis, so as to determine various kinetic parameters like energy of activation of edible oils were done by various other workers[152-155].

Various other scientists have done thermal analysis of various alkaline earth and transition soaps of fatty acids like laurate, caprate, caprylate, stearate and palmitate [156-160].

Kishita, Inoue and Kubo[161] studied the structures of Urea complex of Copper alkanoates. Potts and Hadson[162] used Copper soaps in the polymerization of vinyl derivatives of pyridine. Several workers described the uses of Copper soaps as stabilizers for nylon threads, synthetic polyamide and polyesters[163]. The protection of fabrics, nets, cordage etc. from fungi and decay by impregnating them in ammoniacal solution of Copper soaps was described by several workers[164-165]. The effectiveness of Copper soaps as fungicides, bactericides, insecticides and herbicides were also studied[166].

Varkonj and Sz'ell[167] studied the water repellency of Copper soaps, and it was observed that treating the heavy fabrics with Copper napthenate formed waterproofing and water repellant coating. It was observed by Zahardniuk *et al.*[169] that Copper soaps were more effective for protection of stored sugar beets. It was pointed out by Leyland and Stanford[170], Gebhardt[171] and by Pederson[172] that oxidation of natural rubber increased rapidly by the addition of Copper stearate.

Bartleson and Hughes[173] used Copper soaps in lubricants, which were stable to oxidative deterioration. To decrease wear and tear of drawing dies, lubricant containing Copper soap was observed to be more effective[174]. Mattiello[175] described the use of Copper soaps as driers for the preparation of paint, varnishes and other protective coating. It was observed that the addition of Copper soaps to fuel oil reduced the smoke and fumes of burning oil[176].

The use of Copper linoleate as heavy-duty wood preservative, and many other biological activities of Copper metal containing surfactants have also been studied[177-187].

Due to the presence of nitrogen and sulphur atom, the application of benzothiazole and its various derivatives as ulcer inhibitor, antiglutamate, fungicidal agents, antibacterial, anti-tubercular agents, herbicidal agents, intermediates in agrochemical and pharmaceutical fields and their uses in diabetic complications have been reported recently by various workers[188-195].

Survey of literature shows that Copper soaps and their complexes with nitrogen and sulphur containing ligands play a vital role in biological activities and have sufficient pharmaceutical, industrial and analytical applications. Biocidal studies have been conducted on Copper soaps and complexes derived from edible oils to assess their comparative toxicity on fungi *Alternaria alternata*.

To investigate the thermal behaviour, nature and type of micelles formed by various surfactants, the significance of present work cannot be ignored. Thermal stability, kinetic parameters, solute – solvent and solute – solute interactions, critical micelle concentration and other fundamental studies will play a significant role in the selection of synthesized Copper soaps and their complexes in various industries. The possibility cannot be denied that these synthesized Copper soaps and their complexes may be biodegradable and hence environment friendly, thus they may have a vital role to play in wood preservation and in other biological activities.

EXPERIMENTAL

All the chemicals used were of LR/AR grade. Solvent was purified according to standard procedures before use. Elemental analysis was done for soaps and complexes for their metal content following standard procedures[7]. The complexes that are studied were prepared in two steps.

In the first step, Copper soap was prepared and in the second step complexation of Copper soap was done with ligands like Urea and Benzothiazole.

(a) Purification of Benzene

Benzene was dehydrated by storage over sodium wire for 2-3 days and by refluxing for about twenty hours, it was then distilled and redistillation was carried out azeotropically with ethanol (B.P. – 80° C)[8].

(b) synthesis of Copper (II) Soaps

Copper soap was prepared by refluxing the edible oils i.e. Mustard oil and Soyabean oil of a reputed brand available in the Indian market, with alcohol and 2N KOH solution for 3 hours (Direct metathesis). The neutralization of excess KOH present was done by IN HCl. Saturated solution of copper sulphate was then added to it for conversion of neutralized soap into Copper soap. Copper soap so obtained was then washed with hot water and dried. The soap was recrystallized using hot benzene.

(c) Synthesis of Ligand

The ligand 2-amino-6-chloro Benzothiazole was synthesized using thiocyanation method[9]. 2- amino-6-chloro Benzothiazole was prepared by thiocyanation of para substituted arylamine, in the presence of thiocyanogen gas, which was generated in-situ by the reaction of cupric chloride and sodium thiocyanate[10-13]. The purity of Benzothiazoles has been checked by thin layer chromatography in various non-aqueous solvent systems.

(d) Synthesis of Complexes

The purified Copper soap derived from edible oil was refluxed with ligand (Urea/2-amino-6-chloro Benzothiazole) in 1:1 ratio using benzene as a solvent for one hour. It was then filtered hot, dried, recrystallized and purified in hot benzene. TLC using silica gel was used to check the purity of the complex.

In general, all the four solid complexes obtained are green in colour and sticky in nature. They are soluble in benzene and other organic solvents but insoluble in water. All the complexes are stable at room temperature, their physical parameters are discussed in table 5.1. On the basis of their elemental analysis, 1:1 (metal:ligand) type of stoichiometry has been suggested.

(e) Determination of Molecolar Weights of Copper Soaps

Molecular weights of Copper soaps are determined from saponification value[14]. The saponification equivalent or saponification value is a measure of the average chain length of the fatty acid that makes up a fat. The saponification equivalent (S.E.) is the amount of material saponified by one gram equivalent of potassium hydroxide, whilst the saponification value (S.V.) is the number of milligrams of KOH required to hydrolyse one gram of material; the two being related by the expression

$$S.E. = \frac{56100}{S.V.}$$

Table 5.1: Energy of activation (in kj mole^{-1}) for the decomposition reaction of copper soaps derived from mustard and soyabean oil using various equations for different steps

Soap ↓ / Step and Equation →	Coats – Redfern			Horowitz – Metzger			Broido		
	I	II	III	I	II	III	I	II	III
CM	77.3	98.4	251.3	100.9	110.7	238.4	91.4	124.7	171.4
CS	85.1	102.1	170.1	99.3	103.7	121.4	88.0	106.8	166.2

Thus, S.E. may be taken as average molecular weight of the oil. Value of S.E. is determined by experiment; from these values average molecular weights of the Copper soaps are calculated. The value of S.V. and molecular weights are recorded in table 5.2.

Table 5.2: Energy of activation (in KJ mole^{-1}) for the decomposition reaction of urea complexes of copper soaps derived from mustard and soyabean oil using various equations for different steps

Complex ↓ / Step and Equation →	Coats – Redfern			Horowitz – Metzger			Broido		
	I	II	III	I	II	III	I	II	III
CMU	112.8	126.1	214.4	112.0	124.0	188.8	93.1	105.8	232.7
CSU	112.8	134.0	178.7	108.1	133.3	188.8	130.6	152.4	203.2

Table 5.3: Energy of activation (in KJ mole^{-1}) for the decomposition reaction of Benzothiazole complexes of copper soaps derived from mustard and soyabean oil using various equations for different steps

Complex ↓ / Step and Rquation →	Coats – Redfern			Horowitz – Metzger			Broido		
	I	II	III	I	II	III	I	II	III
CMB	95.7	111.6	167.5	100.9	104.1	149.9	124.7	152.4	171.4
CSB	88.8	103.7	138.2	117.8	129.1	231.7	97.9	124.7	228.6

The Copper soaps and complexes are abbreviated as follows:

1. Copper – Mustard soap (CM)
2. Copper – Soyabean soap (CS)
3. Copper – Mustard soap – Urea complex (CMU)
4. Copper – Mustard soap – Benzothiazole complex (CMB)
5. Copper – Soyabean soap – Urea complex (CSU)
6. Copper – Soyabean soap – Benzothiazole complex (CSB)

THERMOGRAVIMETRIC ANALYSIS

Since thermogravimetric methods have been used in characterization of oils and fats; this technique has been employed to study the kinetics of thermal decomposition of soaps and complexes derived from these oils.

The edible oils deteriorate when processed inadequately, with the principal reaction being oxidation. Oxidation of the oils occur through a free radical mechanism i.e. decomposition of hydroxides and peroxides in low molecular weight acids and aldehydes occur[1-2]. The peroxide or other oxidation products formed can be determined by spectral or chemical analysis. Currently, thermoanalytical methods such as differential scanning colorimetry (DSC) and thermogravimetry/derivative thermogravimetry (TGA/DTA) are receiving considerable attention. TGA/DTA curves can be used to determine the kinetic parameters and the oxidative induction period [3-4]. On the other hand, as oxidative thermal decomposition involves exothermic and endothermic reactions, it is possible to estimate the energy involved in the process i.e. energy of activation. Therefore, this method is more advantageous than the conventional method, because it is more precise and sensitive; and require a smaller sample mass and results are obtained more rapidly[5-6].

Thermogravimetry has been employed to study the kinetics of thermal decomposition of CM, CS, CMU, CMB, CSU and CSB. The samples were sent to CSMCRI, Bhavnagar for thermogravimetric analysis. The TGA curves of the above mentioned compounds were obtained by Metter – Toledo system (TGA/SDTA 851e) Module. The analysis was done on STARe software system. TGA was done on nitrogen (N_2) atmosphere between 50°C – 750°C at the rate of 10°C per minute. The results were obtained as plots of 'weight loss v/s temperature' and '% weight loss v/s temperature'.

RESULTS AND DISCUSSION

(i) Thermal decomposition

Literature survey reveals that several methods of kinetic analysis, which have been proposed, are based on hypothesis that from single thermogravimetric trace, meaningful values may be obtained for parameters such as activation energy pre-exponential factor and reaction order[7-11]. Various other scientists have done TGA studies to evaluate various kinetic parameters for metal soaps of Zn [12], Rb[13], Pr[14], Cs[15], Li[16], Cd[17], Mg[18] and other transition metals like Cu[19-20], Mn[21] and Ni[22-23]. The various kinetic parameters evaluated included rate constants, order of reaction and energy of activation.

The thermal decomposition profiles for CM and CS have similar characteristics as can be observed from figure 5.1 and 5.2, where all the non-isothermal TGA curves have three decomposition steps in the range of 473 to 823 K (200 to 550° C). The Copper soaps then finally decompose into parent ketones, cupric oxide and carbon dioxide. The results of TG curves show that the final residue is metal oxide (cupric oxide) and the weight of the residue is in agreement with the theoretically calculated weight of metal oxide from the molecular formula of the corresponding soap.

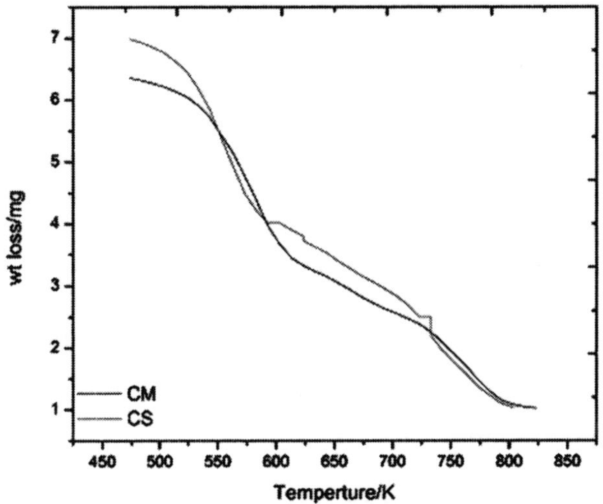

Fig. 5.1: Plot of % wt loss v/s temperature for CM and CS

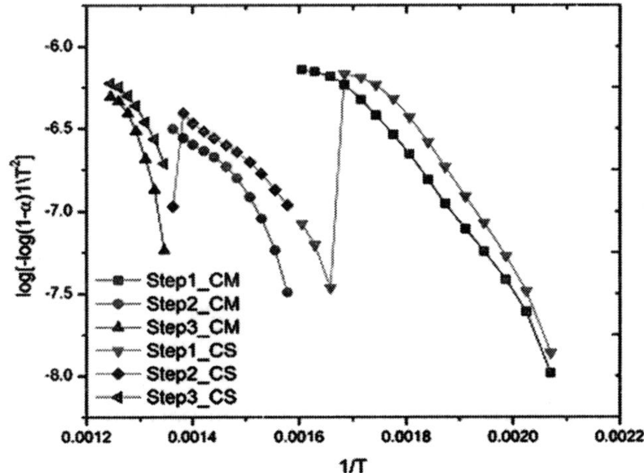

Fig. 5.2: Plot of Coats and Redfern equation for CM and CS

Thermal decomposition of these soaps derived from Mustard oil and Soyabean oil occurred in three stages, related to the decomposition of polyunsaturated, monounsaturated and saturated fatty acids respectively.

In relation to the thermal decomposition steps, it was observed that the first step (473 to 623K) corresponds to the decomposition of the polyunsaturated fatty acids. The long chain fatty acids produce volatile compounds, which are constantly removed by vapour generated during heating. These products (dimers, trimers, polymers) are formed principally by thermal reactions of unsaturated fatty acids such as linoleic acids. The first step is the most important for the thermal stability of the soaps derived from edible oils, because this is the step where decomposition of the unsaturated fatty acids begins.

The second step in the thermal decomposition of soaps derived from edible oils lie in the range of 573 to 733 K (320 to 460 °C) and corresponds to the decomposition of monounsaturated fatty acids, such as oleic acid. During this reaction, the double bonds are broken, causing the long chain fatty acid molecules in the edible vegetable oil to become saturated.

The third step in the thermal decomposition, which occurs in the temperature range of 723 to 823 K (450-550 °C), corresponds to the thermal decomposition of the saturated fatty acids such as palmitic acid. As already mentioned earlier, the weight of the remaining residue is found to be nearly equal to the theoretically calculated weight of cupric oxide.

In our referred systems, i.e. CM and CS, have same thermal stability as the first step thermal decomposition begins at 473K in both the cases. An interesting observation noted on perusal of figure 5.1 is that the first step for CM lies in the range of 473K to 623K, while CS undergoes first step degradation in the range of 473K to 593K. Hence, the possibility cannot be denied that CM, which is derived from mustard oil, takes longer time and need higher temperature to completely decompose its polyunsaturated fatty acid (PUFA) content as compared to CS, which is derived from soyabean oil.

Similarly, for second step decomposition of CM the range is 623K to 733K, and for CS the range lies between 593K and 723K. Thus again it may be suggested that CM needs longer time and higher temperature to completely decompose its monounsaturated fatty acid (MUFA) content as compared to CS, which is derived from soyabean oil.

For the third step, for CM the decomposition range lies between 733K and 803K. Therefore, it can be again be suggested that CM needs longer time and higher temperature to completely decompose its saturated fatty acid content as compared to CS. Thus, the possibility cannot be denied that CM possesses higher thermal stability in comparison to CS.

(ii) Kinetic parameters

These results have been applied on various equations like Coats – Redfern equation, Horowitz – Metzger equation and Broido equation to evaluate the energy of activation (E) for thermal degradation of each of the three steps of these soaps.

Of the various methods of kinetic analysis, Coats – Redfern[24] equation has been found to be the most appropriate in calculating the energy of activation. The method follows the rate low mentioned as follows:

$$\frac{d\alpha}{dt} = k\,(1-\alpha)^n \qquad (1)$$

A temperature dependent Arrhenius equation of the type holds valid is:

$$K = A\,e^{-E/RT} \qquad (2)$$

Where 'α' stands for the fraction of soap decomposed, 'n' for the order of the reaction, 'K' for the rate constant, 'E' for the energy of activation of the reaction, 'R' the gas constant (R = 8.314 J mol^{-1} K) and 'A' for the pre – exponential or frequency factor and is usually assigned to be independent of absolute temperature 'T'.

On integrating a combination of equations (1) and (2), and further using approximate expression for inexact integral, Coats and Redfern derived the equation:

$$\frac{\log f(\alpha)}{T^2} = \log \frac{AR}{aE}\left(1 - \frac{2RT}{E}\right) - \frac{E}{2.303RT} \qquad (3)$$

Where 'α' is the linear rate of heating and f (α) = – log (1-α) for n=1

Hence, this equation can be rewritten as:

$$\log \frac{[-\log(1-\alpha)]}{T^2} = \log \frac{AR}{aE}\left(1 - \frac{2RT}{E}\right) - \frac{E}{2.303RT} \qquad (4)$$

The values of energy of activation using Coats–Redfern equation for each of the three steps have been evaluated from the plots of 'log {[– log (1-α)]/T^2} v/s 1/T' (Fig. 5.2).

The values of the parameters a, log {[– log (1-α)]/T^2} and 1/T for CM and CS are (Fig. 5.2) are linear. The values of activation energies evaluated from the slope of these plots are recorded in table 5.1. The values of energy of activation are observed to be in following order for both CM and CS.

Step III > Step II > Step I.

Mention may also be made of the fact that although decomposition of CM and CS is continuous with respect to time and temperature, but Freeman – Caroll method is not applicable as the plots of '[log (dw/dt)]/[log W_r] v/s 1/T' do not pass through the origin confirming that the order of reaction is not zero.

To confirm the energy of activation Horowitz – Metzger[25] equation has been used to evaluate the value of 'E'. The Horowitz – Metzger equation is as follows.

$$\ln [\ln (1 - \alpha)^{-1}] = \frac{E.\ \theta}{RT_s^{\ 2}} \tag{5}$$

Where 'α' is the fraction of soap decomposed at time 't', 'T_s' is the temperature at which the rate of decomposition is maximum and 'θ' is equal to $(T - T_s)$. The energy of activation is obtained from the slope of the plot between ln [ln (1– α)$^{-1}$] v/s q (Fig. 5.3).

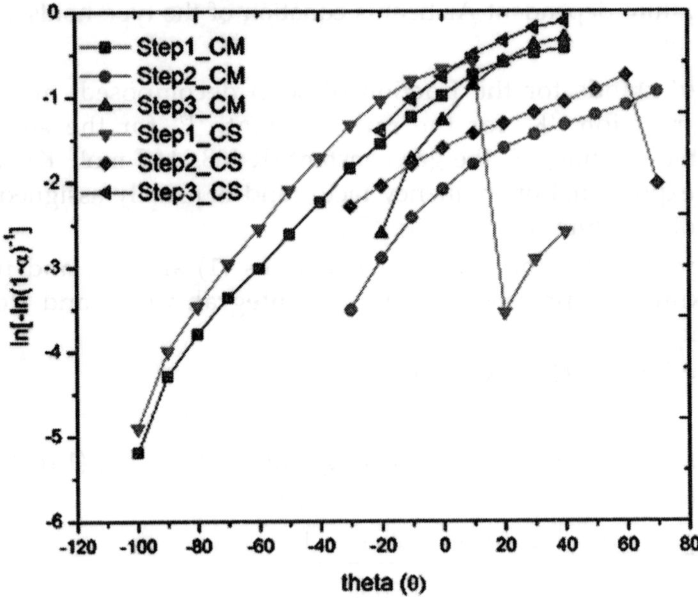

Fig. 5.3: Plot of Horowitz – Metzger equation for CM and CS

The plots of ln [ln (1–α)$^{-1}$] against q are depicted in figure 5.3 And the values of energies of activation calculated from the slopes of these plots are recorded in table 5.1. For Horowitz – Metzger equation the values of each step are in the order:

Step III > Step II > Step I

The energy of activation for the stepwise thermal decomposition of CM and CS has also been calculated by using Broido's[26] equation which is as follows:

$$\ln [\ \ln (1/y)] = - \frac{E + C}{RT} \tag{6}$$

Where 'y' is fraction of weight at temperature 'T', 'E' is the activation energy and 'R' is the gas constant in joule mol $^{-1}$ K^{-1}. The energy of activation for each step is calculated from the slope of plot between ln [ln (1/y)] and (1/T) as depicted in figure 5.4. The values of activation energies for different steps of thermal decomposition of CM and CS are recorded in table 5.1 and are found to be in the following order.

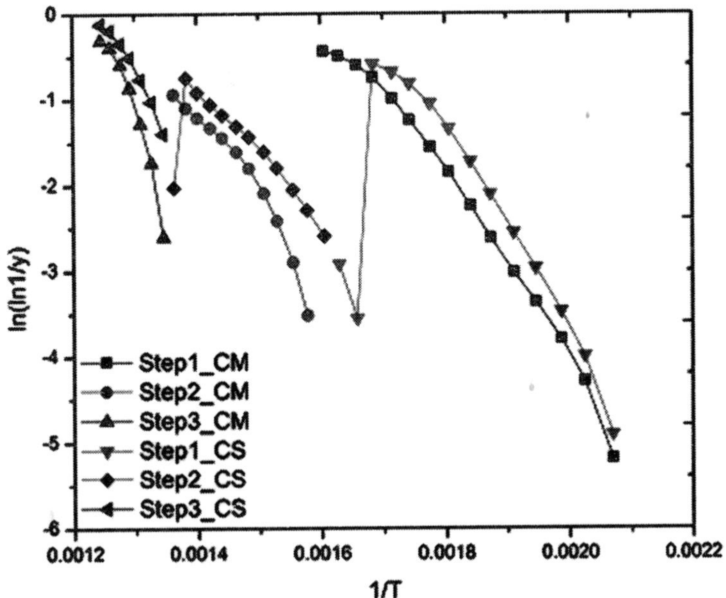

Fig. 5.4: Plot of Broido'sequation for CM and CS

Step III > Step II > Step I

A perusal of table 5.1 reveals that the value of activation energy is highest for the third step and smallest for the first step, irrespective of the equation applied signifying that saturated fatty acids require highest activation energy for decomposition.

GENERAL PROFILE OF THE REFERRED SYSTEMS

(i) Thermal decomposition

Of the six referred systems studied, three (CM, CMU and CMB) are derived from Mustard oil, and three (CS, CSU and CSB) are derived from Soyabean oil. The results of thermogravimetric analysis reveal that all the referred systems undergo stepwise thermal degradation in three steps corresponding to the decomposition of polyunsaturated, monounsaturated and unsaturated fatty acid components of their corresponding edible oil. The graphical representation of the three step thermal degradation profiles, where all the referred systems have similar characteristics are depicted in figure 5.5 (CMU and CSU) and figure 5.6 (CMB and CSB) where all the non-isothermal TGA curves reveal the three step thermal degradation in the temperature range of 473-823K (200 °C – 550 °C). The Copper soaps and complexes decompose into parent ketones, cupric oxide and carbon dioxide. For all the referred systems, the weight of final residue is observed to be in agreement with the theoretically calculated weight of metal oxide from the molecular formula of the corresponding soap/complex.

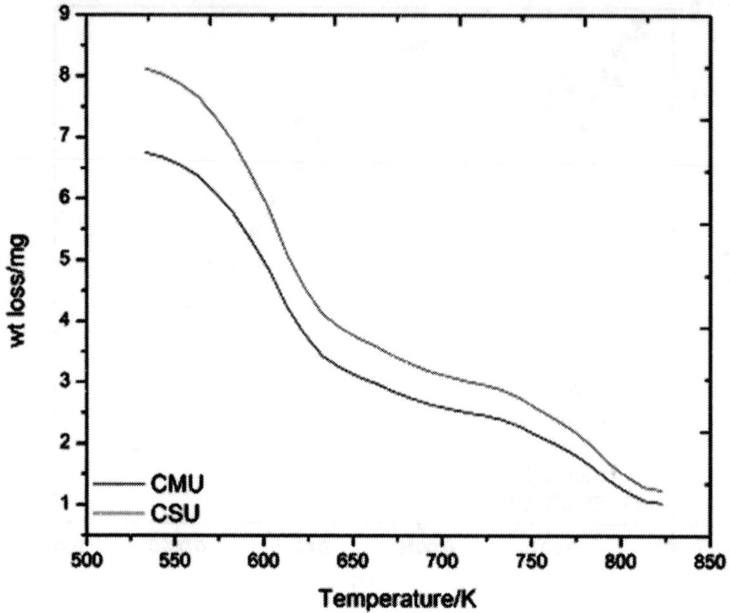

Fig. 5.5: Plot of % wt loss v/s temperature for CMU and CSU

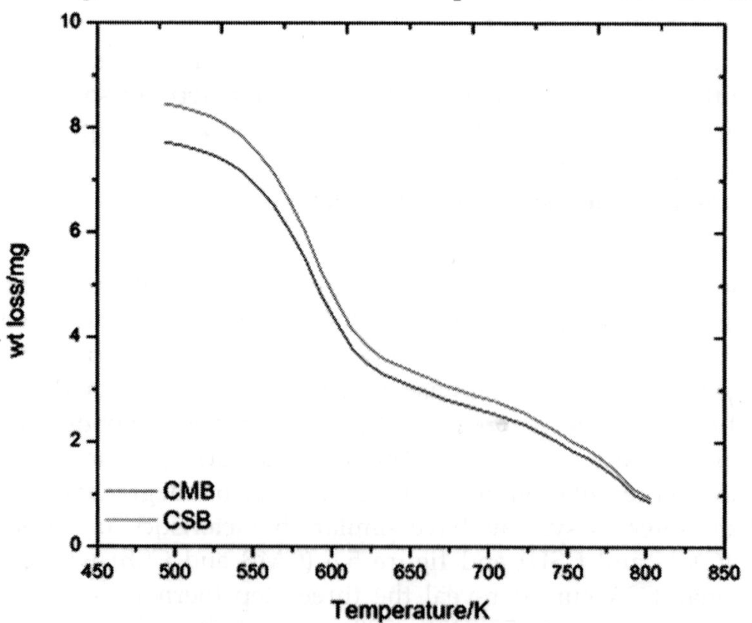

Fig. 5.6: Plot of % wt loss v/s temperature for CMB and CSB

On the basis of the temperature at the beginning of thermal decomposition i.e. initial temperature of step–I, it is clear from tables that the thermal stability is highest for Urea complexes and least for soaps; their thermal stability is in the following order.

Urea complex > Benzothiazole complex > Soap

The higher stability of Urea complex may be ascribed to the fact that Urea ligand being smaller than Benzothiazole moiety, fits more compactly within the soap moiety on complexation, resulting in a compact structure which is harder to break.

(ii) Kinetic parameters

The energy of activation 'E' has been evaluated for thermal degradation of each of the three steps for all our referred systems, using various equations like Coats – Redfern, Horowitz – Metzger and Broido equation (Figures 5.7 to 5.12).

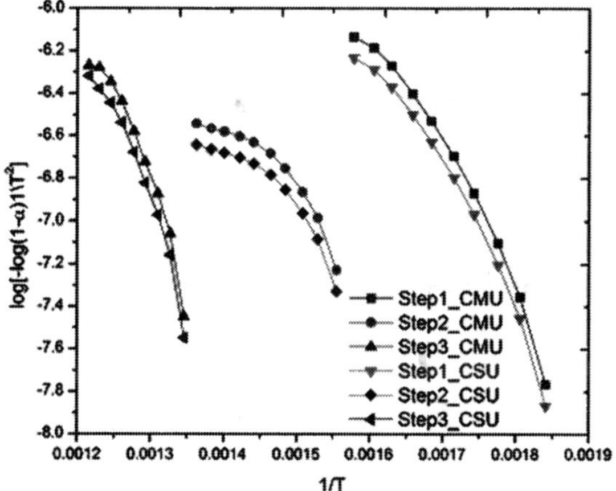

Fig. 5.7: Plot of Coats and Redfern equation for CMU and CSU

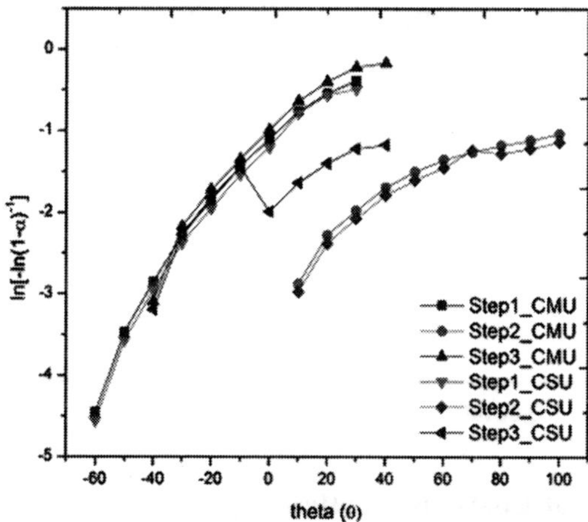

Fig. 5.8: Plot of Horowitz – Metzger equation for CMU and CSU

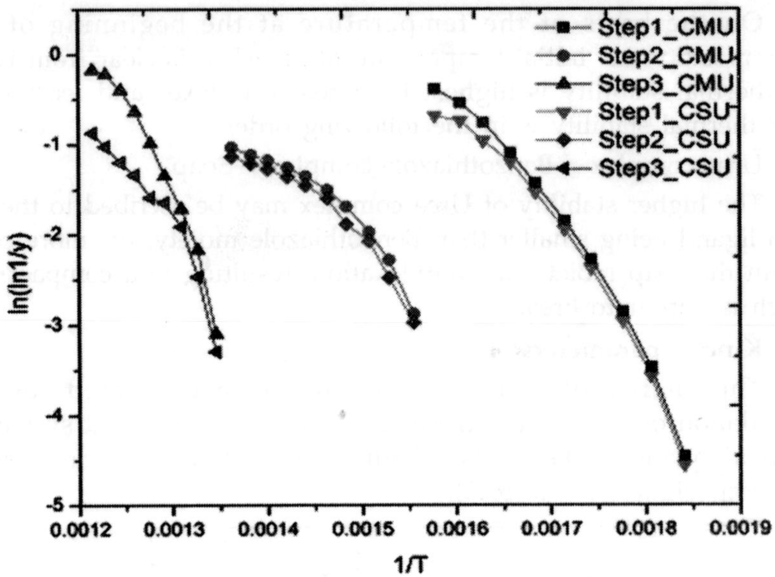

Fig. 5.9: Plot of Broido's equation for CMB and CSB

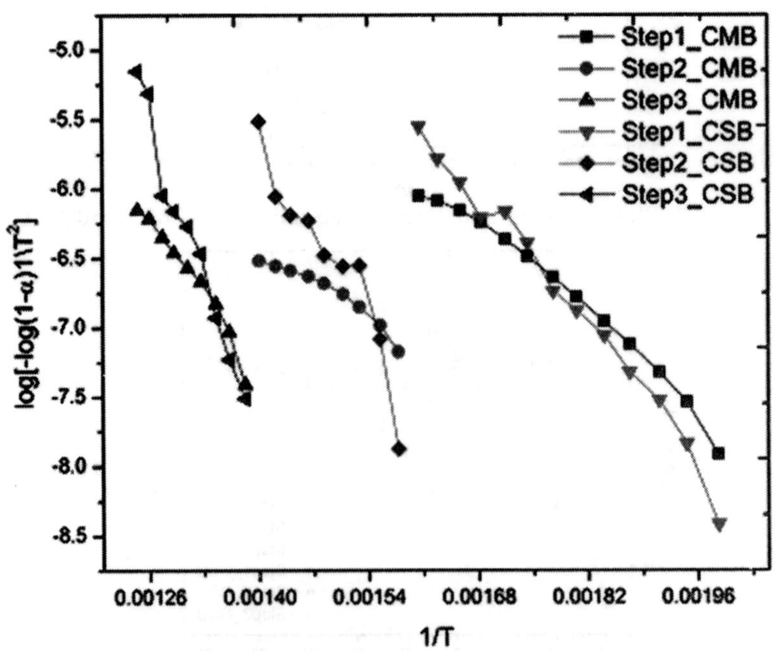

Fig. 5.10: Plot of Coats and Redfern equation for CMB and CSB

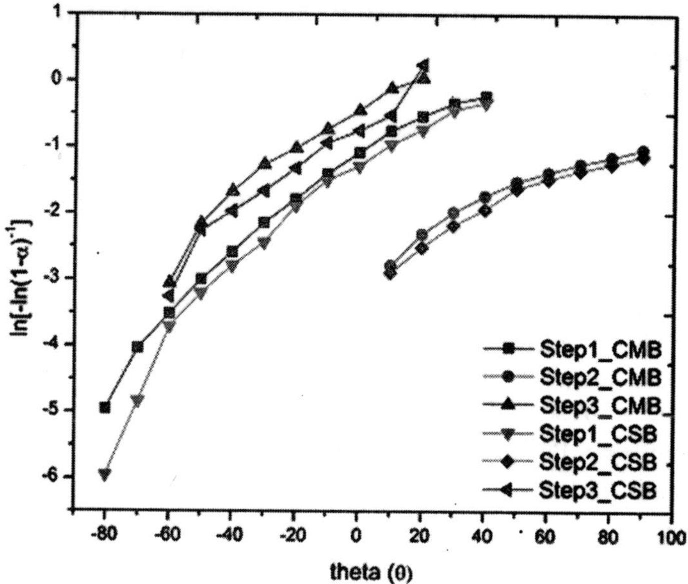

Fig. 5.11: Plot of Horowitz – Metzger equation for CMB and CSB

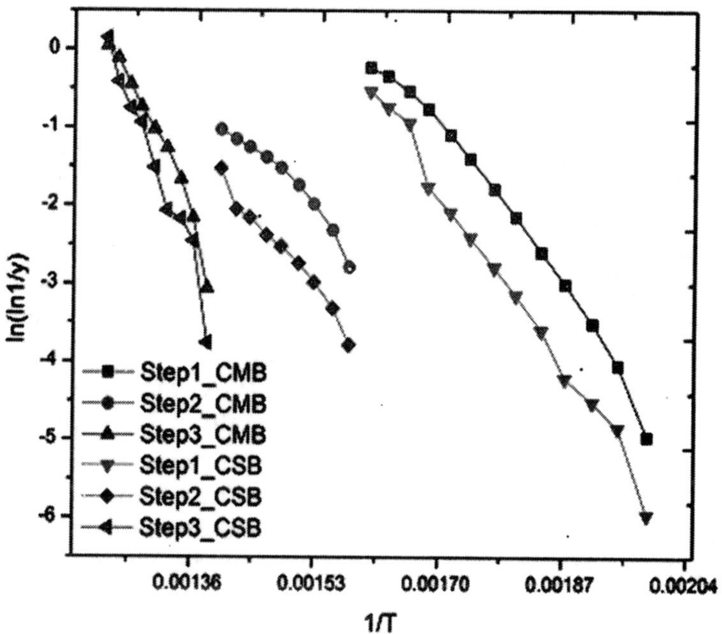

Fig. 5.12: Plot of Broido's equation for CMB and CSB

On perusal of this tabulated data, it is observed that for all the equations applied, the stepwise energy of activation follow the order:

Step III > Step II > Step I

The increase in activation energy in relation to the steps in thermal decomposition of the systems studied, occurred due to the possible break in the molecular bonds of unsaturated fatty acids, which are less stable than the molecular bonds of stable saturated fatty acids requiring higher activation energy for degradation[1].

On studying tables 5.2-5.3 with a comparative overview, it has been observed that Urea complexes, in general, have the highest value of energy of activation and the soaps have the least. The general order of activation energies can be represented as:

Urea complex > Benzothiazole complex > Soap

Mustard oil derivative > Soyabean oil derivative

There was a good correlation between the activation energies evaluated by various integration and approximation methods, however, the values obtained by the approximation methods were higher than the values obtained by integration methods, which can be ascribed to the different mathematical treatments of the methods[1].

CONCLUSON

The Copper soap derived from Mustard oil and their complexes with nitrogen and sulphur containing ligands such as Urea and Benzothiazole have been synthesized and studied for their structural aspects, which were confirmed using various techniques like IR, NMR and ESR spectroscopy. Thermogravimetric analysis (TGA) has been used to study the thermal decomposition of Copper soaps and their complexes to evaluate their energy of activation. Thermogravimetry has been employed to study the kinetics of thermal decomposition of CM, CS, CMU, CMB, CSU and CSB. Since all the above-mentioned compounds are derivatives of edible oils (Mustard and Soyabean), the nature of thermal degradation is found to be same as that of these edible oils. The TGA curves of the above mentioned compounds were obtained by Metter – Toledo system (TGA/SDTA 851e) Module. The analysis was done on STARe software system. TGA was done on nitrogen (N_2) atmosphere between 50 °C - 750 °C at the rate of 10 °C per minute.

Thermal degradation of these oils occurred in three stages, related to the decomposition of polyunsaturated, monounsaturated and saturated fatty acids respectively. The Copper soaps and complexes then finally decompose into parent ketones, cupric oxide and carbon dioxide. The final residue is cupric oxide, and the weight of the residue has been found to be almost equal to the theoretical value of cupric oxide calculated from the molecular weights of the respective soaps and complexes.

Of the various methods for kinetic analysis, Coats - Redfern equation, Horowitz – Metzger equation and Broido equation have been used to calculate the energy of activation for various soaps and complexes. The values of energy of activation for all the applied equations, for each step of thermal degradation, follow the order:

Step III > Step II > Step I

The increase in activation energy in relation to the successive steps in thermal decomposition of the systems studied, occurred due to the possible break in the molecular bonds of unsaturated fatty acids, which are less stable than the molecular bonds of stable saturated fatty acids requiring higher activation energy for degradation.

REFERENCES

1. Jurij J., Hostynek H. and Oward I. *Maibach Taylor &Fromics* 5 (2006) 16.
2. Czeslawk and Kajdas *Elsevier Ltd. Rolavel* 3 (2006) 38
3. Ratomahenina A., Galzy P., Graitte J. and Pina M., *Riv. Ital. Sostanze Grasse (Eng)* 60 (11) (1985) 673.
4. Singh, Verma S.B., Jordan J. and Sossna R., *Ger. Offen. D.E. 3, 703, 258* Cl. 4 Feb (1987) C.A. 110, 101192, Jan (1987)
5. Mukherjee P. and Meysels K.J. (U.S. Natl. Bur. Stand.) No. 36 (1971), *Natl. Stand. Ref. Data. Ser.*
6. Moroi Y., *"Micelles :Theoritical and Applied Aspects"* Springer (2005)
7. Mukherjee G.N. and Chakrborty P.K. *J. Indian Chem. Soc.* 79 (2002) 137.
8. Patel R.N., Kumar Subodh and Pandeya K.B. *Indian J. Chem.* 39A (2000) 1124.
9. Rafalski L. and Zawadzki J. *Pol. PL 144, 961,* 2 Aug 1985 C.A. 112 1211635 Mar-Aug (1990)
10. Crop K. *Kokai Tokkyo Koho Jp.* 59 193129 18 Apr (1983) C.A. 102, 168691z (1985)
11. Filov V.A., Bandman A.L. and Ivin B.A. *"Harmful Chemical Substances"* Vol. 1, 66, Eills Horwood Lmtd., Eng (1988).
12. Reed P.D. *J. Am. Perfumer Aromat.* 76 (3) (1961) 49.
13. Koeing A.E., *J. Am. Chem. Soc.* 36 (1914) 951.
14. Levy J. *Fatty Acids: Their Ind. Appl.* (1968) 200-20
15. Gunstone F.D. *"An Introduction to the Chemistry of Fats and Fatty Acids"*, Chapmann and Hall Ltd., London (1950).
16. Playfair L. *Ann.*, 37 (1841) 152.
17. Fremy E. *Ann.*, 36 (1840) 44.
18. Voelcker A. *Ann.*, 64 (1848) 342.
19. Noller C.R. *J Am Chem. Soc.* 56(1934) 1563.
20. Sacc *Ann.*, 51 (1844) 213.
21. Hilditch T.P. *J. Soc. Chem. Ind.* 58 (1934) 233.
22. Raphael R.A. *Nature* 165 (1950) 235.
23. Shinowara G.Y. *J. Biol. Chem.* 134 (1940) 331.
24. Arens C.L. *et al, Biochem. J.* 37 (1943) 1.

25. Kumar N. and Kachroo Pant, P.L., *J. Indian Chem. Soc.* VII 98 (1980) 1.
26. Mukherjee G.N. and Das A., *J. Indian Chem. Soc.* 78 (2001) 78.
27. Singh N., Sangwan N.K. and Dhindsu K.S., *Pest Manag. Sci.* 56 (2000) 284.
28. Mehrotra K.N., Mehta V.P. and Nagar T.N., *Cellulose Chem. Technol.*1 (1973) 38.
29. Ojha K.G., Jaisinghani N. and Tahiliani H., *J. Indian Chem. Soc.* 79 (2002) 191.
30. Gupta A., Sharma R. and Prakash L., *J. Indian Chem. Soc.* 74 (1994) 635.
31. Gupta R.R., *"Phenothiazines and 1,4-benzothiazines : Chemical and Biomedical Aspects"*, Elsevier, Amsterdam (1988).
32. Valli G., Sivakolunthu S. Muthusubramanian S, and Sivasubramanian S., *J. Indian Chem. Soc.* 77 (2000) 252.
33. Kulkarni K.G. and Fingerman M., *Gen. Pharmacol.* 17(6) (1986) 671.
34. Vishwavidhyalaya, GourHar Singh and Chaurasia Sunita Shrivastava Savitri, *Indian Drugs* 28 (1991) 474 Chem. Abst. 116 (1992) 15347f.
35. Sawhney S.S., Phindsa S.S. andVir D., *J. Indian Chem. Soc.* 65(9) (1988) 643.
36. Burch E.A. and Ayd. F.J., *J. Clin. Psychiatry* 44 (1983) 242. Chem. Abst. 95 (1983) 133118.
37. Koland F.P., *IRCS Med. Sci. Libr. Compound* 9(6) (1981) 546 Chem. Abst. 95 (1981) 9085.
38. Marvini F.P., *Mech. Ageing Dev.*, 36 (3) (1986) 295.
39. Shukla I.C., *J. Inst. Chem. (India)* 62(4) (1990) 159 Chem. Abst. 114 (1991) 1503075.
40. Raknew N., *Farmatsi* (Sofia), 37(3) (1987) 10.
41. Vorontsov Y.V., Lerner I.M., and Shchelkunov E.L., *Farmacol. Toksikol.*, 43(1) (1980) 81 Chem. Abst. 92 (1980) 157547.
42. Schacht E., Vandorpe J., Dejardin S., Lemmouchi Y. and Seymour L., *Biotechnology and Bioengineering* 52 (1996) 102.
43. Schacht E., Dejardin S. and Lemmouchi Y., *Bioactive and Compatible Polymers* 13 (1998) 4.
44. Morgan R.J., Eaddy L.B., Solie T.N. and Turbes C.C., *Lab. Anim.*, 15(1981)281 Chem. Abst. 95 (1981) 214987.
45. Dave A.M., Bhatt K.N., Vndania N.K. and Trivedi P.B., *J. Indian Chem. Soc.*, 65(5) (1988) 365.
46. Pinto A.C., Dasilva R.S. and Hollins R.A., *J. Heterocycl Chem.* 16(5) (1979) 1085 Chem. Abst. 92 (1980) 58705.
47. Thirumalaikumar M., Sivakolunthu S., Punuswamy A and Sivasubramanian S. *Indian J. Chem.* 38A (1999) 720.
48. Sastry C., Reddy V., Ram B. Jogibhukta M., Krishnan V.S.H., Singh A.N., Reddy J.G., Chaturvedi S.C., Rao S.P. and Sridher D.R., Indian J. Chem. 28B (1989) 52.
49. Jogibhukta M., Krishnan V.S.H., Singh A.N., Rao K.S. Sridher D.R., Rastogi K. and Jain M.L. *Indian IN 158,841 (1987)* Chem. Abst. 107 (1987) 154344.
50. Gupta R.R., Kumar R. and Goutam R.K., *J. Fluor. Chem.* 28(4) (1985) 381 C.A.: 105 (1986) 6467r.
51. Mitsuaki T. and Masonori W., *Kokai Tokkyo Koho Jp.*, 02,101, 068 pp 7 (1988) C.A.: 113 (1990) 73019.
52. Ishinge S., Usni H. and Sacki K., *GerOffen 2, 704, 724, (1977)* C.A.: 87 (1977) 144134.
53. Fengler G., Arlt D., Grohe K Zeiler H.I and Metzger K., *Ger. Offen 3,229,125 (1984)* C.A.: 101 (1984) 7176.

54. Filacchioni G., Nacci V. and Stefancich G., *Farmaco. Ed. Sci.*, 31 (7) (1976) 478., C.A. : 85 (1976) 143048.
55. Mahapatra B.B. and Ray Puspa, *J. Indian Chem. Soc.* 79 (2002) 536.
56. Patel R.N., Kumar and Pandeya K.B., *Indian J. Chem.* 39A (2001) 1124.
57. Kriza A., Reiss A. Blejoice S. Brujan L. and Stanica N., *J. Indian Chem. Soc.* 77 (2000) 488, 76 (1999) 406.
58. Mahapatra B.B. and Mishra R.R, *J. Indian Chem. Soc.* 78 (2001) 395.
59. Patel R.N., Patel A.P. and Pandeya K.B., *J. Indian Chem. Soc.* 76 (1999) 362.
60. Mane P.S., Shirodhar S.G. and Chondhekar T.K., *J. Indian Chem. Soc.* 79 (2002) 376.
61. Mishra V., *J. Indian Chem. Soc.* 79 (2002) 374.
62. Bhave N.S., Bahad P.J., Sorrparote P.M. and Aswar A.S., *J. Indian Chem. Soc.* 79 (2002) 342.
63. Kaur M.P., Kanungo B.K. and Sandhu J.S., *J. Indian Chem. Soc.* 79 (2002) 46.
64. Madved A. and Filliporic I., *Croat. Chem. Acta.* 35 (1963) 51.
65. Fisel S., *Zhur. Neorg.Khim.* 5 (1955) 1090.
66. Kaufman H.P. and Lissling, *Fette U. Seifen* 55 (1953) 90.
67. Fisel S., *Acad. Rep. Popular Romaine Filialalaji Studic Careetaxi Stiint* 7(2) (1956) 13, 6(3/4) (1955) 295.
68. Chandra Sulekh and Sharma, S.D., *J. Indian Chem. Soc.* 79 (2002) 495.
69. Hussain Reddy K. and Radhakrishna Reddy M., *J. Indian Chem. Soc.* 79 (2002) 219.
70. Kumar Devendra and Sharma R.C., *J. Indian Chem. Soc.* 79 (2002) 284.
71. Singh Bihari, Singh G.P., Kumar Madanjeet, Kumar Brajesh and Kumari Priya, *J. Indian Chem. Soc.*, 79 (2002) 278.
72. Pal S., Das D., Chattopadhyay P. Sinha C. and Panneerselvam, K., *Lu T-H., Polyhedron* 19 (2002) 1263.
73. Gad, *Arch. Anat. Physiol.*, (1978) 181.
74. Mc Bain J.W. and Green A.A., *J. Am. Chem. Soc.*, 68 (1946) 1731.
75. Mc Bain J.W. and Morrill R.C. Jr., *J. Am. Chem. Soc.*, 63 (1941) 670.
76. Mc Bain J.W. and Laing M.E., *J. Am. Chem. Soc.*, 58 (1936) 2610.
77. Lawerence A.S.C., *Trans Faraday Soc.* 35(70) (1935) 2 *Ann. Reports (Chem. Soc. London)* 37 (1940) 102, *J. Phys. Colloid Chem.* 52 (1948) 1504.
78. Mc Bain J.W. and Morrill R.C.Jr., *J. Phys. Chem.* 46 (1942) 10.
79. Von Hann F.V., *Kolloid* 2 (1932) 62, 202.
80. Lindan G., *Naturwiss.* 20 (1932) 396.
81. Winsor P.A., *Trans Faraday Soc.* 44(1948) 376, 382, 387, 390.
82. Demchenko P.A., *DopovidiAkad. Nauk, Ukrain USSR* (1959) 496, *Masloboino-Zhirovaya Prom.* 25(10) (1959) 22, *Ibid* 28(2) (1662) 23, *Kolloid-Zhur* 23 (1961) 36, *Ukraine Khim.Zhur* 23 (1962) 46, 203, *KolloidZh.* 24(1) (1962) 11 *J. Phys. Chem.* 36 (1932) 1401, 1672, 2455.
83. Chatterjee B.K. and Palit S.R., *J. Indian Chem. Soc.* 39 (1962) 571.
84. Relph C.L., *J. Colloid Interface Sci.* 21(3) (1966) 266.
85. Jain A.K. and Singh R.P.B., *J. Colloid Interface Sci.* 77 (1) (1980) 274.
86. Dobry A., *J. Phys. Chem.* 58 (1950) 576.
87. Nobel R.W., Scalane T.J. and Eisher A., *J. Am. Oil. Chem. Soc.* 35 (1962) 31.
88. Matuura R. and Nagasue K, *Mem. Fac. Sci. Kyusha Univ. Ser.* C_3 (1958) 49.

89. Nelson S.M. and Pink R.C., *J. Indian Chem. Soc.* (1952) 1744.
90. Wolf J.P., *Olegineucu*, 5 (1950) 20.
91. Mehrotra R.C. and Rai A.K., *J. Inorg. Nucl.Chem.* 21($^3/_4$) (1961) 311.
92. Mehta V.P., Hasan M. and Mathur S.P., *An. Quim* 74 (1978) 1016.
93. Mc Bain J.W., *Trans Faraday Soc.* 9 (1913) 99.
94. Hartle G.S., *Aqueous Solutions of Paraffin-Chain salts*, Hermann, Paris (1936).
95. Mc Bain J.W., *Colloid Chemistry, Theoretical and Applied* (J. Alexander, ed.) Reinhold New York (1944).
96. Mattoon R.H. Stearns R.S. and Harpins W.D., *J. Phys. Chem.* 15 (1947) 209.
97. Debye P. and Anacker E.W., *J. Phys. Colloid Chem.* 5 (1951) 644.
98. Preston W.C., *J. Phys. Chem.* 52 (1948) 84.
99. Kreschek G.C., *Water: A Comprehensive Treatise* Vol. 4, Aqueous Solutions of Amphiphiles and Macromolecules (F.Franks, ed) pp. 96-98, Plenum Press, New York (1975).
100. Shinoda K., *Colloidal Surfactants*, Chapter 1 Academic press, New York (1963).
101. Corrin M.L., *J. Colloid Sci.* 3 (1948) 333.
102. Williams R.J., Phillips J.N. and Mysels K.J., *Trans Faraday Soc.* 51 (1955) 728.
103. Mehrotra K.N., Mehta V.P. and Nagar T.N., *J. Prakt. Chem.* (1970) 312.
104. Mehrotra K.N. and Jain M., *Indian J. Chem.* 31A (1992) 452.
105. Malik W.U. and Ahemad S.I., *J. Polarog. Soc.* 12(2) (1966) 50.
106. Malik W.U. and Haque R., *J. Analyt. Chem.* 189 (1962) 179.
107. Popov A., Yanishileva N. and Iuanova B., *Maslo – Sapuena Prom. Byal* 6(4) (1967) 13.
108. Mehrotra K.N., Mehta V.P. and Nagar T.N., *J. Prakt. Chem.* 313 Heft 4 (1971) 607.
109. Malik W.U. and Haque R., *J. Am. Oil Chemists Soc.* 41(6) (1964) 168.
110. Malik W.U. andAhemad S.I., *Indian J. Chem.* 2(4) (1964) 168.
111. Ayers W.C., *Anal. Chim.Acta* 15(1956) 77.
112. Yokolshi H. and Yogi S., *Bunseki Kagaku* 17(1) (1968) 17.
113. Hattiandi G.S., Vold M.I. and Vold R.D., *Ind. Eng. Chem.* 41 (1949) 2320.
114. Guha B.C., *Proc. Roy. Soc.* A 206 (1951) 353.
115. Foex G. and Karantases J., *Compt. Rend.* 237 (1953) 982.
116. Figgis B.N. and Marin R.L., *J. Indian Chem. Soc.* 35 (1956) 37.
117. Herron R.C. and Pink R.C., *J. Indian Chem. Soc.* (1956) 3948.
118. Gilmour A. and Pink R.C., *J. Indian Chem. Soc.* (1953) 2198.
119. Satake I. and Matuura R., *Chem. Fac. Sci. Kyushu Univ. Ser.* C_5 1(1962) 13.
120. Kishita M., Inoue M. and Kubo M., *Nippon Kagaku Kaishi* 84 (1963) 758.
121. Martin R.L. and Waterman H., *J. Indian Chem. Soc.* (1957) 2545.
122. Mehrotra R.C. and Rai A.K., *J. Inorg. Nucl.Chem.* 21 (¾) (1961) 311.
123. Kokot R. and Martin R.L., *Inorg. Chem.* 3(9) (1964) 1306.
124. Martin R.L. and Whitelay A., *J. Indian Chem. Soc.* (1952) 1394.
125. Banarjee B.C. and Palit S.R., *J. Indian Chem. Soc.* 27 (1950) 385.
126. Mehta V.P., Talesara P.R., and Sharma R., *Indian J. Chem.* 39A (2001) 383.
127. Mehta V.P. Talesara P.R. and Sharma R., *Indian J. Chem.* 40A (2001) 399.
128. Sherwani M.R.K., Sharma R., Gangawal A. and Bhutra R., *Indian J. Chem.* 42A (2003) 2527.

129. Schulman J.H. and Riley D.P., *J. Colloid Sci.* 3 (1948) 383.
130. Anacker E.W., *J. Colloid Sci.* 8 (1953) 402.
131. Mc Bain J.W. and Johnson K.E., *J. Am Chem. Soc.* 66 (1944) 9.
132. Shinoda K., *Bull. Chem. Soc. Jpn.* 26 (1953) 101.
133. Ooshika v., *J. Colloid Sci.* 9 (1954) 254.
134. Mc Bain J.W., *"Frontiers in Colloid Chemistry"* Vol. VIII, Interscience Publishers Inc. (1950).
135. Mc Bain J.W. and Huff H.M., *J. Colloid Sci.* 4 (1949) 383.
136. Mc Bain J.W. and Mc Hon H., *J. Am Chem. Soc.* 70 (1948) 3838.
137. Kolthoff I.M. and Stricks W., *J. Phys. Colloid Chem.* 52 (1948) 915, 53 (1949) 424.
138. Matuura R., *Nippon Kagaku Kaishi* 82(1961) 1624.
139. Barclay G.A. and Kennard C.H.L., *J. Indian Chem. Soc.* (1961) 3289.
140. Yoko Kurodo, *Nippon Kagaku Kaishi* 86 (1965) 560.
141. Grant R.F., *Can J. Chem.* 42(4) (1964) 951.
142. Mehta V.P., Hasan M. Mathur S.P. and Rai G.L., *Tenside Surf. Det.* 16 (1979) 2.
143. Manhas B.S., Kalia S.B. and Sardana A.K., *J. Indian Chem. Soc.* 83 (2006) 652.
144. Reddy R.K., Reddy K.M. and Mahendra K.N., *Indian J. Chem.* 45A (2006) 377.
145. Lal R.A., Basumalary D., Chakraborty J., Bhaumik S., and Kumar A., *Indian J. Chem.* 45A (2006) 619.
146. Patel R.N., Singh N. and Gundla Y.L.N., *Indian J. Chem.* 45A (2006) 614.
147. Mijanuddin M., Gangopadhyay S., Mondal S., Mukharjee M. and Ali M., *Indian J. Chem.* 45A (2006) 858.
148. Ali A., Salunke S. Gawali, Rao P. and Linares J., *Indian J. Chem.* 45A (2006) 853.
149. Erden I., Demirhan N. and Avciata U., *Indian J. Chem.* 45A (2006) 1395.
150. Sharma V.K. and Shrivastava S., *Indian J. Chem.* 45A (2006) 1368.
151. Souza A.G., Santos J.C.O., Conceicao M.M., Dantas Silva M.C. and Prasad S., *Brazilian J. Chem. Engg.* 21(2) (2004) 265.
152. Souza A.G., Conceicao M.M. and Macedo R.O., *An. Assoc. Bras. Quim* 47 (1998) 361.
153. Santos J.C.O., Santos A.V. Souza A.G., Prasad S. and Santos I.M.G., *J. Food. Science* 67(4)(2002) 1393.
154. Santos J.C.O., Santos A.V. and Souza A.G., *Europ J. Pharm. Sci.* 13 (supp.1) (2001) 523.
155. Santos J.C.O., Santos M.G. Conecicao M.M. *et al*, *J. Thermal Anal. Colorimetry* 75(2) (2004) 419.
156. Rasheed A. and Bhobe R.A., *J. Indian Chem. Soc.* 53 (1976) 442.
157. Adeoson S.O., *J. Therm. Anal.* 14(3) (1978) 235.
158. Kambe H., Ozania T. Onoue M. and Igarashi S., *Bull. Chem. Soc. Jpn.* 35 (1962) 81.
159. Mehrotra K.N., Saroha S.P.S. and Kachhwaha R., *Tenside Surf. Det.* 18(1) (1981) 28.
160. Mehta V.P., Heda L.C. and Gupta R., *Asian J. Chem.* 4(4) (1992) 791.
161. Kishita M., Inoue M. and Kubo M., *Nippon Kagaku Zasshi* 84 (1963) 758.
162. Potts M.F. and Hadson P.H., *U. S. 2 767,159, (1956).*
163. Imperial Chemical Industries Ltd., *Brit. 1, 033 999, (Cl. C08g)* (1966).
164. Marsh B.P., *Ind. Eng. Chem.* 36 (1944) 176.
165. Samsonova O.A., *TekStil Prom* (1/2) (1943) 15.

166. Singh H., Srivastava U.K., Shukla S.N. and Upadhayay M.K., *Indian. J. Chem.* 31A (1992) 472.
167. Varkonyi B. and Sz'ell T., *Acta Univ. SzagadiensisActa Phys. et. Chem.*, 5 (1959) 73.
168. Duren Fabrik Chemisch G.M. B.H., *Ger. 1 062, 664, (1959).*
169. Zahradniuk J., Schmidt L. and Havranek A., *Listy Cukrov* 83(9) [Czech] (1967) 193.
170. Leyland B.N. and Stanford R.L., Trans Inst. Rubber Ind. 35 (1959) 25.
171. Gabhardt H.L., *Foundary* 74 (1946) 110, 198, 200, 202, 204, 206.
172. Pedersen L.H., *Acta. Chem. Scand.* 4 (1950) 487.
173. Bartleson D.J. And Hughes C.E., *U.S. 2 560, 542 (1951).*
174. Yokouldev V.M., Pershina N.Y., Bekrenev A.V. and Masalkina C.N., *Polytechnic Ins. Samara U.S.S.R.* Su 1, 715-835 [CICIOMI 73/00], (1992) Appl. 4. 747, 084, 08 Jan, (1990).
175. Mattiello J.J., *Protective and Decorative Coatings* Vol. 1 Wiley, New York, (1941).
176. ESSO Research and Engg. Co., *Fr. 1 381, 305[CI.C. 109], (1964).*
177. Reddy K.H., Reddy P.S. and Bahu P.R., *Transition Met. Chem.* 25 (2000) 154.
178. Kriza A., Spinu C. and Plemiceanu M., *J. Indian Chem. Soc.* 76 (2000) 82.
179. Malik A.K., Kaul K.N., Lark B.S., and Rao A.L.J., *Bibliographic Citation, Pesticide - Science India,* 53:1(1998) 104-106.
180. Agnihotri N.K. Singh V.K. and Singh H.B., *Bibliographic Citation, Talanta - Oxford, India* 45:2 (1998) 331-341.
181. Goff M.D., Sumack R.L., Tilt K.M. and Hagan A.K., *Bibliographic Citation, J. of Arboriculture, U.S.A.* 22:5 (1996) 201-205.
182. Buick T.A., Stall W.M., Kostewicz S.R. and Smith K., *Bibliographic citation, Hort.-Science, U.S.A.* 25:11 (1990) 1407-1408.
183. Demes H., Gaudchau M and Burow R.F., *Bibliographic Citation, Pesticide - Science, Germany,* 38:2-3 (1993) 278-280.
184. Soyez J.L., *Brighton Crop Protection Conference Pests and Diseases, France* Vol. 1 (1992) 451-456.
185.Sarricolea M.L., Villa-Elizaga I. and Lopez J., *Bibliographic Citation, Biology of the Neonate, Spain,* 63:1 (1993) 14-25.
186. Villa – Elizaga I., Sarricolea M.L. and Lopez J., *Bibliographic Citation, 8th International Symposium on Trace Elements in Man and Animals, Spain,* 23 (1993) 558-561.
187. Blenis P.V., Nadeav L.B., Knowles N.R. and Logue G., *Bibliographic Citation, Hort-Science* 32(6) (1997) 1077-1084.
188. MezzinaElisabetta, Frenna Vincenza and Chimichi Stefano, *Magn. Reson.Chem.* 34(12) (1996) 1019.
189. Salman Salman R., *Spectrosc. Lett.* 29(8) (1996) 1573.
190. StetinovaJarmila and Krublora Marcela, *Khim. Geterotsikl.Soedin.* C(0) (1995) 1402-4.
191. Kutty N., Go-Palari and Bhatt A.R., *J. Inst. Chem. (India)* 67(1) (1995) 22.
192. AotsukaTomoji, Abe Naoki and Ashizawa Naoki, [Grelan Pharmaceutical Co.Ltd., Japan] *Eur. Pat. Appl. EP 714 893* (Cl. C07D277/64) (1996) *Jp Appl. 94/317, 809, 41pp* (1994).
193. Tanabe Yoo, Yoshida Yoshihiro and Okumura Hitorni. *Heterocycles Jp,* 45(8) (1997) 1579.
194. CustelceanuRadu, Silberg I.A. and FarcasSorinI., *Heterocycl. Commun, Rom,* 3(4) (1997) 317.
195. Malik A.K. Kaul K.N. Lark B.S. and Rao A.L.J., *Bibliographic Citation, Pesticide - Science India,* 53:1 (1998) 104-106.

Pages: 99-127

Metals Distribution in Environment
Edited by: **Dr. Deep Mala & Dr. Pawan Kumar 'Bharti'**
ISBN: 978-93-86841-91-9
Edition: **2019**
Published by: **Discovery Publishing House Pvt. Ltd., New Delhi (India)**

Cadmium Enrichment in Agro-ecosystem

Prasann Kumar[1]
Shweta Pathak[2]

ABSTRACT

Metals are a natural part of terrestrial ecosystem. Out of the 10 most abundant elements in earth's crust, seven are metals (Mason, 1953). Heavy metal refers to all metals having a specific gravity greater than 4 (Anonymous, 1964). Only those lower (metal) members of the periodic table which are (1) relatively abundant in earth's crust, (2) extracted and used in reasonable amounts, (3) used in places where the public may come into contact with them, and (4) toxic to human beings, are generally referred to as heavy metals (Sahu *et al.*, 2004). Under physiological condition 17 heavy metals have been classified based on their solubility and given as they may be available for living cells and are of importance for organisms and ecosystem. Among these metals, Fe, Mo, Zn and Mn are important as micronutrients and Ni, Co, Cu, V etc, possess importance as trace elements. Hg, As, Cd and Pb have no known function and seem to be more or less toxic to plants and microbial population (Godbold and Huttermann, 1985). Heavy metals enter the food chain from industrial sources, natural sources and geochemical cycle.

Keywords: Agriculture, Biotic, Cadmium, Density, Environement, Forage, Gap, Toxicity

INTRODUCTION

Heavy metals are important environmental pollutants and their toxicity is a problem of increasing significance for ecological, evolutionary,

1 Department of Agronomy, School of Agriculture, Lovely Professional University, Jalandhar - 144 411 Punjab, (India)
2 Department of Plant Physiology, I.Ag. Sci., BHU., Varanasi - 221 005, U.P., (India)

nutritional, and environmental reasons. Of all non-essential heavy metals, cadmium (Cd) is perhaps the metal that has attracted the most attention in soil science and plant nutrition due to its potential toxicity to humans, and also its relative mobility in the soil-plant system. Friedrich Stromeyer and Karl Hermann discovered cadmium (Cd) almost simultaneously in 1817 in samples of zinc oxide obtained by roasting zinc carbonate from Salzgitter (Germany). Cadmium, a group II B transition element, was discovered by a German chemist freidrich strohmeyer in 1817. It is considered a non-nutrient element since it has no known function in plant development and life, with the exception of Cd-carnomis anhydrase of marine diatoms (Lane and morel, 2000). The average natural abundance of Cd in the earth's crust has most often been reported from 0.1 to 0.5 ppm. And non-polluted soil solutions also contain Cd concentrations ranging from 0.04 to 0.32 mM (Wagner 1993). Because Cd is a naturally occurring component of all soils, all food stuffs will contain some Cd and, therefore, all humans are exposed to natural levels of Cd. It has been known that leafy vegetables and potato tubers naturally assemble higher levels of Cd than fruits and cereals.

Maize (*Zea mays* L.) is a suitable crop for tropics and subtropical regions of the world. Maize can be an excellent model plant to study the physiological changes responsible for reduced productivity under stressful conditions. Being a rich source of nutrition (72% starch, 10% protein, 8.5% fiber, and 4.8% edible oil), maize is a major source of food, sugar, cooking oil, and animal feed all over the globe. Maize is preferred in poultry feed because of its easy availability; maize constitutes to about 60 per cent of the feed in the poultry feed industry and, therefore, is a critical raw material. With its wide applications, maize is also referred to as the Queen of Cereals. Maize also finds application in food containers, plastic food packaging, baby powder, diapers, medicine, vitamin tablets, textile products, candies and so on. Maize rich breakfast cereals, cooking oils, snacks and popcorn have also become popular. Internationally, maize has been processed to produce bio-ethanol in a big way for blending with auto fuels. In fact, maize is the only cereal that has such diverse uses. Keeping the value of maize crop in mind, cadmium stress being the harmful menace to its crop growing, the experiment was performed to assess the effect of various cadmium concentrations on different agronomical, physiochemical attributes of maize seedlings at different time intervals in the present study.

Effect of Heavy Metal Toxicity on Plants

Gisbert *et al.* (2003) examined that the heavy metal stress is one of the major abiotic stresses that causes environmental pollution in recent decades. These metals unlike other organic pollutants are not degraded and converted into harmless compounds via biological processes. Liu *et al.* (2003) reported that the cadmium (Cd) pollution in agricultural farmland has become a serious problem in many parts of the world, due to industrial development and the heavy use of chemical fertilizers, pesticides and herbicides, which produce serious threats to human health through the food chain. Arduini *et al.* (2004) found that changes in root morphology did not affect Cd translocation to the above ground parts of the plant. The distribution of Cd in leaves bulbs and roots of *M. plumbea* differed with increasing Cd concentrations. Cadmium accumulation in the leaves increased with increasing Cd. Bavi *et al.* (2006) has been shown that isolated chloroplast of 21 days old bean plants grown in nutrient solution containing different concentration of cadmium did not show a significant change in the rate of Hill reaction. This indicates that during the 7 days of treatment any cadmium ion taken up by plants may have been localized in root cell vacuoles thus have been kept away from photosynthesis sites, protecting photosynthesis from the harmful effects of cadmium. Wu *et al.* (2006) reported that Zn^{2+} concentration of rice genotypes increased with Cd levels up to 0.1mM for the shoot and 0.5mM for roots, while at Cd levels exceeding these levels, Zn^{2+} concentrations were reduced; Fe concentrations increased up to 0.1mM Cd in both shoot and roots, while higher Cd levels resulted in a sharp decrease of Fe. Krupper and Kroneck (2007) found that the increasing industrial production led to elevated release of heavy metals into the environment, thus increasing risk for human health, if accumulated in crop plants. Among others, nickel (Ni) and cadmium (Cd) are potentially dangerous because of their toxic effects and their accumulation in the food chain. Ni abundance in soils worldwide is >5 kg ha^{-1}, and in terms of plant metabolism, Ni is an essential ultra micronutrient found to be the active centre of urease and the cofactor of one superoxide dismutase isoforms.

Krantev *et al.* (2008) noticed that cadmium (Cd) is a highly toxic trace element that enters the environment mainly from industrial processes and phosphate fertilizers. It can reach high levels in agricultural soils and is easily assimilated by plants. When taken up by plants, it induces various visible symptoms of phytotoxicity e.g. leaf roll, chlorosis, growth reduction in root and shoot, browning of root tips and eventually death. Khan *et al.* (2008) elucidated that the concentration of heavy metals determined in selected plants are well below the critical limit. Maximum concentration of Mn (52.94 ppm), Ni (4.35 ppm) and Cu (9.65 ppm) were found in *A.vulgaris,* Zn (47.18ppm) in *S.rebaudiana*, Fe (206.69 ppm) in *W.somnifera* and Cr (5.89ppm) in *G. aparine*. Lead and cadmium were below the detection limits. The implication of findings may be taken into consideration whilst using the herbs for human consumption.

Bharadwaj *et al.* (2009) found that the higher concentration of Cd is responsible for the complete inhibition of germination and growth was also decreased as concentration of heavy metals was increased as compared to control plants; minimum morphological growth occurred in the plants in which Pb concentration was 8g/kg soil while for Cd, it was 2.5g/kg soil when compared with control plants. Monteiro *et al.* (2009) reported that Cd in the nutrient solution produced growth inhibition in lettuce plants, the growth of lettuce shoots was significantly reduced after 14 days when compared to the control. Root growth was also lower in Cd exposed plants, but difference was not significant and there were macro and micronutrient imbalances in leaves and roots of lettuce.

Wang *et al.* (2009) reported that accumulation of metals in crops including medicinal plants such as chamomile is a global problem owing to health risk for human. Therefore selection of cultivars with reduced root to shoot metal translocation is of great importance. Auda *et al.* (2011) concluded that Cd toxicity was more abvious than Pb toxicity and these symptoms were more severe in foliar treated than in root treated plants. Cd application decreased the dry weight of whole plants, shoot and roots, when compared with untreated contol plants.

Effect of Cd on Mineral Nutrition

It has been reported that uptake, transport and subsequent distribution of nutrient elements by the plants can be affected by the presence of Cd ions. Cd has been shown to interfere with the uptake, transport and use of several elements (Ca, Mg, P, and K) and water by plants (Das *et al.*, 1997). Chang *et al.* (2003) reported Cd induced iron deficiency in sugar beet. In pea plants, the uptake of P, K, S, Ca, Zn, Mn, and B was inhibited strongly after Cd exposure (Metwally *et al.*, 2005). Treatment of barley plants with 1.0 μM Cd decreased the concentrations of P, K, Ca, Mg, Cu, Fe, Mn, Zn, Mo, and B in roots, whereas the concentrations of these elements in shoots were not decreased in comparison with the control (Guo *et al.*, 2007). Cd also reduced the absorption of nitrate and its transport from roots to shoots, by inhibiting nitrate reductase activity in the shoots (Hernandez *et al.*, 1996). Appreciable inhibition of the nitrate reductase activity was also found in plants of *Silenecucubalus* (Mathys, 1975). Nitrogen fixation and primary ammonia assimilation decreased in nodules of soybean plants during Cd treatments (Karina *et al.*, 2003).

Effect of Cadmium on Plants

Cd does not have any beneficial physiological role in plants, but when accumulated, it affects all aspects of growth and development. In plants, Cd is one of the most readily absorbed and most rapidly translocated heavy metals, and can cause numerous morphological and physiological changes even at low concentrations (Seregin and Ivanov, 1998). At the morphological level, an excessive amount of Cd causes inhibition of plant growth, photosynthesis, enzyme function and cell metabolism in addition to disturbances in plant-water relationships (Mobin and Khan, 2007; Shi and Cai, 2008; Shi *et al.*, 2010). These effects are strongly dependent upon the plant species and the level of Cd applied.

Symptoms of Toxicity

Plants exposed to Cd can show many symptoms such as chlorosis, leaf roll, and necrosis (Benavides *et al.*, 2005). Chlorosis, leaf roll and stunting are the main and most easily observed toxic symptoms in the presence of excessive amounts of heavy metals. Toxicity may result from the binding of metals to sulphydryl groups in proteins leading to disruption of structure, inhibition of activity and deficiency of essential elements (Van Assche and Clijsters, 1990). The excess amount of heavy metal may stimulate free radical production and reactive oxygen species resulting in oxidative stress (Dietz *et al.*, 1999). Studies have indicated that the effect of cadmium toxicity depends on the applied concentration, the age of leaves, phenological development, plant species and cultivar (Baszynski *et al.*, 1980; Becerril *et al.*, 1989; Costa and Morel, 1994; Lang *et al.*, 1995; Vassilev *et al.*, 1995). As reported by Singh *et al.*, (2003) cadmium induced changes in water status of plants viz., total water content, specific water content, water saturation deficit (WSD) and transpiration when subjected to 250 ppm concentration of Cd.

Effect of Cadmium on Plant Physiological and Biochemical Parameters

Chen and Kao (1995) showed that proline accumulation can be induced in rice roots by treating seedlings with Cd. Proline has been reported to play important role in osmo-regulation, protecting enzyme denaturation, acting such as a source of carbon and nitrogen, stabilizing the machinery of protein synthesis, regulating the cytosolic acidity and/or scavenging hydroxyl radicals. Galli *et al.* (1996) reported a strong reduction in root dry weight for a root cadmium concentration of 562 mg kg^{-1} DM. Being highly mobile in phloem, cadmium can accumulate in any part of the plant causing stunted growth, chlorosis (Chaffei *et al.*, 2004) and leaf epinasty (Zhao *et al.* 2006). It also induces biochemical change in roots and leaves, such as lignification of cell walls in root tissues and leaf main vein. Larsson *et al.* (1998) performed an experiment in *Brassica napus* plants and showed that cadmium lowered total chlorophyll content, carotenoid content, and increased the non-photochemical quenching. Furthermore, cadmium inhibited the oxidative mitochondrial phosphorylation, probably increasing the passive permeability to H^+ of the mitochondrial inner membrane. Measured as CO_2 uptake, the photosynthetic rate in spruce (*Picea abies*) was significantly decreased by cadmium. With the enhanced cadmium accumulation, as a characteristic visual symptom, the reduction of the chlorophyll content of leaves could be observed. This fact is supported by the experiment done by Hegedus *et al.* (2001). Sandalio *et al.* (2001) reported that the chloroplasts, the major component of photosynthetic organ, are highly sensitive to damage exposed Cd toxicity. Oncel *et al.* (2000) observed that the two wheat varieties to which Cd and Pb were applied, total chlorophyll decreased. Cho and Kim (2003) noticed that cadmium has a great mobility in soil as compared with other metals, and easily taken up by roots and is translocated to different plant parts. Singh *et al.* (2003) showed that both growth and photosynthetic pigments are affected by the presence of heavy metals. The stronger effect, after Hg was that of Cd and the smaller inhibitor effect was tomato leaf. In the case of Cd $(NO_3)_2$ the inhibitory effect of Cd was smaller than $CdCl_2$, probably due NO_3 anion, which is used as chemical nutrient. Claussen (2005) reported increase in the level of proline in plants such as heavy metals, temperature and drought. Hayat *et al.* (2007) also determined that proline level increased the physiological drought stress generated by cadmium. Zengin and Munzuroglu (2005) reported that the heavy metals inhibit metabolic processes by inhibiting the action of enzymes, and this may be the most important cause of inhibition. Decreased chlorophyll content associated with heavy metal stress may be the result of inhibition of the enzymes responsible for chlorophyll biosynthesis. Cadmium was reported to affect chlorophyll biosynthesis and inhibit protochlorophyll reductase and aminolevulinic acid (ALA) synthesis (Stobart *et al.* 1985). The chlorophyll content declined progressively with increasing concentration of heavy metals. A significant increase of proline and ascorbic acid content was detected in primary leaves after 10 days exposure to heavy metals.

Jain and Srivastava (2006) found that the effect of different level of Cd (0, 10, 100, 200 ppm) as cadmium chloride, on growth, cell division, chlorophyll content, activity of catalase, peroxidase enzymes, foliar anatomical characters and essential nutrient content in sugarcane, and found that Cd effect being less pronounced in variety CO 64 in terms of lower decrease in growth attributes. Bavi *et al.* (2006) noticed that the cadmium has a great mobility in soil as compared with other heavy metals and is easily taken up by roots and is translocated to different plant parts, the uptake of heavy metals by plants is controlled by both soil and plant factors cadmium causes perturbations in various plant processes such as photosynthesis, sulfate assimilation and respiration. Plant growth inhibition and alteration in metabolism are mainly due to direct effects of cadmium on various enzymes activities and on growth processes. The selective accumulation of intracellular amino acids often occurs in response to environmental stresses such as drought, flooding, low temperature, or salinity. Jhon *et al.* (2008) also demonstrated the vivid results of cadmium stress on chlorophyll quantity that eventually affect photosynthesis. It was observed that 1 mg/l of each Cd and Pb used individually marginally increased the chlorophyll (chl a, chl b and total chlorophyll).The prolonged exposure to high concentration of cadmium (40 mg/l) reduced chl a significantly to about 82% of the control, and Pb showed the decline of 77% of the control after 30 days. Similarly, chl b decreased from 0.36 to 0.01 and 0.04 mg/g FW after 24 days of exposure to 40 mg/l of cadmium and 40 mg/l of Pb, respectively. Thus heavy metal alters chloroplast ultrastructure and reduces net photosynthetic rate, stomatal conductance and leaf transpiration (Souza *et al.*, 2011). Krantev *et al.* (2008) examined that net photosynthesis is also sensitive to Cd because it directly affects chlorophyll biosynthesis (Stobort *et al.* 1985; Padmaja *et al.* 1990; Gadallah 1995) and the proper development of the chloroplast ultrastucture (Stoyanova and Merakchiiska-Nikolo 1992, Stoyanaova and Tchakalova 1997). The negative effect of Cd can also be observed in the carboxylating phase of photosynthesis. The main targets of the influence of Cd are two key enzymes of CO_2 fixation, ribulose 1,5-bisphosphate carboxylase (RuBPC) and phosphoenol pyruate carboxylase (PEPC). It has been shown that Cd^{2+} ions lower the activity of RuBPC and damage its structure by substituting for Mg^{2+}ions, which are important cofactors of carboxylation reactions, and may also shift RuBPC activity towards oxygenation reactions (Siedlecka *et al.* 1998). Bharadwaj *et al.* (2009) reported that along with the growth of plants under increasing concentration of heavy metals, the entire metabolic activity of the plants under metal stress was affected resulting in reduced metabolic activities. Under the metal stress, the levels of photosynthetic pigments, namely chlorophyll 'a' and chlorophyll 'b' and carotenoids decreases as the concentration of Pb and Cd in soil increases. Chlorophyll 'a' was more affected in comparison to carotenoids.

Effect of Cadmium Toxicity on Maize Plant

Keltjens *et al.* (1998) reported that heavy metal contaminated soils often show increased levels of more than one metal, e.g. copper (Cu), cadmium (Cd), zinc (Zn), lead (Pb) or nickel (Ni). In case such soils are used for crop production, prediction of yield reduction or quality decline due to heavy metals in the soil is inadequate when based only on chemical soil analysis. The use of biomarkers such as phytochelatins (PC), non-protein thiols specifically induced in plants upon exposure to heavy metals, may be an additional indicator. Copper and Cd uptake and induction of PC synthesis were studied with hydroponically grown maize and wheat plants exposed to mixtures of the two metals. A close positive relationship was observed between the concentrations of Cd and PC in the plant shoot material. A decreased shoot concentration of Cd after addition of Cu, due to metal competition at common root absorption sites, coincided with lower shoot PC levels. The observed direct relationship between shoot PC concentration and the degree of metal-induced growth inhibition makes the use of PC promising. Abdul Ghani (2010) conducted a pot experiment to determine the toxic effects of some heavy metals on the plant growth and seed yield of maize (*Zea mays* L.). Heavy metals Mn, Pb, Cd, Cr and Co individually and in combinations were added as chloride salts in solutions to the pots before sowing. Heavy metals caused significant decreases in growth and protein content. Cd was the most toxic metal followed by Co, Hg, Mn, Pb, and Cr. Protein content decreased from 16.0-68.4% in metal exposed plants. Metal accumulation by seeds was directly related to the applied heavy metal with greater concentrations of metals found in cases where metals were added individually rather than in combinations. The toxic effects on the plant growth, nitrogen content in different plant parts, and protein content in seeds, exerted by two metals in combination were only as harsh as for the most toxic metal individually probably due to their antagonistic effects. Tian Yong *et al.* (2012) investigated phytoremediation potential of the bioenergy crop maize (*Zea mays* L.) in Cadmium-contaminated soil. Pot experiments with cadmium concentration gradients of 0, 5, 10, 30, 50 and 100 mg/kg were performed, and the growth parameters, photosynthetic activity and cadmium accumulation characteristics were evaluated during the entire growth period. The experimental results indicated that the maize germination was not sensitive to elevated cadmium stress, and that the photosynthetic activity only declined due to cadmium stress during the early growth stage. Cadmium concentrations greater than 30 mg/kg inhibited maize growth and reduced biomass production. The experiments demonstrated that maize has a great potential for phytoremediation in Cadmium-contaminated soil, where 1025.03 or 117.67 µg cadmium per plant was accumulated when the cadmium concentration in the substrate was 47.17 or 3.80 mg/kg. The bioconcentration factors of the roots (BCF>2.7) were greater than that of the aerial organs, and the translocation factors (TF) were all less than 1, which indicated that Cadmium readily accumulated in the root but was not readily transported to the aerial part. Due to its high biomass production and Cadmium accumulation capacity, maize is a good candidate for use in bioenergy production on Cadmium-contaminated soil.

Abbasi *et al.* (2015) conducted a hydroponic experiment to investigate single and combined effects of 5 micro mol/L cadmium and 100 mM NaCl on growth, root morphology, photosynthetic parameters, leaf and root ultra-structure of two maize hybrids (26204 and 8441) differing in salt tolerance. Indicated that 8441 was more sensitive than 26204 to both Cadmium and NaCl stresses. The reduction in growth and photosynthetic parameters were associated with severe disorganization of nucleus, chloroplast, mitochondrial damage, vacuolation, and increased number and size of pastoglobuli. Interestingly, the combined stress of both NaCl and cadmium had obvious beneficial effect on the plant growth, photosynthetic parameters and cell ultra-structure relative to cadmium or Na stress alone in the two maize hybrids. The study suggested that there is involvement of same genetic and physiological mechanisms in response to both cadmium and NaCl stresses. Wahid and Khaliq (2015) investigated that the influence of cadmium on some germination, morphological, biochemical and histological characteristics of developing embryonic tissue of maize. Cd stress reduced cortical cell size and vascular tissues, and deformed xylem and phloem parenchyma in all plant parts. The main reason for reduced germination was the influence of Cd on architecture of the coleorhiza and coleoptile, which was the result of oxidative stress and other physiological changes taking place in these tissues. Deng *et al.* (2016) reported that the effects of heavy metals (Cu^{2+}, Cd^{2+} and Hg^{2+}) on maize seed germination were investigated at 20°C and 40°C. Compared with 20°C, heat stress induced thermodormancy. However, this thermodormancy could be significantly alleviated by the addition of a low concentration of heavy metals. Heavy metals, as well as heat stress induced H_2O_2 accumulation in germinating seeds. Accordingly, H_2O_2 addition reinforced this promoting effect on seed germination, which was induced by a low concentration of heavy metal. However, this alleviation or aggravation could be partly attenuated by a low concentration of heavy metals. In addition, germination that was inhibited by high concentrations of heavy metals was also partly reversed by fluridone. The obtained results support the idea that heavy metal-mediated ROS and hormone interaction can finally affect the thermodormancy release or not.

Efficacy of Mycorrhiza on Heavy Metal Toxicity in *Zea Mays* and others

Griffioen *et al.* (1994) investigated the possible natural development of heavy metal tolerance in VA-mycorrhizal fungi, plants of *Agrostis capillaris* from an uncontaminated, a copper-contaminated and a zinc/cadmium contaminated area were examined for VA-mycorrhizal infection. A detailed analysis of the surroundings of the copper-enriched site revealed the presence of VA-mycorrhizal fungi and a negative correlation between the infection rate of *A. capillaris* and the copper content of the soil. In contrast to the copper-contaminated soil, the abundant presence of VA-mycorrhizal fungi in the area contaminated by zinc and cadmium indicated that these fungi have evolved a zinc and cadmium tolerance and that they may play a role in the zinc and cadmium tolerance of *A. capillaris*. Weissenhorn *et al.* (1995) conducted two pot-culture experiments with maize in a silty loam contaminated by atmospheric deposition from a metal smelter, root colonization with indigenous or introduced arbuscular mycorrhizal (AM) fungi and their influence on plant metal uptake (Cd, Zn, Cu, Pb, Mn) were investigated. suggesting a protection against metal toxicity. The results showed that the influence of AM on plant metal uptake depends on plant growth conditions. It is suggested that metal-tolerant mycorrhizal inoculants might be considered for soil reclamation, since under adverse conditions, AM may be more important for plant metal resistance. Zahir (1997) observed that in a pot experiment conducted in a growth cabinet, maize cv. LG-11 plants were grown for two weeks in sterilized sand with and without VAM (*Glomus caledonium*) inoculation at 3 phosphorus application levels (3, 10 and 30 mg kg-1). Inoculation significantly suppressed seedling growth, particularly in roots. Phosphorus inhibition of mycorrhizal infection increased with increasing rates of P application. Plant weight increased with increasing P rate.

Physiological Function of Polyamines (Putriscine)

Heby (1981) reported that the aliphatic polyamines, putrescine (1,4 diaminobutane), spermidine, and spermine, are normal cell constituents that play an important role in cell proliferation and differentiation. Pegg *et al.* (1982) Polyamines are ubiquitous organic cations of low molecular weight. The content of these amines is closely regulated by the cell according to the state of growth. The reactions responsible for the biosynthesis and interconversion of the polyamines and their precursor putrescine are described and the means by which polyamine content can be varied in response to exogenous stimuli are discussed. The role of polyamines in the cell cycle, cell division, tissue growth, and differentiation is considered. Recent studies using highly specific inhibitors of polyamine biosynthesis such as alpha-difluoromethylornithine to prevent accumulation of polyamines have indicated that the synthesis of polyamines is intimately associated with these processes. Such inhibitors have great potential for investigation of the cellular role of polyamines. Galston *et al.* (1990) The diamine putrescine, the triamine spermidine, and the tetramine spermine are ubiquitous in plant cells, while other polyamines are of more limited occurrence. Their chemistry and pathways of biosynthesis and metabolism are well characterized. In cereals, the activity of one of the major polyamine biosynthetic enzymes, arginine decarboxylase, is rapidly and dramatically increased by almost every studied external stress, leading to 50-fold or greater increases in putrescine titer within a few hours. Polyamines produced through the action of ornithine decarboxylase, by contrast, seem essential for DNA replication and cell division. The application of exogenous polyamines produces effects on patterns of senescence and morphogenesis, suggesting but not proving a regulatory role for polyamines in these processes. Groppa *et al.* (2001) reported the role of polyamines antioxidant properties in sunflower leaf discs under cadmium and copper induced oxidative stress. Both metals induced oxidative damage in the studied tissue, as evidenced by an increment in lipid peroxidation and a decrease in antioxidant enzymes ascorbate peroxidase (APOX), glutathione reductase (GR) and superoxide dismutase (SOD) activities. Polyamines concentrations were differently affected according to the metal used. Putrescine (Put) was reduced 52% by Cd^{2+} and 39% by Cu^{2+}, spermidine (Spd) was decreased to 21 and 59% of the control by $Cd^{2+}$and Cu^{2+}, respectively and spermine (Spm) content was not modified by any of the metals. Pretreatment with exogenously added polyamines (1 mM) showed that Spm reverted the effect of Cd^{2+} and Cu^{2+} on lipid peroxidation almost to control values. This work suggests that polyamines are undoubtedly related to the protection against metal-induced oxidative stress. Anthropogenic perturbations of biosphere manifested in a broad array of global phenomena, including accelerated rate of industrialization, intensive agriculture, and extensive mining accompanied by burgeoning population and rapid urbanization have not only wreaked the havoc on the availability of natural resources but also caused widespread and grave contamination of the essential components of life on the planet. Of the implications of human-induced disturbance of natural biogeochemical cycles, accentuated accumulation of heavy metals (HMs) is a problem of paramount importance for ecological, nutritional, and environmental reasons. HMs belong to a group of nonbiodegradable, persistent inorganic chemical constituents with the atomic mass over 20 and the density higher than 5-3 g/cm that have cytotoxic, genotoxic, and mutagenic effects on humans or animals and plants through influencing and tainting food chains, soil, irrigation or potable water, aquifers, and surrounding atmosphere. Heavy metals (HM) are conventional elements with properties like ductility, conductivity, stability as cations, ligand specificity, etc., and an atomic number. HM such as Cu, Zn, Mn, Fe, Ni, and Co are essential micronutrients for plant metabolism but when present in excess, these, as well as low levels of non-essential HM such as Cd, Hg, and Pb, can become extremely toxic. There are two kinds of metals found in soils, which are referred to as essential micronutrients for normal plant growth (Fe, Mn, Zn, Cu, Mg, Mo, and Ni) and nonessential elements with unknown biological and physiological function (Cd, Sb, Cr, Pb, As, Co, Ag, Se, and Hg). Both underground and aboveground surfaces of plants are able to receive HMs. The essential elements play a pivotal role in the structure of enzymes and proteins. Tolerance to HM in plants may be defined as the ability to survive in a soil/water that is toxic to other plants and is manifested by an interaction between a genotype and its environment. To protect themselves from metal poisoning, plants must develop mechanisms by which the HM entering the cytosol are either immediately excluded or complexes and neutralized, thus preventing the metal from inactivating catalytically active or structural proteins, presumably by adopting mechanisms that may also be involved in the general homeostasis of essential mineral ions and to tolerate them. The strong effect of HM on oxidative processes is the base for other connections with signaling response and genetic diversity. Plant tolerance to HM depends largely on plant efficiency in uptake, translocation, and further sequestration of HM in specialized tissues or in trichomes and cell organelles. Metals which are complexed and sequestered in cellular structures become unavailable for translocation to the shoot.HM binding to the cell wall is not the only plant mechanism responsible for metal immobilization into roots and subsequent inhibition of ion translocation to the shoot. The vacuole is generally considered to be the main storage site for metals in yeast and plant cells and there is evidence that phytochelatin-metal complexes are pumped into the vacuole in plants. Plants require them in tiny quantities for their growth, metabolism, and development; however, the concentration of both essential and nonessential metals is one single important in the growing process of plants so that their presence in excess can lead to the reduction and inhibition of growth in plants. HMs at toxic levels hamper normal plant functioning and act as an impediment to metabolic processes in a variety of ways, including disturbance or displacement of building blocks of protein structure, which arises from the formation of bonds between HMs and sulfhydryl groups, hindering functional groups of important cellular molecules, superseding or disrupting functionality of essential metals in biomolecules such as pigments or enzymes, and adversely affecting the integrity of the cytoplasmic membrane, resulting in the repression of vital events in plants such as photosynthesis, respiration, and enzymatic activities. On the other hand, elevated levels of HMs are associated with the increased generation of reactive oxygen species (ROS), such as superoxide free radicals (O_2 ·–d), hydroxyl free radicals (OH ·–d), or non-free radical species (molecular forms) such as singlet oxygen (O_2^*) and hydrogen peroxide (H_2O_2) as well as cytotoxic compounds like methylglyoxal (MG), which can cause oxidative stress via disturbing the equilibrium between prooxidant and antioxidant homeostasis within the plant cells. This condition implicates the causation of multiple deteriorating disorders such as, oxidation of protein and lipids, ion leakage, oxidative DNA attack, redox imbalance, and denature of cell structure and membrane, ultimately resulting in the activation of programmed cell death (PCD) pathways. Plants employ various inherent and extrinsic defense strategies for tolerance or detoxification whenever confronted with the stressful condition caused by higher concentrations of HMs. As a first step towards dealing with metal intoxication, plants adopt avoidance strategies to preclude the onset of stress via restricting metal uptake from soil or excluding it, preventing metal entry into plant roots. This can be achieved by some mechanisms such as immobilization of metals by mycorrhizal association, metal sequestration, or complication by exuding organic compounds from the root. At next stage, if these strategies fail and HMs manage to enter inside plant tissues, tolerance mechanisms for detoxification are activated which include metal sequestration and compartmentalization in various intracellular compartments (e.g., vacuole), metal ions trafficking, metal binding to cell wall, biosynthesis or accumulation of osmolytes andosmoprotectants, for example, proline (Pro), intracellular complexation or chelation of metal ions by releasing several substances, for example, organic acids, polysaccharides, phytochelatins (PCs), and metallothioneins (MT), and eventually if all these measures prove futile and plants become overwhelmed with toxicity of heavy metal (HM), activation of antioxidant defense mechanisms is pursued. The study also focuses on underlying functions and detoxification capabilities of two important ligand peptides including PCs and MTs that are typically used by plants to enhance tolerance to HM toxicity. Moreover, another line of plant defense strategy to combat against toxicity of HMs which involves the utilization of primary metabolite molecule Pro and the instigation of AM symbiotic system as well as their possible collaboration with one another or with plant antioxidant system is discussed and surveyed. Lastly, some suggestions will be made in terms of pursuing ways to have a better understanding of metal-plant causality involving action and reaction between these two abiotic and biotic entities in everchanging natural environments and climate. Some directions for future works will also be provided.Plants possess a sophisticated and interrelated network of defense strategies to avoid or tolerate HM intoxication. Physical barriers are the first line of defense in plants against metals. Some morphological structures like thick cuticle, biologically active tissues like trichomes, and cell walls as well as mycorrhizal symbiosis. The Scientific World Journal can act as barriers when plants are faced with HM stress. Trichomes for instance, can either serve as HM storage site for detoxification purposes or secrete various secondary metabolites to negate hazardous effects of metals. On the other hand, once HMs overcome biophysical barriers and metal ions enter tissues and cells, plants initiate several cellular defense mechanisms to nullify and attenuate the adverse effects of HMs. Biosynthesis of diverse cellular biomolecules is the primary way to tolerate or neutralize metal toxicity. This includes the induction of a myriad of low-molecular weight protein metallochaperones or chelators such as nicotianamine, putrescine, spermine, mugineic acids, organic acids, glutathione, phytochelatins, and metallothioneins or cellular exudates such as flavonoid and phenolic compounds, protons, heat shock proteins, and specific amino acids, such as proline and histidine, and hormones such as salicylic acid, jasmonic acid, and ethylene. When the above-mentioned strategies are not able to restrain metal poisoning, equilibrium of cellular redox systems in plants is upset, leading to the increased induction of ROS. To mitigate the harmful effects of free radicals, plant cells have developed antioxidant defense mechanism which is composed of enzymatic antioxidants like superoxide dismutase (SOD), catalase, (CAT), ascorbate peroxidase (APX), guaiacol peroxidase (GPX), and glutathione reductase (GR) and nonenzymatic antioxidants like ascorbate (AsA), glutathione (GSH), carotenoids, alkaloids, tocopherols, proline, and phenolic compounds (flavonoids, tannins, and lignin) that act as the scavengers of free radicals. As previously indicated some of the biological molecules involved in cellular metal detoxification can be multifunctional and have antiradical, chelating, or antioxidant activities. Exploitation and upregulation of any of these mechanisms and biomolecules may depend on plant species, the level of their metal tolerance, plant growth stage, and metal type. Cadmium (Cd2+) is toxic for humans, animals, and plants. This heavy metal enters the environment mainly from industrial processes and phosphate fertilizers; it is taken up by plants and transferred to animals and humans through the food chain. In higher plants, cadmium is strongly phytotoxic and is usually accompanied by an oxidative stress, as reported earlier. In fact, Cd causes a transient depletion of GSH and an inhibition of antioxidative enzymes giving rise to an H_2O_2 accumulation, and if the metal is not detoxified rapidly it may trigger the growth inhibition, stimulation of secondary metabolism, lignification, and finally cell death. Arbuscular mycorrhizal fungai have repeatedly been demonstrated to alleviate heavy metal stress of plants. Only few plants can cope with the adverse conditions on heavy metal soils.

Metals are a natural part of terrestrial ecosystems. Also out of the 10 most abundant elements in the earth's crust, seven are metals (Mason, 1953). Heavy metal refers to all metals having a specific gravity greater than 4 (Anonymous, 1964). Only those lower (metal) members of the periodic table which are (1) relatively abundant in the earth's crust, (2) extracted and used in reasonable amounts, (3) used in places where the public may come into contact with them, and (4) toxic to human beings are generally referred to as heavy metals (Sahu *et al.*, 2004). Based on their solubility under physiological conditions, 17 heavy metals may be available for living cells and are of importance for organisms and ecosystem. Among these metals, Fe, Mo, Zn and Mn are important as micronutrients and Ni, Co, Cu, V etc. possess importance as trace elements. Hg, As, Cd and Pb have no known function and seem to be more or less toxic to plants and microbial population (Godbold and Huttermann, 1985). Heavy metals enter the food chain from industrial sources, natural sources and geochemical cycle. Heavy metals are important environmental pollutants and their toxicity is a problem of increasing significance for ecological, evolutionary, nutritional, and environmental reasons. Of all non-essential heavy metals, cadmium (Cd) is perhaps the metal that has attracted the most attention in soil science and plant nutrition due to its potential toxicity to humans, and also its relative mobility in the soil–plant system. Friedrich Stromeyer and Karl Hermann discovered cadmium (Cd) almost simultaneously in 1817 in samples of zinc oxide obtained by roasting zinc carbonate from Salzgitter (Germany). Cadmium, a group II B transition element was discovered by a German chemist freidrich strohmeyer in 1817. It is considered a non-nutrient element, since it has no known function in plant development and life, with the exception of Cd-carnomis anhydrase of marine diatoms (Lane and morel, 2000). The average natural abundance of Cd in the earth's crust has most often been reported from 0.1 to 0.5 ppm. According to Wagner (1993), non-polluted soil solutions contain Cd concentrations ranging from 0.04 to 0.32 mM. Because Cd is a naturally occurring component of all soils, all food stuffs will contain some Cd and therefore all humans are exposed to natural levels of Cd. It has been reported that leafy vegetables and potato tubers naturally accumulate higher levels of Cd than do fruits and cereals.

Maize (*Zea mays* L.) is a suitable crop for tropics and subtropical regions of the world. Maize can be an excellent model plant to study the physiological changes responsible for reduced productivity under stressful conditions. Being a rich source of nutrition (72% starch, 10% protein, 8.5% fiber, and 4.8% edible oil), maize is a major source of food, sugar, cooking oil, and animal feed all over the globe. Maize is preferred in poultry feed because of its easy availability; maize constitutes about 60 per cent of the feed in the poultry feed industry and therefore is a critical raw material. With its wide applications, maize is also referred to as the Queen of Cereals. Maize also finds application in food containers, plastic food packaging, baby powder, diapers, medicine, vitamin tablets, textile products, candies and so on. Maize rich breakfast cereals, cooking oils, snacks and popcorn have also become popular. Internationally, maize has been processed to produce bio-ethanol in a big way for blending with auto fuels. In fact, maize is the only cereal that has such diverse uses. Keeping the value of maize crop in mind, cadmium stress being the harmful menace to its crop growing, the experiment was performed to assess the effect of various cadmium concentrations on different agronomical, physiochemical attributes of maize seedlings after different time intervals. Abedin *et al.* (2002) studied the uptake kinetics of arsenic species, arsenite and arsenate, in rice plants and found that arsenate uptake was strongly suppressed in the presence of arsenite. Ackerson and Krieg (1977) reported that sorghum stomata are relatively less sensitive to Vapor Pressure Deficit as compared with other C4 species like maize. Akdeniz *et al.* (2006) reported that there was a relationship among Cr, Zn and P concentrations. In the leaf, there was a significant relationship between Ni and Zn, Pb and Cd, but the relation between Mg and Cu concentration was negative. Similarly, there was a significant and positive correlation for P, K, Mg and Ca concentrations in seed. It can be suggested that sewage biosolids application did not cause any significant increase in heavy metal levels in leaf and seed of grain sorghum. Metals have toxic effects on living organisms when they exceed a certain concentration. Al-Enezi *et al.*(2005) reported that the propagation of heavy metals in biological food chain is one of the important issues of this behavior, as increasing the amount of several heavy metals in higher stages of the food chain is many times more than initial levels Al-Jaloud *et al.* (1995) reported that, sorghum crop is important to provide livestock forage, and forage health has a direct effect on human health. Arduini *et al.* (2004) found that changes in root morphology did not affect cadmium translocation to the above ground parts of the plant. The distribution of the Cd in leaves, bulbs and roots of plants differed with the increasing concentration of the cadmium concentration. Bavi *et al.* (2006) studied that isolated chloroplast of 21 days old plants grown in nutrient solution containing different concentrations of cadmium did not show a significant change in the rate of Hill reaction. Bhardwaj *et al.* (2009) studies that higher concentration of Cd is responsible for the complete inhibition of germination and growth also decreased as concentration of heavy metals was increased as compared to control plants. Bhardwaj *et al.* (2009) reported that along with the growth of plant under increasing concentration of heavy metals, the entire metabolic activity of the plants under metal stress was affected resulting in reduced metabolic activity. Bi *et al.* (2003) reported that, the metal concentration in plants has been shown to be higher or lower compared to the control (non-bioaugmented soil), depending on the metal (Bi *et al.*,2003 and/or its concentration in the soil. Nevertheless bio-augmentation almost always increases the rate of metal extracted from plants. Bjerrum's (1959) definition of heavy metals is based upon the density of the elemental form of the metal, and he classifies heavy metals as those metals with elemental densities above 7 g cm^{-3} Brooks (1998) reported that the hyperaccumulator can accumulate large amounts of element in their above ground biomass from the surrounding soils and tolerate high soil concentration. Therefore, Hyperaccumulator usually contain over 1000 mg kg^{-1} of elements in their above ground biomass, or the enrichment factor (EF) (the ratio of element concentrations in Hyperaccumulator to those in the surrounding soil) should be above one. The most common method to identify hyperaccumlating plants is to collect plant species that are growing in contaminated sites, and determine the concentrations of elements in the biomass. Caddel and Weibel (1971) reported that under long day condition the number of leaves increased with the increase in temperature. This happening is not common in all but reported in some genotypes.Cao *et al.* (2007) reported that microbial performances cannot be compared with each other because the methods used to estimate the bioavailable fractions of metals vary from one experiment to other experiment. Indeed several extractants are used such as water, $MgCl_2$, NH_4NO_3, DTPA, KNO_3 and HCl. Bioavailability of metals is even divided into three different pools: immediately soluble metals (with water), exchangeable metal forms (with KNO_3) and complexes or adsorbed metal form (EDTA).Chander and Brookest (1991) reported that the when *Scirpus sp., Phragmites karka* and *Bacopa mannieri* were grown in tannery effluent and sludge containing 2.3μg ml^{-1} and 214 mg kg^{-1} Cr, respectively, there was significant reduction in Cr concentrations. While there was an increase in biomass, no visible phytotoxic symptoms were shown by treated plants.

Cho and Kim (2003) Noticed that cadmium has a great mobility in soil as compared with other heavy metals and is easily taken up by roots and is translocated to different pats of the plants. Clark *et al.*(1968) reported that seed pericarp and tests may contain the germination inhibitor and which lead to the dormancy in the sorghum and when this pericarp was removed from the seed surface then it is observed that germination rate will enhance. Dormancy in seed is associated with ABA because the hormone can be detected in both developing and mature seeds and is proved to be inhibited when applied exogenously. In general dormancy is defined in a functional sense. Seeds that do not germinate given optimal conditions of temperature, water and oxygen are considered dormant, whereas those that do germinate are considered non-dormant.Cramer and Quarric (2002) reported that excessive concentrations of the various essential micronutrients had reported to affect initiation of the leaf primordial but did not depict any decline in the leaf number of concerned plants. Da Lin *et al.* (2011) reported some important changes in growth and physiological characteristics of the sorghum plant under cadmium stress, such as height, chlorophyll content, root activities and MDA content. They concluded that Cd effect was the manifestation of oxidative stress. Low concentration of cadmium can promote the growth of hard wheat, while under a relatively high concentration, the growth of wheat and tillering were both inhibited. Delavari *et al.* (2010) reported that the analysis of the variance of photosynthetic pigments is shown in salinity. Devitt *et al.* (1984) reported that sorghum root growth in saline media was repressed in an exponential relationship to a build up in the root. Eastein (1993) reported that the physiological maturity of the sorghum grain can be established by the dark placental region at the end of the grain. Elobeid *et al.* (2012) elucidated that Cd treatment caused significantly growth reductions in leaf formation, shoot height growth, stem radial growth and root elongation compared with controls, which significant decrease in plant biomass. However, the growth reductions differed between the different tissues; shoot elongation and leaf formation almost stopped after one week of Cd exposure, whereas stem radial growth was reduced from two weeks of Cd exposure onwards from the beginning. Falkowski and Raven (2007) observed that chloroplast contains many different parts that respond to heavy metal stress, therefore any changes in chlorophyll synthesis and activity used as the index of the direct toxic effects of heavy metals. Galavi *et al.* (2010) conducted an experiment in order to investigate the effect of treated municipal wastewater on soil chemical properties and heavy metal uptake by sorghum. Galvez and Clark (1991) reported that silicon mitigates the aluminum toxicity produced in the plants. Gisbert *et al.* (2003) reported that the heavy metal stress is one of the major abiotic stresses that cause environmental pollution in recent decades. These metals unlike other inorganic pollutants are not degraded and converted into harmless compounds via biological processes. Glass (2000) reported that phytoremediation is eco-friendly approach for the removal of contamination of agricultural soils. After the treatment the soil health going to improve and it allows sustaining crop production. If you have considering the economics incurred in the treatment, then these are supposed to be generally cheaper than physical ones.Haussmann *et al.*

(2000) showed that heterosis in yield is well expressed under a wide range of the stress condition. Scientist after exhaustive research reaches to the conclusion that heterosis in grain sorghum productivity is based on unique development events in the formation of the panicle structure and most likely involved in the stability of some important physiological parameters like photosynthesis, and other under diverse environmental conditions. Izadiyar and Yargholi (2010) reported that the maximum cadmium accumulation in sorghum was less than the UN standard set of agricultural and nutritional materials which permits at most a daily use of 35 micro-grams of cadmium by human beings, the standard set by the American Food Industries which permits a daily use of at most 92 micro-grams of cadmium by human. Jackson (1993) reported that the root may have a role in affecting shoot senescence. He suggests that soil conditions may be sensed by the shoot via. three major endogenous plant hormones, which are produced in the root, such as ABA, Ethylene and Cytokinins.Jalil *et al.*(1994) reported that low concentration of cadmium can promote the growth of hard wheat, while under a relatively high concentration, the growth of wheat and tillering were both inhibited and the degree varied among different varieties. Kayser *et al.* (2001) reported that low availability of the metals in the soil solution is the one of the major significant factors for the lower amount of metals extracted from plants from the soil. In general, scientist reported that, they oftenaccount for less than 1% of the total metal in soil and the rate of availability is influenced by the several soil physical and chemical characteristics such as pH, CEC and organic matter. Kennedy and Filippis (1999) reported that the anthocynin pigments increased with salt stress in both salt tolerant and salt sensitive plant. Krantev *et al.* (2008) reported that the net photosynthesis is also sensitive to Cd because it directly affects chloroplast biosynthesis and the proper development of the chloroplast ultrastructure. Ku *et al.* (2001) has successfully transformed rice with maize genes encoding two key enzymes of C4 photosynthesis: PEPC (Phosphoenol Pyruvate Carboxylase) and PPDK (Pyruvate Dikinase). Evidence after the extensive research suggests that both PEPC and PPDK play a key role in organic acid metabolism in the guard cells to regulate stomatal opening. Kumar and Dwivedi (2014) reported that, the Increasing growth of world population along with the expansion of the agricultural and industrial activities for improving supply of nutritional materials and the occurrence of several consecutive years of drought, are the reason why available water resources in most countries located in the dry-region zone have been used with the highest degree; such a condition may naturally exert a great deal of pressure on water resources. Kumar *et al* (2011) reported that the cadmium (Cd) is a divalent heavy metal cation and is one of the most toxic heavy metals. It is supplied to soil, air and water mainly by effluent from industries, mining burning, leakage waste, by fertilization with phosphate and sewage sludge. Cd is readily taken up by plants, leading to toxic symptoms such as peroxidation of lipids, decreasing the glutamic acid, protein, potassium ion level & chlorophyll content, damaging cell's photosynthetic machinery, inhibiting stomatal opening, increasing aspartic acid concentration and growth. Kupier *et al.* (2004) reported that a potential alternative option consists of optimizing the synergistic effect of plants and microorganism by coupling phytoextraction with soil bio-augmentation, also called rhizoremediation. Kusano *et al.* (2008) polyamines including putrescine are small ubiquitous nitrogenous compounds which are involved in several plant growth and development processes. This is considered as the recent additions to the class of plant growth regulators, and as a secondary messenger in signaling pathways.Lewis (1993) suggested that forming soap with fatty acids is an important criterion of "heaviness". Thus, again we have no consistent basis for defining the term. Another group of definitions is based on atomic number. A fourth group of definitions is based on other chemical properties, with little in common, density for radiation screening, density of crystals, and reaction with dithizone.LIU Da-lin *et al.* (2010) reported that the regulatory mechanism of the soil cadmium (Cd) on antioxidants in sorghum was studied using three sorghum species viz., sweet sorghum and sorghum hybrid sudangrass. Liu *et al.* (2003) reported that the cadmioum (Cd) pollution in agricultural farmland has become a serious problem in many parts of the world, due to industrial development and the heavy use of the chemical fertilizers, pesticides and herbicides, which produce serious thrust to human health through the food chain. Major *et al.* (1990) proposed the basic concepts for predicting leaf number on the basis of photoperiodic response.McBridee (1995) heavy metals represented a portion of important environmental pollutants which cause pollution problems by increasing their use in products in recent decades. In spite of gradual accumulation of heavy metals in the soil, the stability of heavy metals in the environment will lead to pollution since they could not be decomposed like organic pollutants by biological or chemical processes. Miller *et al.* (1968) established the five groups of sorghum genotype on the basis of their critical photoperiodic requirements. Molla-hoseini *et al.* (2005) reported that the accumulation of cadmium in different plant parts suggests that with a high degree of movement which this metal has in soil, it can be easily absorbed by the root and then transferred to different organs of the plant. It means accumulation of this element in soil and consequently the undesired increase in the amount of this metal in plants in the long term endangers the health of affected plants and consequently, the health of farm animals and humans. Monterio *et al.* (2009) reported that membrane permeability was assessed by measuring electrolyte leakage. No significant were observed between control and Cd exposed leaves. Cd induced senescence was not significantly reflected in solute leakage. Nalini and Chandra (2002) reported that heavy metals by inhibiting cell division or decreased cell expansion in the elongation zone or both of them reduce root length.Ozdener and Kutbay (2011) reported that the chlorophyll a and b contents were decreased under Cd treatment, chlorophyll a and b contents decreased due to increased Cd concentration. Pal *et al.* (2002) reported that the phytochelatin (PC) levels increased in the roots after 1 days of Cd treatments. The PC synthase activity decreased in all cases compared to the control in the roots. Parry and Kelso (1975) reported that sorghum accumulates the silicon in various tissues including the root.Pescord (1992) reported that, the storage of heavy metals severely threaten human health, but due to their long half-life (e.g. 1460 days for lead and 200 days for cadmium), tendency for storing such elements is dramatic. Premachandra *et al.*(1995) reported that the main solutes accounting for osmotic adjustment are due to sugars and potassium. Qin *et al.* (2000) heavy metal caused a reduction in plant photosynthesis, thereby reducing the plant water and nutrient adsorption, which affected the normal growth and development of sorghum.Qin *et al.* (2004) reported that the heavy metal, poisonous effects caused a reduction in plant photosynthesis, thereby reducing the plant water and nutrient absorption, which affected the normal growth and development of plants. Quinby (1974) developed the F1 hybrid in sorghum through the use of cytoplasmic genetic male sterility system. He also reported the increasing biomass production with little or no effect on harvest index. Rainbow (1985) reported that the various industries of electroplating, pigments, paints, stainless steel, mine tailing, battery, coal combustion, etc. are continuously causing soil pollution by adding different heavy metals viz. Cd, Cr, Pb, Ni, Zn and Cu, etc. Sandalio *et al.* (2001) reported that the chloroplast the major component of photosynthesis organ is highly sensitive to damage exposed Cd toxicity. Schmidt (2003) reported that elevated heavy metal concentrations in the soil can lead to enhanced crop uptake and negative effect on plant growth. Senthil *et al.* (2003) reported that the increased chlorophyll content in the green gram plants when sprayed with 40 ppm of NAA at flowering stages. Serafini-Fracassini and Mossetti (1986) reported that PAs are associated with cell wall polysaccharides or membranous fraction indicating thereby their prospects for a function information and anchoring of the plant cell wall polysaccharides, or in coupling membrane proteins in cytoplasmic structural protein. Several reports indicated that the response to abiotic injury and mineral nutrient deficiency is associated with the production of conjugated Pas.Sharma (1998) increased polyamines level in stressed plants have adaptive significance because of their involvement in the regulation of cellular ionic environment, maintenance of membrane integrity, prevention of chlorophyll loss and stimulation of protein, nucleic acid and protective alkaloids.Sharma *et al.* (2010) reported that the higher the magnitude of reduction in photosynthesis rate in increasing concentrations of Cd is caused by inhibition of PSII activities. Singh *et al.* (2003) showed that both growth and photosynthetic pigmentation system are affected by the presence of heavy metals. Souza Rauser (2003) reported that plants are seldom exposed in nature to the effect of a single heavy metal since excess metal ions exist mostly in mixtures in various polluted soils and irrigation water worldwide. Subba Rao (1982) the biofertilizers means the input of plant nutrients of biological origin for the growth of plants. Biofertilizers are also known as 'microbial inoculants' or 'microbial preparations'. They themselves do not increase the soil fertility directly, but instead they exercise their biological effects on improving the nutritional conditions. This has led to the mass production of *Rhizobium, Azotobacter, Cyanobacteria, Azospirillum,* phosphate solublizing bacteria and VAM. Takeda *et al.* (1983) reported that the polyamines are basic in nature, having positive charge at physiological pH. They have been shown to bind strongly *in vitro* to negatively charged nucleic acids acidic phospholipids and types of enzymatic and non-enzymatic proteins whose activity can be affected by the presence of polyamines. These interactions of ions are important for maintenance of the biological function of cells under *in vivo* condition. As in the case of other plant growth regulators, the polyamine pool depends on its [a] synthesis; [b] oxidative damage; [c] conjugation and transport. PAs transport is the energy dependent process and calcium is involved in the corresponding mechanisms. Tomsett and Thurman (1986) reported that the hyper-accumulation is an eco-physiological adaptation of plants to metalliferous soils. The mechanism of metal accumulation, which involves extra-cellular and intracellular metal chelation, precipitation, compartmentalization and translocation in the vascular system, are poorly understood. Wilson (1975) reported the negative association between grain number per panicle and weight per gram in sorghum.Wilson (1988) reported that the effect of the most common environmental factors, such as water, available nutrients, perception of light and ambient CO_2 concentration, root growth can be explained reasonably well by its relationship to shoot growthYang *et al.*(2005) researched the effect of sewage irrigation accelerated the decline of wheat seedlings and root, reducing the root number and the root activities significantly. Yusuf *et al.* (2011) Suggested that a different pattern of response was observed for the marker of oxidative stress, i.e., lipid perioxidation and H_2O_2 content and electrolyte leakage. Zengin and Munzuroglu (2005) reported that the heavy metals inhibit metabolic processes by inhibiting the action of enzymes and this may be the most important causes of inhibition. Decreased chlorophyll content associated with heavy metal stress may be the result of inhibition of the enzymes responsible for the chlorophyll biosynthesis. Cadmium was reported to affect chlorophyll biosynthesis and inhibit protochlorohyll reduction. Zornoza *et al.* (2002) reported that alter the plant's biochemical, metabolic functions, and pathways and also affects their physiological functions such as plant growth, development, cell differentiation, elongation, photosynthesis, nutrition, water transport, respiration, absorption of minerals from the soil. Van Nostrand's International Encyclopedia of Chemical Science 1964 and in 1987, the editors of Grant and Hackh's Chemical Dictionary included metals with a density greater than 4 g cm^{-3}. Heavy metals are metals and metallolids, which have atomic weight between 63.5 and 200.6 $gmol^{-1}$ and density is greater than 4.5 gcm^{-3}. Heavy metals are conformist in nature, meaning they persist in the environment for longer periods. Heavy metals such as mercury (Hg), lead (Pb), arsenic (As), cadmium (Cd), selenium (Se), copper (Cu), zinc (Zn), chromium (Cr) and vanadium (V) are measured potentially hazardous (Late and Rohindra 2002) to the plants, human being and the environment. According to Pekey (2006), heavy metal are deemed grave pollutants for the reason that of toxicity, perseverance and non-biodegradability in the environment and efforts are being made to reduce the harmful effect of the heavy metal pollutants around the globe. Pollutant is any substance which due to its high concentration in environment shows deleterious effect on living being, however a minute quantity of those substance are needed for overall development of living being. Indispensable trace metals such as Cu, Zn and Fe are imperative components of enzymes, respiratory proteins and certain structural elements of organism, but higher than certain threshold concentrations they are considered potentially toxic to both humans and plants, also heavy metals have grater detrimental environmental effects when a water body has low pH (Brown and Depladge 1985).Heavy metals are as expected occurring elements in the bedrock from where they are incorporated in minerals and ores together with other metals and they can be released through weathering and mining. Other than the natural source major inputs of heavy metals pollutant to the aquatic and terrestrial environment include urban storm, water runoff, industrial effluents, mining operations and atmospheric contaminants in particulate and dissolved form (Reichelt and Jones 1994). Toxic heavy metals such as Cd, Cu, Zn, Ni and Pb are frequently present in high concentrations in sewage sludge, ash and use of antifouling paints on marine vessels and structure yield appreciable concentrations of heavy metals to the sea (Kennish 1997) also sedimentations from natural as well as anthropogenic source contributes as significant sources of heavy metals to the marine environment. The sediments can be terrestrial origin such as run- off from logging catchments or from poor farming practices or of riverine inputs. By means of indication to the chemistry of heavy metals the solubility of heavy metals increases as pH decrease, Cd, Cu, Pb and Zn are all reasonably soluble at low pH. At higher pH values they are immobilized in complexes or mineral structure.

Below reducing conditions they form insoluble complexes with sulphides in the midst of very low mobility as a result. In oxidizing conditins they are precipitated in concert with carbonates or adsorbed onto iron or manganese oxy hydroxides (Brady 2002). A number of heavy metals are volatile in temperament while those heavy metals that do not volatilize or evaporate the ultimate sink are soils and sediments (Baird *et al.*, 1998). Mining and ore processing also leave go of heavy metals. The sensitivity of plants to heavy metals depends on an interrelated network of physiological and molecular mechanisms such as:

1. Uptake and accumulation of metals through binding to extracellular exudates and cell wall constituents.
2. Efflux of heavy metals from cytoplasm to extra-nuclear compartments including vacuoles.
3. Complication of heavy metal ions inside the cell by various substances, for example, organic acids, aminoacids, phytochelatins and metallothioneins.
4. Accumulation of osmolytes and osmoprotectant and induction of anti-oxidative enzymes.
5. Activation or modification of plant metabolism to allow adequate functioning of metabolic pathways and rapid repair of damaged cell structure (Cho *et al.*, 2003).

Cadmium is a malleable, ductile metal which is typically obtained as a by-product from the smelting of lead and zinc ores. The principal use of cadmium is as constituents in alloys and in the electroplating industry. Other uses of cadmium include paints and pottery pigments, corrosion resistant coating of nails, screws, etc, in process engraving, in cadmium-nickel batteries, and as fungicides (Stoeppler 1991). Cadmium is also naturally present in soils and mineral fertilizers. Origin of cadmium in soil is described as agricultural wastes (20 %), sludge (38%), fertilizers (2%) and atmospheric fallouts (40%)

Cadmium is one of the most toxic elements with reported carcinogenic effects in humans (Goering *et al.*, 1994). Cadmium and cadmium compounds are, compared to other heavy metals, relatively water soluble and mobile compound in most soils, generally more bio- available and tends to bio-accumulate. It induces cell injury and death by interfering with calcium (Ca) regulation in biological system. Cadmium is not essential for plant or animal life (IPCS monographs/WHO1995a; WHO1995b). It is more mobile than zinc but less mobile than nickel. Cadmium is voluntarily accumulated by several organisms, predominantly by microorganism and mollusks where the bio-concentration factors are in the order of thousands. Its mobility basically depends on the pH; the metal's adsorption to the soil's solid phase can be multiplied threefold for every unitary increase in pH in a range from 4 to 8.

Terrestrial plants may build up cadmium in the roots and cadmium is found bound to the cell walls (AMAP 2000). As told very beigning in the introduction chapter that, the pH level is one of the most important factors controlling cadmium absorption. Compared with other micropolluants such as Cu or Pb, transfer of Cd to the above ground parts of the plant may be measured as significant. Accumulation of cadmium in roots shows only 2 to 5 times compared with the above ground parts but cadmium is transferred only with difficulty to reproductive or storage organs of the plant. No deficiency level for cadmium is known. On the opposing, cadmium is well known as a highly phytotoxic element. Besides decreasing growth and development, phytotoxicity also occurs above 5.0-30.0 mg/kg dry weight, though chlorosis, which can be followed in the case of acute cadmium poisoning by necrosis (Browen 1979). Other compounds including Fe, Se, Mn and particularly Zn are antagonistic to Cd.

A draft commission regulation practice to set maximum level for some heavy metals in foodstuff as 0.05 mg kg^{-1} in fish, vegetables and fruits, excluding leafy vegetables, root vegetables and potatoes; 0.1 mg kg^{-1} cereals, except wheat grain and rice; 0.2 mg kg^{-1} in wheat grain and rice, leafy vegetables and mushrooms.

CONCLUSION

Numerous standards and a great deal of suggestions persist all over the world regarding the amount of heavy metals in different plant types, which can be consumed by humans. Also, there are many values consequent to the amount of heavy metals in sewers which may be released into environment. There are some standards showing permitted levels of the heavy metal, cadmium:

(a) The WHO has presented the highest allowable concentration of cadmium accumulation in human diet 0.1mg/l.

(b) United Nation standard for nutritional and agricultural materials has determined a max level of 0.01ppm for cadmium accumulation in irrigational waters and maximum level of 7 µg kg^{-1} body weight for humans' daily diets.

(c) The United States Environmental Protection Agency (USEPA) has presented a standard which permits a maximum amount of 85ppm for cadmium in ooze which may be deposited in agricultural lands.

REFERENCES

Abeledo, L.G., D.F. Calderini and G.A Slafer. 2002. Physiological Changes Associated with the Breeding Process. In: Slafer GA, Molina-Cano JL, Savin R, ArausJL, Romagosa I. Eds. Barley Science: Recent Advances from Molecular Biology to Agronomy of Yield and Quality. New York-Food Production Press. 2002: 361-386.

Ackerson, R.C. and Krieg, D.R. 1977. Stomatal and Nonstomatal Regulation of Water-use in Cotton. Corn and Sorghum. Plant Physiol., 60: 850-853.

Alloway, B.J. 1990. Heavy Metal in Soils. John Wiley and Sons Inc. New York, pp. 20-27.

Akdeniz, H., Yilmaz, I., Bozkurt, M.A. and Keskin, B.2006. The Effects of Sewage Sludge and Nitrogen Applications on Grain Sorghum Grown (*Sorghum vulgare* L.) in Turkey. Polish J Environ. Stud., 15(1): 19-26.

Al-Enezi, G., Hamodam, M.F. and Fawzi, N. 2005. Heavy Metal Content of Municipal Wastewater and Sludges in Kuwait. J Environ. Sci. Health, 39: 397-407.

Al-Jaloud, A.A., Hussain, G., Al-Saati, A.J. and Karimulla, S.1995. Effect of Wastewater Irrigation on Mineral Composition of Corn and Sorghum Plants in a Pot Experiment. J Plant Nut., 18: 1677-1692.

AMAP 2000. AMAP. AMAP Assessment (2002). Heavy Metals in the Arctic-Pre-print Files. Arctic Monitoring and Assessment Programme; Oslo, Norway, pp. 870.

Arduino, E., Barberis, E., Carraro, F. and Forno, M.G.1984. Estimating Relativeages from Iron-oxide/totaliron Ratios of Soils in the Western Povalley, Italy. Geoderma 33: 39-52.

Baird *et al.*, 1998. Baird, E., Booth, A., Broers, L., Hayes, L., Powell, W., Thomas, W., Vivar H., Young, G. (1998). Introgression of Quantitative trait loci (QTLs) Determining Strip Rust Resisitance in Barley: An Example of Marker-assisted Line Development. *Theor. Appl. Genet.*, 96: 123-131.

Bavi, K., Kholdebarin, B. and Moradshahi, A. 2011. Effect of Cadmium on Growth Protein Content and Peroxidase Activity in Pea Plants. Pak. J Bot., 43: 1467-1470.

Bhardwaj, P., Chaturvedi, A.K., and Prasad, P. 2009. Effect of Enhanced Lead and Cadmium in Soil on Physiological and Biochemical Attributes of *Phaseolus vulgaris* L. Nature and Sci., 7(8): 63-75.

Bi, Y.L., Li, X.L. and Christie, P. 2003a. Influence of Early Stages of Arbuscular Mycorrhiza on uptake of Zinc and Phosphorus by Red Clover from a Low Phosphorus Soil Amended with Zinc and Phosphorus. Chemosph., 50: 831-837.

Bjerrum J. 1959. Metal Amine Formation in Aqueous Solution. In: *Treatise on analytical Chemistry*. Vol. I. J. Elving (eds.). New York: The Interscience Encyclopedia.

Brady, N.C. In: The Nature and Properties of Soils, 13th edition, Prentice Hall (2002). pp. 456-464.

Brooks, R.R., Chambers, M.F., Nicks, L.J. and Robinson, B.H. 1998. Phytomining Perspect., 3(9): 359-361.

Browen 1979. Brown, M.T., Depledge, M.H. (1985). Determination of Trace Metal Concentrations in Marine Organisms. In: Metal Metabolism in Aquatic Environment. (Ed Langston, W.J., Bebianno, M.J.).

Brown, M.T., Depledge, M.H. (1985). Determination of Trace Metal Concentrations in Marine Organisms. In: Metal Metabolism in Aquatic Environment. (Ed Langston, W.J., Bebianno, M.J.).

Caddel, J.L. and Weibel, D.E. 1971. Effect of Photoperiod and Temperature on the Development of Sorghum. Agron. J. 63: 799-803.

Cao, A., Carucci, A., Lai, T., La Colla, P. and Tamburini, E. 2007. Effect of Biodegradable Chelating Agents on Heavy Metals Phytoextraction with *Mirabilis jalapa* and on its Associated Bacteria. Europ. J Soil Biol., 43: 200-206.

Chander, K. and Brookest, P.C. 1991. Effect of Heavy Metals from Past Applications of Sewage Sludge on Microbial Biomass and Organic Matter Accumulation in a Sandy Loam and Silty Loam UK Soil. Soil Biol. Biochem., 23(10): 927-932.

Channappagoudar, B.B., Hiremath, S.M., Biradar, N.R., Koti, R.V. and Bharamagoudar, T.D. 2008. Physiological Basis of Yield Variation in Foxtail Millet Karnataka. J Agric. Sci., 20(3): 481-486.

Chaney, W.R., Kelley, J.M. and Strickland, R.C. 1978. Influence of Cadmium and Zinc on Carbondioxide Evolution from Litter and Soil from a Black Oak Forest. J Environ. Qual., 7: 115-119.

Cho, D.H. and Kim, E.Y. 2003. Bioprocess Biosysytem. Eng. 25(5): 271-277.

Cho *et al.*, 2003. Cho, M., Chardonnens, A.N., Dietz, K.J. (2003). Differential Heavy Metal Tolerance of Arabidopsis halleri and Arabidopsis thalina: A Leaf Slice Test. New Phyto., 158: 287-293.

Clark, L.E., Collier, J.W. and Langston, R. 1968. Dormancy in *Sorghum bicolor* (L.) Moench. II. Effect of Pericarp and Testa. Crop Sci., 8: 155-158.

Da-Lin, L., Shu-pan, Z., Zheng, C. and Wei-wei, Q. 2011. Soil Cadmium Regulates Antioxidases in Sorghum. Agri. Sci. China, 9(10): 1475-1480.

Devitt, D., Stolzy, L.H and Jarell, W.M. 1984. Response of Sorghum and Wheat to different K/Na Ratio at Varying Osmotic Potential. Agron. J. 76: 768-788.

Elobeid, M.,Gobel, C., Feussher, P. and Polle, A.2012. Cadmium Interferences with Auxin Physiology and Lignifications in Poplar. J Exp.Bot., 63(3): 1413-1421.

Ethanol fuel from biomass, In: Advances in Agricultural Microbiology, pp.585-641. Oxford and IBH publishing, CO, New Delhi.

Falkowski, P.G and Raven, J.A. 2007. Aquatic Photosynthesis. 2nd edu, Blackwell Sciences, London.

Galavi, M., Jalali, A., Ramroodi, M., Mousavi, S.R. and Galavi, H. 2010. Effects of Treated Municipal Wastewater on Soil Chemical Properties and Heavy Metal uptake by Sorghum (*Sorghum bicolor* L.). J Agric. Sci., 2: 235-241.

Galvez and Clark, R.B. 1991. Effect of Silicon on Growth and Mineral Composition of Sorghum (*Sorghum bicolor*) Grown with Toxic Levels of Aluminium. Dev. Plant Soil Sci. 45: 815-823.

Gisbert, C., Rus, A.M., Bolarin, M.C., Lopez-Coronado, J.M., Arrillage, I., Montesinos, C., Caro, M., Serrano, R. and Moreno, V. 2003. The Yeast HAL1 Gene Improves Salt Tolerance of Transgenic Tomato. Plant Physiol., 123: 393-402.

Glass D.J. 2000. Economic Potential of Phytoremediation. In: Raskin I., Ensley B.D. (eds): Phytoremediation of Toxic Metals: Using Plants to Clean up the Environment. John Wileyand Sons, New York: 15-31.

Goering *et al.*, 1994. Goering, P.L., Waalkes, M.P., Klaassen, C.D. (1994). Toxicity of Cadmium. *In* "Handbook of Experimental Pharmacology: Toxicity of Metals, Biochemical Effects" (Ed) By Goyer R.A.C., Herian M.G. Springer Verlag, New York. pp. 189-213.

Haussmann, B.I.G., A.B. Obilana, P.O. Ayiechno, A. Blum, W. Schipprack and H.H. Geiger. 2000. Yield and yield Stability of Four Population Types of Grain Sorghum in a Semi-arid Area of Kenya. Crop Sci., 40: 319-329.

Jackson, M.B. 1993. Are Plant Hormones Involved in the Root to Shoot Communication? Adv. Bot. Res., 19: 103-187.

Jalil, A., Selles, F. and Clark, J.M. 1994. Effects of Cadmium on Growth and the uptake of Cadmium and other Elements by Durum Wheat. Plant Nutr., 17: 1839-1895.

Kayser, G., Korckritz, T. and Markert, B. 2001. Bioleaching for the Decontamination of Heavy Metals. Wasser and Boden., 53: 54-58.

Kennedy, B.F. and De Filippis, L.F. 1999. Physiological and Oxidative Response to NaCl of the Salt Tolerant *Grevillea ilicifolia* and the Salt Sensitive *Grevillea arenaria*. J PlantPhysiol., 155: 746-754.

Kennish 1997. Kennish, M.J. (1997). Practical Handbook of Estuarine and Marine Pollution. pp. 253-256.

Khudsar, T., Mahmooduzzafar and M. Iqbal. 2001. Cadmium-induced Changes in Leaf Epidermis, Photosynthetic Rate and Pigment Concentration in *Cajanus cajan*. Biol. Plant., 44: 59-64.

Krantev, A., Yordanova, R., Janda, T., Szalai, G. and Popova, L. 2008. Treatment with Salicylic Acid Decreases the Effect of Cadmium on Photosynthesis in Maize Plants. J PlantPhysiol., 165: 920-931.

Ku, M.S., Cho, D.I., Li, X., Jiao, D.M., Pinto, M., Miyao, M. and Matsuoka, M. 2001. Introduction of Genes Encoding C4 Photosynthesis Enzymes into Rice Plants: Physiological Consequences. Novartis Founds Symp. 236: 100-111.

Kumar, P and Dwivedi, P. 2014. Phytoremediation of Cadmium through Sorghum. In Recent Advances in Crop Physiology (Ed. Amrit Lal Singh). Daya Publishing House, 2014, pp. 311-342.

Kumar, P., Mandal, B. and Dwivedi, P. 2011. Heavy Metal Scavenging Capacity of *Mentha spicata* and *Allium cepa*. Medicinal Plant, 3(4): 315-318.

Kuiper, I., Lagendijk, E.L., Bloemberg, G.V. and Lugtenberg, B.J.J. 2004. Rhizoremediation: A Beneficial Plant Microbe Interaction. Mol. Pla. Micr. Inter., 17: 6-15.

Kusano, T., Berberich, T., Tateda, C. and Takahashi, Y.2008. Polyamines: Essential Factors for Growth and Survival, Planta, 228: 367-381.

Late, R., Rohinder, D. (2002). Heavy Metal in Major Environmental Issues. *Sci.* 56: 756-762.

Liu, Q., Diamond, M.L., Gingrich, S.E., Ondov, J.M., Maciejczyk, P. and Stern, G.A. 2003. Accumulation of Metals, Trace Elements and Semivolatile Organic Compounds on Exterior Window Surfaces in Baltimore. Environ Pollu., 122(1): 51-61.

Liu, J.X. 2004. Effects of Cadmium and Zinc Interaction on Corn Seedlings Physiological and Biochemical Characteristics. Yi Chun College J, 26(6): 55-57.

Major D.J., Rood, S.B. and Miller, F.R. 1990. Temperature and Photoperiod Effects Mediated by the Sorghum Maturity Genes. Crop Sci., 30: 305-310.

McBride, M.B. 1995. Toxic Metal Accumulation from Agricultural use of Sludge: Are the USEPA Regulations Protective? J Environ. Quality, 24: 5-18.

Molla-hoseini, H., M. Harati, A. Akbari and M. Hariri. 2005. Accumulation of Heavy Metals in Sorghum Irrigated with Sewage. Proceeding of 9th of Iranian Soil Sciences Conference.

Monteriro, C.M., Castro, P.M.L. and Malcata, F.X. 2009. Use of Microalgae *Scendesmus oliquusto* Remove Cadmium cations from Aqueous Solutions. World J Microbial. Biotechnol. 25: 1573-1578.

Nalini, P. and Chandra, P.S. 2002. Effect of Heavy Metals Co, Ni and Cd on Growth and Metabolism of Cabbage. Plant Sci., 163: 753-758.

Ozdener, Y. and Kutbay, H.G. 2011. Physioloical and Biochemical Responses of the Leaves of Verbascum Wiedemannianum Fisch and May to Cadmium. Pak. J Bot., 43: 1521-1525.

Pal A., Kulshreshtha K., Ahmad K.J. and Behl, H.M. 2002. Do Leaf Surface Characters Play a Role in Plant Resistance to Auto-exhaust Pollution. Flora, 197: 47-55.

Parry, D.W. and M. Kelso.1975. The Distribution of Silicon Deposits in the Root of *Moliniacaerulea* (L) Moench and *Sorghum bicolor*(L.) Moench. Ann. Bot., 39: 995-1001.

Pekey, H. (2006). The Distribution and Sources of Heavy Metals in Izmit Bay Surface Sediments Affected by a Polluted Stream, Marine Pollution Buletin, 52: 1197-1208.

Pescod, M. B. 1992. Wastewater Treatment and use in Agriculture. FAO Irrigation and Rainage Paper 47 Rome: Food and Agriculture Organization of the United Nations.

Premachandra, G.S., Hahn, D.T., Rhodes D. and Joly, R.J. 1995. Leaf Water Relation and Solute Accumulation in Two Grain Sorghum Lines Exhibiting Contrasting Drought Tolerance. J Exp. Bot., 46: 1833-1841.

Qin, T.C., Ruan J.L.J and Wang, L.J. 2000. Effects of Cadmium on Plant Photosynthesis. Environ. Sci. Technol., 13: 33-35.

Qin, H, Diener, D.R., Geimer, S., Cole, D.G. and Rosenbaum, J.L.2004. Intraflagellar Transport (IFT) Cargo: IFT Transports Flagellar Precursors to the Tip and Turnover Products to the Cell Body. JCell Biol. 164(2): 255-266.

Quinby, J.R. 1974. Sorghum Improvement and the Genetic of Growth. College Station: Texas A & M University Press, p. 108.

Rainbow, P.S. 1985. The Biology of Heavy Metals in the Sea. Intl. J Environ. Studies, 25: 195-211.

Reichelt and Jones 1994. Reichelt, A.J., Jones, G.B. (1994). Trace Metals as Tracers of Dredging Activity in Cleveland Bay-field and Laboratory Studies. *Aust. J. Marine and Freshwater Res.*, 45: 1237-1257.

Sandalio, L.M., Rodríguez-Serrano, M., Romero-Puertas, M. and del Río, L.A. 2008. Imaging of Reactiveoxygen Species and NO in vivo in Plant Tissues. Methods Enzymol. 440: 399-409.

Schmit, U. 2003. Enhancing Phytoextraction: The Effect of Chemical Soil Manipulation on Mobility, Plant Accumulation and Leaching of Heavy Metals. J Environ Quality 32(6): 1939-54.

Senthil, T., Sachdev, S. and Vojta, M. 2003. Phy. Rev.Lett. 90: 216403.

Serafini-Fracassini, D. and Mossetti, U. 1986. What is the Function of Conjugated Polyamine in Plants? In: C.M. Calderara, C. Clo. C. Guarmieri (Eds), Biochemical Studies of Natural Polyamines, Cooperativa Libraria Universitaria Editrice, Bologna, 1986, pp. 157-202.

Setia, R.C. and Bala. R.1994. Anatomical Changes in Root and Stem of Wheat (*Triticum aestivum*L.) in Response to different Heavy Metals. Phytomorph. 44: 95-104.

Shah, D., Horsch, R., Klee, H., Kishore, G.,Winter, J., Tumer, N., Hironaka, C., Sanders, P., Gasser C. and Aykent. S. 1986. Engineering Herbicide Tolerance in Transgenic Plants. Sci., 233: 478-481.

Sharma, S.S., Schat, H. and Vooijis, R.1998. *In vitro* Alleviation of Heavy Metal-induced Oxidative Enzymes Inhibition by Proline. Phytochem. 49: 1531-1535.

Shi, W., Bischoff, M., Turco, R. and Konopka, A. 2002. Long-term Effects of Chromium and Lead upon the Activity of Soil Microbial Communities. Appl. Soil Ecol., 21: 169-177.

Singh, R.P., Tripathi, R.D., Dabas, S., Rizvi, S.M.H., Ali, M.B., Sinha, S.K., Gupta, D.K., Mishra, S. and Rai,U.N. 2003. Effect of Lead on Growth and Nitrate Assimilation of Vigna radiata (L.) Wilczek seedlings in a Salt Affected Environment. Chemo., 52: 1245-1250.

Soudex, P., Petrova, S. and Vanek, T. 2012. Phytostabilization or Accumulation of Heavy Metals by using of Energy Crop Sorghum sp., Intl. Proc. Biol. Environ. Eng., 46: 25-29.

Souza, J.F. and Rauser, W.E. 2003. Maize and Radish Sequester Excess Cadmium and Zinc in Different Ways. Pl. Sci., 165: 1009-22.

Stoeppler, M. 1991. Cadmium. In: Merian E (ed.) Metals and their Compounds in the Environment: Occurrence, Analyses and Biological Relevance. VCH, New York, pp. 803-851.

Stoeppler 1991. Stoeppler, M. (1991). Cadmium. In: Merian E (ed.) *Metals and their Compounds in the Environment: Occurrence, Analyses and Biological Relevance*. VCH, New York, pp. 803-851.

Takeda, Y., Samejina, K., Nagano, K., Watanable, M, Sugeta, H. and Kyogoku, Y., 1983. Determination of Protonation site in Thermospermine and in other Polyamines by 15N and 13C Nuclear Magnetic Resonance Spectroscopy, Eur. J. Biochem., 130: 383-386.

Tomsett, A.B. and Thurman, D.A. 1988. Molecular Biology of Metal Tolerances of Plants, Plant CellEnviron., 11: 383-394.

Van Nostrand's International Encyclopedia of Chemical Science 1984. Van Nostrand's Encyclopedia of Chemistry, 5th Edition. Glenn D. Considine (Editor). ISBN: 978-0-471-61525-5, 1856 Pages January 2005.

Wilson, J.B. 1986. A Review of Evidence on the Control of Shoot: Root, in Relation to Model. Ann. Bot., 61: 433-449.

Yang, J.F., Bu, Y.S. and Guo, X.Y. 2005. Research on Effects of Soil Exogenous Cadmium and Lead Pollution on Rape Growth. Shanxi. Agric. Sci., 3: 26-28.

Zareim, M., Kong, S., Hempels, S., Nekonei, M.K., Savaghebi, G. and Buscoff. 2008. Comunnity Structure of Arbuscular Mycorrhiza Fungi Associated to *Venonic rechingeri* at the Anguran Zinc and Lead Mining Region. Envron Poll., 156: 1277-1288.

Zengin, F. and Munzuroglu, O. 2005. Effect of Some Heavy Metals on Content of Chlorophyll, Proline and some Antioxidant Chemicals in Bean (*Phaseolus vulgaris L.*) Seedlings. Acta Biol. Crac., 47(2): 157-164.

Zornoza, P., Vázquez, S., Esteban, E., Fernández -Pascual, M. and Carpena, R. 2002. Cadmium-stress in Nodulated White lupin: Strategies to Avoid Toxicity. Plant Physiol. Biochem. 40: 1003-1009.

Pages: 128-139

Metals Distribution in Environment
Edited by: **Dr. Deep Mala & Dr. Pawan Kumar 'Bharti'**
ISBN: 978-93-86841-91-9
Edition: **2019**
Published by: **Discovery Publishing House Pvt. Ltd., New Delhi (India)**

7

Seasonal Variation of Physicochemical Properties and Heavy Metals Content of Leachate in Obio/Akpor L.G.A Rivers State, Nigeria

Andy William Asukwo
Osu Charles Ikenna
Iwuoha G.N.; AdoweiP

ABSTRACT

The paper discusses the seasonal variation of physicochemical properties of leachate generated from active and inactive municipal solid waste dumpsites and its negative impact on the underground water in Obio/Akpor L.G.A, Rivers State. This study investigated the levels of leachate contamination and the effects on borehole water close to selected dumpsites. Leachate and borehole water samples were collected and analyzed for various physicochemical parameters and heavy metals during dry and wet-season. Parameters measured were pH, NH_3-N, COD, BOD_5, NO_3^-, Odour, ColourPb, Cu, and Cd. The sampling locations were Alakahia dumping site along East-West road (SLA), Choba dump site along East-West road (SLB) and Chinda borrow pit, off chinda road Mile 4 (SLC). The result from the analysis showed that pH values were within FEPA recommended limit for both seasons and that of water samples were below the specified range. NH_3-N (2.64mg/l, 7.92mg/l, 2.40mg/l), COD (130mg/l, 128mg/l, 156mg/l), Pb (0.175mg/l, 0.12mg/l, 0.40mg/l) were most polluted during dry season. For wet-season, Nitrate (5.44mg/l, 4.550mg/l, 5.89mg/l) recorded very high values while BOD_5, Cu, and Cd were below permissible limit for both seasons with values ranging from 3.25mg/L to

Department of Pure and Industrial Chemistry, Faculty of Science, University of Port Harcourt, Nigeria

2.80 mg/L (dry season),3.00mg/L to 3.70mg/L(wet-season); <0.001mg/L (dry season), 0.062mg/L to 0.057mg/L, (wet-season) and 0.010mg/L to 0.014 mg/L (dry season), 0.049mg/L to 0.066 mg/L (wet-season) respectively.

Keywords: Leachate, Solid waste, Dump sites, Borehole water

INTRODUCTION

Solid waste management has become a significant environmental problem in our society today particularly in Rivers State and Nigeria as a whole due to illegal dumping of both hazardous and non-hazardous solid wastes in dumps. Open dump method of waste disposal although illegal, is the most widely practiced form of solid waste disposal in Nigeria (Horsfall and Spiff, 2013).

Increased industrial, commercial activities as well as demographic expansion have caused an astronomical rise in the volume and diversity of solid waste generated in the country and this remarkable growth rate has not been matched in order to improve the quality of the urban environment (Aluko *et al.,* 2003).

Management of municipal solid waste (MSW) still remains one of the most neglected areas of urban development especially in Nigeria with rapid migration of people from villages to cities and anthropogenic activities which degrade the status of our environment on a daily basis leading to more land being required for ultimate disposal of these solid waste making issues related to solid waste disposal a major challenge (Bhalla *et al.*, 2013).

An open dump is an illegal solid waste disposal site, where abandoned piles of waste and debris are left in noticeable quantities example include old barrels, vegetable matter, plastics, bottles, used tyres, pipes, asbestos, abandoned piles of household garbage. In developing countries like Nigeria where open dump disposal method is mostly practiced due to the non-availability of trained manpower, uncontrolled and low budget for waste disposal has led to a rise in the number of dump site and has become a normal method of solid waste disposal such that some open dumps have grown larger and larger as it a threat in our environment with occurrence such as fire and explosion, contamination of streams, rivers, soil, lakes and ground water.

Despite the application of $5R_s$ which are refusal, reduction, reuse, recycle and recovery, waste disposal sites and landfills are still the principal focus for ultimate disposal of residual waste and incineration residues worldwide (Aluko *et al.,* 2003). Leachate is the liquid that is formed as water passes or percolate through a solid waste in a dump site (Ojoawo *et al.,* 2012). It is created when the landfill beds damp content exceeds its retention capacity which is described as the maximum water quality that can be retained in porous material of the landfill (Koc-Jurczyk, 2009). The emitted liquid may contain several mixtures such as inorganic, organic, micro-biological and suspended solid substances which have detrimental effect on surface water and soil. Proper treatment and safe disposal of leachate is one of the major environmental challenges faced worldwide especially in developing nations (Sacky and Meizah, 2015). Characteristics of dump site leachate are extremely variable depending on the composition of the solid waste, precipitation rate, compaction, cover design, site hydrology, dump site age, sampling procedures and interaction of leachate with the environment as well as landfill design and its operations. The basic parameters that characterize dump sites are chemical oxygen demand (COD), biological oxygen demand (BOD), Ratio of BOD/COD, colour, pH, heavy metal, alkalinity and oxidation reduction potentials (Bhalla *et al.*, 2013).

Generally the trend between dump site age and leachate composition has demonstrated that leachate toxicity decreases with time in which the rate of stabilization of waste depends on the movement of water through the dump that is influenced by infiltration (Ojoawo *et al.*, 2012). The impact of dump site leachate on the surface, ground water, soil and human health has become a major issue in solid waste management in that, areas close to landfill or open dump sites have a greater possibility of ground water contamination because of the potential pollution source of leachate originating from the nearby site, such contamination of ground water resources poses a substantial risk to local resource users and to the natural environment. In soil, dump site and its leachate contribute significantly in degradation of soil quality leading to massive destruction ofthe ecosystem and posing a threat to human health with ailments like cancer, organ damage, and even death to man either through direct or indirect contact. It also causes an imbalance to fauna and flora in the soil (Sidhardhan and Kumar, 2014). Therefore managing leachates that come out from solid waste dump sites could be attained by providing impermeable liner to every dump site, then centrally collecting the leachates and treat them before they are discharged into nearby rivers or streams which serve as the major source of water supply for domestic, industrial, agricultural activities. This will go a long way in monitoring the concentration of potential contaminants at specific dump sites.

MATERIALS AND METHODS

Leachate Sampling Analysis

Leachate samples were collected randomly at selected leachates drains at each dump site, since each of the dump sites are low lying land areas, the leachate were collected at the base of the solid waste heaps as the leachate drained out under gravity. Four liters of plastic containers were used to collect the leachate samples but the containers were first cleaned by soaking in 10% nitric acid and rinsed with distilled water.

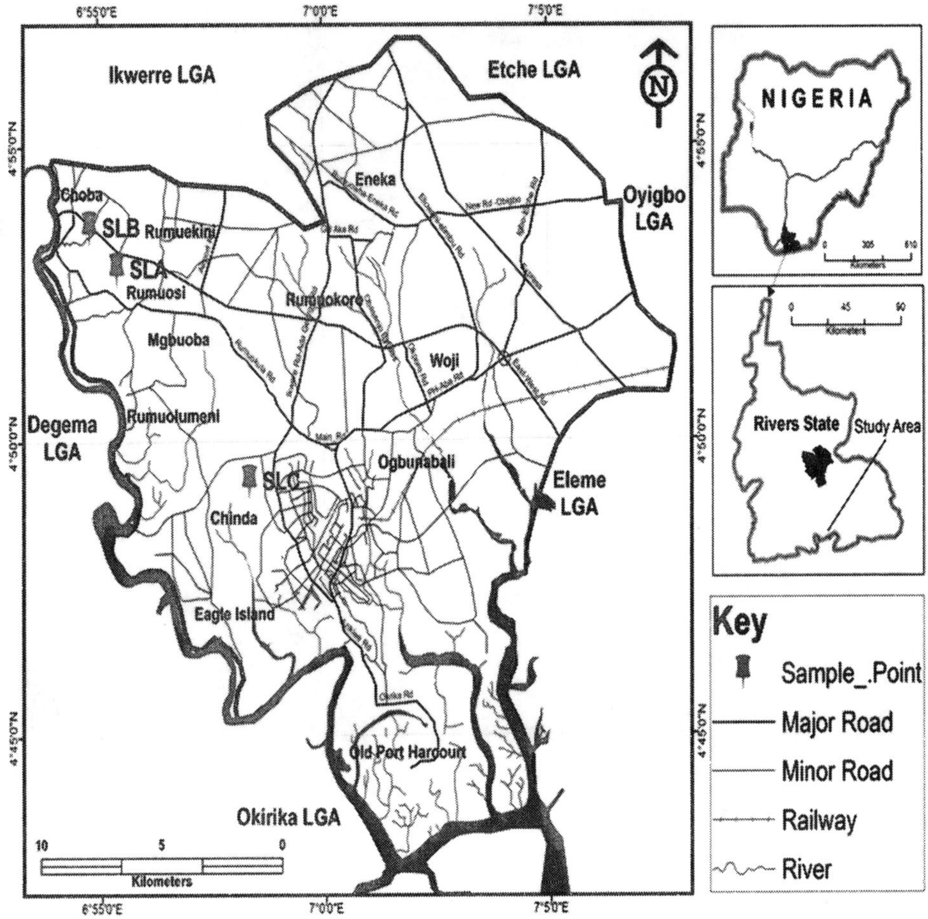

6°55'0"E
7°0'0"E
7°5'0"E
4°55'0"N
4°50'0"N
4°45'0"N
Ikwerre LGA
Etche LGA
N
Eneka
Choba
SLB
Rumuekini
SLA
Rumuosi
Oyigbo LGA
Rumuokoro
Mgbuoba
Woji
Degema LGA
Rumuolumeni
Ogbunabali
SLC
Chinda
Eleme LGA
Eagle Island
Old Port Harcourt
Okirika LGA
10 5 0
Kilometers
NIGERIA
Rivers State
Study Area
Key
Sample_.Point
Major Road
Minor Road
Railway
River

GIS OF THE STUDY AREA

A
B

In each of the sampling site, the containers were rinsed twice with the leachate sample before collection. At Alakahia dump site (SLA), the two leachate sample collection points were labeled A_1 and A_2 with a distanceof 0-10m between the two points and water samples were also collected from boreholes labeled $W_A$whichwere collected at a distance of about 25m from the dump site. For Choba dump site (SLB), the leachate samples collected at the two points were labeled B_1 and B_2 with about 0-6m distance between the two points and borehole water samples at a distance of 30m from the dump site were collected as control and labeled W_B. At chinda dump site (SLC), the leachate samples were collected at two points and labeled C_1 and C_2 with about 0-8m distance between the two points and borehole water samples as control were also collected and labeled Wc at a distance of about 37m from the dump site. The pH of the samples was measured in-situ for each of the sampling locations and the samples were transferred immediately to the laboratory and was stored at 4° C after filtration through glass micro filter (0.47mm). The samples were collected in January and may which represent dry season and wet-season respectively.

Analytical Work

Analytical methods used were according to "Standard methods for examination of water and wastewater" Specified by American Public Health Association (APHA, 2005). The pH was measured by Mettler Toledo portable pH meter using pH standard calibration methods. The Ammonia Nitrogen (NH_3-N) was determined using powder pillows methods (D8155: Standard Methods). Chemical oxygen demand (COD) was determined using open Reflux method followed by titration with Ferrous Ammonium Sulphate (FAS). Biological oxygen demand-Winkler's method was used to estimate initial and final Dissolve Oxygen (DO) in the samples and BOD_5 was determined. Brucine methods were used to analyse Nitrate and concentration was measured using UV-VIS Spectrophotometer (Genesis 10 UV). The colour and odour were observed in situ. Heavy metal viz Lead (Pb), Copper (Cu) and Cadmium (Cd) were determined using a Flame Atomic Absorption Spectrophotometer.

RESULT AND DISCUSSION

Table 7.1: Average values of physicochemical characteristics of Leachate samples during dry season

Parameters	SLA_D (mg/l)	SLC_D(mg/l)	SLC_D(mg/l)
Colour	Light greenish-brown	Light greenish- brown	Light greenish- brown
Odour	Foul smell	Foul smell	Foul smell
pH	6.93	7.02	6.70
NH_3-N	2.64	7.92	2.40
COD	130.0	128.0	156.00
BOD_5	3.25	3.20	2.80
NO_3	5.95	2.51	6.46
Pb	0.175	0.12	0.40
Cu	<0.001	<0.001	<0.001
Cd	0.010	0.014	<0.001

Table 7.2: Average values of physicochemical characteristics of Leachate samples during wet-season

Parameters	SLA_R (mg/l)	SLB_R (mg/l)	SLC_R (mg/l)
Colour	Greenish brown	Greenish brown	Greenish brown
Odour	Foul smell	Foul smell	Foul smell
pH	6.52	6.66	6.47
NH_3-N	0.00	0.730	0.00
COD	7.40	24.30	96.40
BOD_5	3.65	3.00	3.70
NO_3	5.44	4.55	5.895
Pb	<0.001	<0.001	0.001
Cu	0.061	0.062	0.057
Cd	0.064	0.049	0.066

The mean variations of leachate characteristics are shown in table 7.1 and 7.2 where the concentration of pollutants varied based on the season. Leachates were light green-brown in colour during dry season compared to wet-season where the colour was green-brown and it l required high chlorination in order to removed pathogenic organisms. The pH of leachates was neither alkaline nor acidic with average pH values of 6.93, 7.02, 6.70 during dry season and 6.52, 6.66, 6.47 during wet-season for SLA, SLB and SLC respectively. The pH of the leachate depends solely on the age of the dump site, which means the pH of the stabilized leachate (old dumpsite in which the pH value is normally above 7.5) is always higher than that of a young dumpsite which is normally less than 6.5. What causes the initial low pH in a young (<5 years) dump site leachate is due to presence of high concentrations of volatile fatty acid (Acidogenic Phase) and this low pH can increase the solubility hence increasing the amount of metal ions that could be in solution (Chian and Dewalls, 1976). From the results it was deduced that the dump sites are young dump sites and the values were within the acceptable recommended limit. The average value of ammonia nitrogen in the leachate samples (Table 7.1 and 7.2) showed different values during dry and wet-season. The highest value was obtained at SLB with the value of 7.92 mg/L for both seasons. The value indicates the ages of the dump site with SLB found to be the oldest dump site compared to SLA and SLC with evident release of nitrogenous substances from the decomposed refuse. The higher the age of the dump site the more ammonia concentration. Chemical oxygen demand was used to measure the amount of oxygen needed to oxidize the organic constituents chained completely to inorganic constituents. The average values of COD were presented in table 7.1 and 7.2. The highest values were obtained at the SLC with the values of 156 mg/l and 96.40 mg/l whereas the lowest values were obtained at SLB with the value of 128 mg/L and 24.30 mg/L during dry and wet-season respectively. These values were above the recommended limit except that of SLB (24.30 mg/L) during wet-season. The increase in the concentration of COD indicates that the leachates required high amount oxygen for decomposition of organic matter by aerobic bacteria. Average value of Biological Oxygen Demand (BOD_5) in leachate samples presented in table 7.1 and 7.2 vary between 2.80mg/L to 3.25 mg/L, for dry season and 2.80mg/L to 3.70mg/L, for wet-season respectively. The highest value was obtained at SLC during wet-season and lowest value was at the same dump site (SLC) during dry season showing variation of $BOD\text{-}_5$ for both seasons. All the values obtained at the three studied locations were below the permissible limit of 30mg/l specified by FEPA. From the results, the concentration of BOD_5 in leachate samples showed that more of the organic matter is present in the leachate which used up any available dissolve oxygen. However, the average value of nitrate obtained during dry and wet-season is presented in table 7.1 and 7.2 were within the permissible limit. The highest value was obtained at SLC with a value of 6.46 mg/L during dry season with the lowest value of 2.51 mg/L obtained at SLB during the same season. The levels of nitrate contamination were found to be low in the leachates collected from the three studied locations indicating that micro-organism utilized more of the nitrate compounds and de nitrification of ammonia gas resulted in a decrease in the concentration of nitrate in the leachate samples. Concentration of heavy metals in the leachate samples obtained for the two seasons from SLA, SLB and SLC showed great variation. Leachate collected during dry season contained high concentration of lead (Pb) and were above the recommended limit with the average values of 0.175mg/l, 0.12mg/l and 0.4mg/l for SLA, SLB and SLC respectively. During wet-season, the concentrations were below the recommended limit. The high concentration during dry season could be attributed to a higher disposal rate of leaded materials such as Pb based paint, Pb batteries, chemicals for photographic processing, children toys present at the dump site as a result of undisrupted industrial activities ongoing inObio/Akpor L. G. A. For copper (Cu) its distribution in leachates varied. The highest value for Cu was obtained at SLB during wet-season with an average value of 0.062mg/l while the lowest value was 0.001mg/L for SLA, SLB and SLC respectively during dry season. The result presented in table 7.3 showed that all the values were above permissible limit of 0.05mg/l. For Cadmium (Cd), the average values for both dry and wet-season presented in table 7.1 and 7.2 were below recommended limit for SLA, SLB and SLC leachate samples.

Table 7.3: Mean variation of physicochemical characteristics of leachate samples for wet and dry season with overall mean

Parameters	Wet season mean SLA,B,C(mg/l)	Dry season mean SLA, B, C (mg/l)	Overall Mean (mg/l)	FEPA Standard
Colour	Greenish-brown	Light greenish-brown	Greenish-brown	
Odour	Odourless	Odourless	Odourless	
pH	6.551	6.880	6.716	6-7
NH_3-N	0.730	4.320	3.423	
COD	42.70	138.0	90.35	75.00
BOD_5	3.450	3.080	3.267	30.00
NO_3	5.295	4.973	5.134	20.00
Pb	<0.001	0.231	0.12	0.05
Cu	0.060	<0.001	0.031	5.00
Cd	0.059	0.0083	0.034	< 1

Table 7.4: Mean variation of physicochemical characteristics results for borehole water samples close to each of the 3 studies area during wet and dry season with overall mean

Parameters	Wet Season Mean WA B,C(mg/l)	Dry Season Mean WA,B,C(mg/l)	Overall Mean (mg/l)	FEPA Standard
Colour	Colourless	Colourless	Colourless	
Odour	Odourless	Odourless	Odourless	
pH	5.183	5.05	5.11	6-7
NH_3-N		0.75	0.75	
COD	20.0	53.3	36.65	75.00
BOD_5	2.13	2.36	2.245	30.00
NO_3	2.86	3.86	3.36	20.00
Pb	<0.001	0.47	0.236	0.05
Cu	0.066	<0.001	0.034	5.00
Cd	0.055	<0.001	0.028	< 1

MEAN VARIATION OF LEACHATE SAMPLES FOR TWO SEASONS

Mean and overall mean leachate characteristics during wet and dry season presented in table 7.3 shows the average value of measured parameters in the SLA, SLB and SLC and then compared with the Nigerian FEPA standard. The Mean pH values of the leachates during wet and dry season were 6.55 and 6.88 with overall mean value of 6.72. These values fall within the recommended FEPA standard. The mean values of Ammonia nitrogen (4.32mg/l and 0.730mg/l) were above permissible limit when compared to that of FEPA standard. The mean concentration of Nitrate (5.295mg/l) during wet-season was higher compared to mean concentration during dry season (4.97mg/l) with overall mean value of 5.134mg/l, the values obtained were below recommended limit of 20mg/l. The values indicated low nitrate levels for the 3 studied areas. SLA, SLB and SLC are situated within the city with minimal agricultural activities that could led to a traces of residual anions of fertilizers used for agricultural purposes that could leach or run-off into these areas and the values are expected to be more pronounced in the villages than in the cities where fertilizers are not utilized in large quantities for farming. The mean concentration of Chemical Oxygen Demand (COD) for SLA, SLB and SLC presented in table 7.3 were 42.70mg/l and 138mg/l for dry and wet season. These values show the variation of COD over the two seasons in which the mean value for dry season is almost twice as high as the recommended standard while during wet-season the mean value is almost two times lower than the standard limit with the overall mean value above the recommended limit of 75mg/l. This increase in the concentration of COD indicates higher amount of oxygen consumed by aerobic bacteria to breakdown the organic matter in the leachates. The mean concentration of Biological Oxygen Demand (BOD_5) showed that the mean values of BOD_5 during wet and dry season were almost in the same range and the value of the overall mean was 9 times lower than the standard value of 30mg/l specified by FEPA. This implies that more organic matter is present in the leachate samples collected between wet and dry seasons because the lower the value of $BOD_{5,}$ the more the organic matter present in the leachate sample the more the dissolve oxygen that will be needed by aerobic bacteria to breakdown the organic matter. Pollution by heavy metals such as Pb (lead), copper (Cu) and cadmium (Cd), showed great variation between the two seasons for the 3 study areas (SLA, SLB and SLC). Lead (Pb) pollution was highest during dry season with a mean value of 0.281mg/l as against 0.05mg/l recommended standard limit followed by cadmium and copper with mean values of 0.0083mg/l against <1mg/l and <0.001mg/l as against 5.00mg/l recommended limits during dry season. For wet-season, the mean value of Pb (lead) became <0.001mg/l compared to the recommended limit of 0.05mg/l. Cadmium levels increased considerably during this season with a mean value of 0.059mg/l, yet the value was below the recommended limit and copper (Cu) with the mean value of 0.0060mg/l was below the recommended standard during this period.When compared to the overall mean values for both dry and wet season for heavy metals, the result showed that lead (Pb) with the overall mean value of 0.12mg/l was high compared to the standard. This could be as the result of dissolve leaded waste materials dumped in the selected sites such as batteries, paint and paint product (Maiti *et al.,* 2015). Overall mean value for copper (Cu) was below the standard limit and that of cadmium with the overall mean value of 0.034mg/l. Therefore the values of these heavy metals during wet and dry season were observed to be low compared to the result obtained by Ojoawo *et al.,* (2012) and Osu and Okoro (2012) were they observed relatively high values of heavy metals such as lead (Pb) and copper (Cu) in the city than at the surrounding villages due to heavy industrial activities taking place in the city.

COMPARISON OF MEAN VARIATION OF WATER SAMPLES WITH THAT OF MEAN LEACHATE CHARACTERISTICS OVER TWO SEASONS

The mean pH values for water samples during wet and dry season are presented in table 7.4 with the mean pH value of 5.183, 5.05 and overall mean of 5.11. These values were not within the specified range of pH value by FEPA. When compared the mean pH of borehole water samples with that of mean pH values of leachate samples (6.56 and 6.88) during dry and wet season, the mean pH value of the water samples were low and more acidic than the leachate samples. The mean values of chemical oxygen demand (COD) during both wet and dry season in water control samples (20mg/l, and 53.3mg/l) were below the specified standard limit of 75mg/l. These values were lower than the mean concentration of COD in leachate samples during dry and wet-season. For biological oxygen demand, the mean concentration of leachate samples were slightly higher than that of mean concentration of water samples. None of these mean and overall mean concentrations were above the recommended limit during wet and dry season. This decrease in the BOD_5 values in the water samples especially during wet-season showed that more organic matter was present in the water samples than in the leachate samples collected. Mean concentration of nitrate in water samples for both seasons presented in table 7.4 were 2.86mg/l, 3.86mg/l, and 3.36mg/l. For alakahia (WA) being 2.86mg/l was low compared to that of choba (WB) and chinda (WC) water samples although the values were almost 4 times lower than 20mg/l specified by FEPA. When comparing these values with the mean values of leachate samples for the two seasons, the mean concentration of nitrate in leachate samples were higher than mean concentration of nitrate in water samples. For heavy metals, the mean concentration of lead (Pb) was less than 0.001mg/l in water samples during wet season but was 0.47mg/l during dry season with the overall mean value of 0.236mg/l. The mean values obtained were above the recommended limit except during wet-season. The mean value for lead (Pb) in the leachate samples during wet-season was also less than 0.001mg/l and became high during dry season similar to that of mean values of water samples. The mean concentration of copper (Cu) in water samples was high during wet-season and less than 0.001mg/l during dry season and the values were below the specified standard limit. In leachate samples presented in table 7.3 showing that the mean concentration of copper fluctuated betweenthe wet and dry season which was the same for the water samples. The mean values of (Cd) cadmium in water samples were 0.055mg/l and <0.001mg/l during wet and dry season respectively with the overall mean value of 0.028mg/l. These values were below the recommended standard of < 1mg/l. When comparing the mean concentration of cadmium in leachate, table 7.3 showed that only the mean value of leachate samples during dry season were above the mean values of water samples during the dry-season while the mean concentration of cadmium in leachate samples for wet-season and its overall mean value were within the same range with that of cadmium mean concentration in the water samples. The odour and the colour of the water samples collected as control were odourless and colourless compared to the leachate samples which had foul and offensive smell, with greenish brown colour due to microbial growth which is normally enhanced by the leachate temperature.

CONCLUSION

The studied areas in the city of Obio/Akpor were non-engineered low lying open dumps. They had neither any bottom liner nor leachate collection and treatment system which contribute to the contamination of underground water and surrounding environment. From the results there was a great variation in the concentration of the various parameters between the two seasons and the concentration of the measured parameters were higher in control water samples from boreholes close to the dump sites than in the leachate itself indicating high percolation into the underground water table thus significantly impacting ground water quality in the selected study area.

REFERENCES

Aluko, O.O., Sridhar, M. and Oluwander P.A. (2013). Characterization of Leachate from a Municipal Solid Waste Landfill Site. Journal of Environmental Health Research. Volume 2.

APHA, (2005). Standard methods for the Examination of Water and Waste Water. American Public Health Association, American Water Works Association, Water Environmental Federation Publication Washington. 21st Edition.

Bhalla, B., Saini M.S. and Jha M.K. (2012).Characterization of Leachate from Municipal Solid Waste (MSW) Landfilling site of Ludhiana, India. International Journal of Research in Engineering and Technology. Volume 2. pp. 732-745.

Bhalla, B., Saini M.S. and Jha M.K. (2013). Effect of Age and Seasonal Variation on Leachate Characteristics of Municipal Solid Waste Landfill. International Journal of Research in Engineering and Technology. Volume 02. pp. 223-232.

Chain, E.S. and Dewalle, E.B. (1996). Sanitary Landfill Leachate and their Treatment. Journal of Environmental Engineering Division, ASCE, Volume 2 (108) pp. 411.

Federal Environmental Protection Agency (FEPA), (1991). National Interim Guideline and Standards for Industrial Effluents and Water Quality Test FEPA: 246.

Horsfall, M. and Spiff, A.I. (2013). Principles of Environmental Pollution, Toxicity and Waste Management. ISBN 978-8195-59-9.

Koc-Jurczyk. (2009). Contemporary Problems of Management and Environmental Protection. Journal of Sewage and Waste Material in Environment. pp. 59-70.

Maiti, S.K., Hazra, T., De S., Debsarkar A. and Dulta, A. (2015). Characterization of Leachate and its Impact on Surface and Ground Water Quality of Closed Dumpsite. International Journal on Procedia Environmental Science. Volume 3(2016) pp. 391-399.

Ojoawo, S.O., Agbede, O.A. and Sangodoyin, A.Y. (2012). Characterization of Dump site Leachate Case Study of Ogbomosho Land, South-Western Nigeria. Open Journal of Civil Engineering. Volume 2. pp. 33-41.

Osu, C. and Okoro, I.A. (2012). Comparative Study on the Toxicity and Characteristics of Leachate from Municipal Solid Waste Landfills in Umuahia. Journal of Applied Sciences in Environmental Sanitation. Volume 7(1). pp. 55-59.

Sackey, A.L., Meizah, K. (2015). Assessment of the Quality of Leachate at Sarbah Landfill site at Weija in Accra. Journal of Environmental Chemistry and Ecotoxicology. Volume 7(6) pp. 56-61.

Sidhardhan, S. and Kumar, S. A. (2014). Assessment of Groundwater Quality at Municipal Solid Waste Dumpsite. International Journal of Research in Engineering and Technology. Volume 3 pp. 173-178.

Pages: 140-152

Metals Distribution in Environment

Edited by: **Dr. Deep Mala & Dr. Pawan Kumar 'Bharti'**

ISBN: 978-93-86841-91-9

Edition: **2019**

Published by: **Discovery Publishing House Pvt. Ltd., New Delhi (India)**

Analysis of Heavy Metals in Pond Environment near Industrial Area at Panipat (Haryana)

Pawan Kumar 'Bharti'

INTRODUCTION

Water is the most used for industrial, municipal and agricultural purpose. In the last two decades, the rapid growths of industrialization and urbanization have created negative impacts on the environment. The industrial, municipal and agricultural wastes containing pesticides, insecticides, fertilizers residues, organic pollutants and heavy metals in their effluents have been polluted surface and ground water. So, water resources must be managed and conserve on sustainable basis for the most beneficial uses in the future. The present study is aimed for an assessment of surface water quality, ground water and agricultural soil quality affected by textile industrial effluents in Panipat industrial area.

In the last two decades, the rapid growth of industrialization and urbanization has created negative impacts on the environment. The industrial wastes containing organic pollutants and heavy metals in their effluents have been polluted surface and ground water. In India, the industrial effluents have contributed a major source of pollution. In recent years, the rapid growth of industrialization and development pose negative impacts on lithosphere, atmosphere and hydrosphere. The composite effluent from textile industries in Panipat may affect the quality of surface water, ground water and agricultural soil system. In the modern industrialization period, the most of water resources have been affected enormously by seepage, leaching and intermixing of industrial effluents in maximum metropolitan cities and industrial townships. The textile effluents have consisting high

(Member of XXX Indian Expedition to Antarctica) Environmental Scientist, Delhi - 7 (India)

concentrations of heavy metals, organic pollutants and toxic colours, may alter the surface water quality of the region and ultimately causes the health hazards among livestock and human being.

In India, the industrial effluents have contributed a major source of pollution. Different industries of the country contributed to generate about 16% of the total waste water. The treatment facilities have been installed in less than one third of the polluting industries (Gopal, 1994). About 6,34,900 metric tons of dyes are used worldwide each year in textile dyeing industries and nearly 10-15% of them are discharged as effluents. The colours affect the nature of water, inhibit sunlight penetration and reduce the photosynthetic action and may toxic to living organisms. The contaminated waste water without any treatment may cause adverse effect on the health of human, domestic animals, wildlife and environment (Sharma *et al.*, 1999).

Textile effluent when discharged into the pond and through pond they percolated to the ground water. Thus, contaminated ground water has deteriorated immensely the drinking utilities, post agriculture irrigation and impacts on soil systems and crop productivity. The aim of this study is to emphasized on the transfer of heavy metals and extent of heavy metal contamination of vegetation due to irrigation with contaminated ground water affected by textile industrial effluents, on agricultural land. Metal transfer factors from effluent to ground water, from ground water to irrigated agricultural soil and from soil to vegetation are described in a simplified method in water, soil and vegetation.

The textile effluents have consisting high concentrations of heavy metals, organic and inorganic pollutants and toxic colours, which may alter the surface water quality of the region. Toxic pollutants may percolate down via soil profile and reach in ground water, which ultimately cause the health hazards among human being and livestock after consumption as daily drinking requirements. The waste water without any treatment may cause adverse effect on the health of human, domestic animals, wildlife and environment. Thus, contaminated ground water has deteriorated immensely the drinking utilities, post agriculture irrigation and impacts on soil systems and crop productivity.

Textile effluent when discharged into the pond and through pond they percolated to the ground water. When this water is used for irrigation purpose affects our crop health. The textile effluent had consisting high concentration of trace heavy metals and through its accumulation in different trophic levels of ecosystem ultimately cause the health hazards among livestock and human beings via food chain (Malik *et al.*, 2004). So, it is very much essential to assess the quality of wastewater before discharging it and to develop an economical method for prevention and control of ground water pollution.

Ground water contaminated by textile effluents, has deteriorated immensely the post agriculture irrigation, drinking utilities and impacts on soil systems. For prevention of ground water pollution, it is very essential to treat industrial wastewater before discharging in to the surface water, because through the surface water pollutants may reach in ground water by leaching process via soil profile.

It is essential to know the status and functions of heavy metals discarding from textile industries in to surface, ground water, soil and crop plant vegetation for health safety of regional people, which may help in recent research in the field of soil and water pollution by industries and for advance alarming against pollution to public, NGOs and GOs. The present paper deals with the distribution and transfer of heavy metals between water and soil. Regarding human consumption and irrigation practices ground water may cause the human and livestock health hazards and reduce soil fertility and agricultural plant productivity.

STUDY AREA

In Panipat city, Dye houses are situated on Jatal road in industrial area, these are quite famous for handloom business. Textile dying industries in Panipat region consume large quantities of water and discharge it into a common effluent drain, which ends up in to a large pond situated near Binjhole village. Since last five or six years, it was noticed that ground water quality is degrading day by day of the regions and local people think that the dye waste water is the major source of heavy metal pollution in area.

But these heavy metals are traveling from wastewater to ground water and ground water to soil system and from soil system to agricultural crop tissues. In this paper, the route of heavy metals from aquatic environment to soil system is highlighted with proper illustrations and flow diagrams.

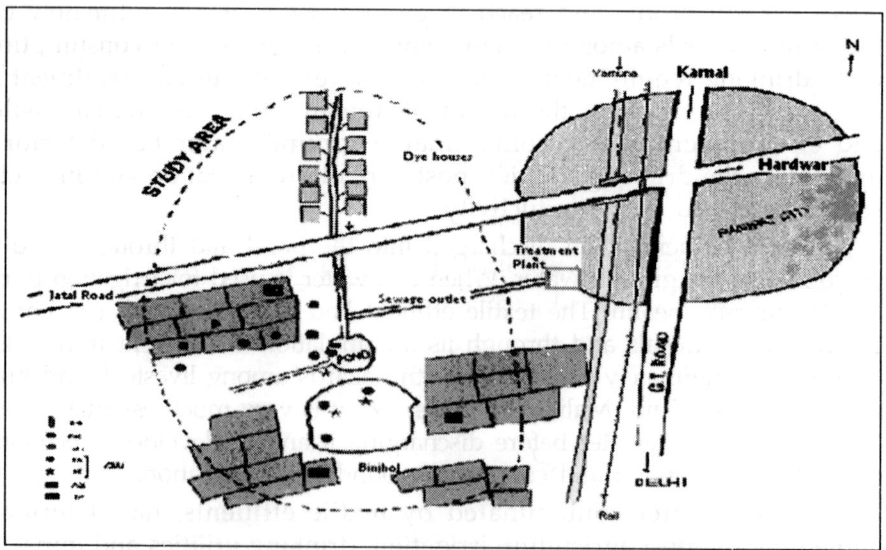

Fig. 8.1: Sampling points of study area at Panipat region

Panipat city is situated on GT road (National Highway 1) in Haryana, which is well known for textile handloom & dye industries. Panipat is situated on the bank of river Yamuna, it lies between 29′ 09′ 50″ and 29′ 50′ North latitude and 76° 31′ 15″ and 77° 12′ 45″ East longitude with a height of 255 masl. Karnal, Sonipat, Jind, Kaithal districts of Haryana and Uttar Pradesh bordered this district. Population of Panipat city is 261874.

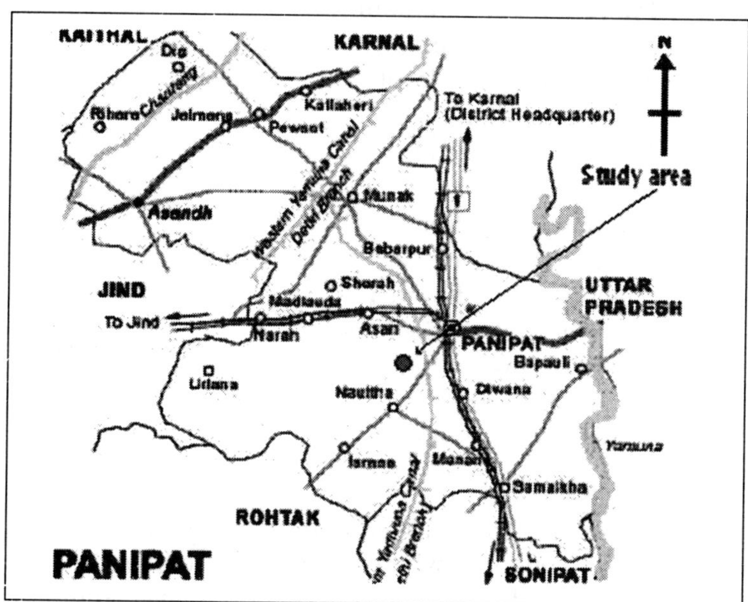

Fig. 8.2: Showing the study point and territory of Panipat district

Source: haryanaonline.com

Topographically, Ground is flat but gently slopes towards south-east. Water table is 5 m BGL (Ground Level). Panipat city is situated on the bank of Yamuna river, which is flowing through the west portion of the city. Agricultural soil is almost of loamy sand type and sandy type. Regarding the atmosphere and temperature, in summer, more summer and in winter the temp goes up to Minimum 4.4 °C in December, January, However in summer it goes up to 42.4 °C in June.

Abbreviations in text and flowchart:

°C	-	Degree Celsius
AGS	-	Agricultural soil
BDL	-	Below detection limit
BGL	-	Below ground level
DGW	-	Deep ground water
DSS	-	Drain sediment soil
ED	-	Effluent drain

EFF - Effluent
Fig. - Figure
GW - Ground water
ha - Hectares
HM - Heavy metals
IAF - Irrigated agricultural fields
mg kg^{-1} - Milligram per Kilogram
Mgl^{-1} - Milligram per liter
masl - Meter above sea level
ppm - Part per million
PSS - Pond sediment soil
PW - Pond water
SD - Standard deviation
Sq. Km - Square Kilometer
SGW - Shallow ground water
TF - Transfer factor (Coefficient)
TIE - Textile industrial effluent
TX - Textile Industry
µg g^{-1} - Microgram per gram

MATERIAL AND METHODS

The effluent samples were collected from the common effluent outlet of dye houses (S_1), large pond (S_2), where the effluent drain ends up, ground water from hand pumps/tube wells (S_3), agricultural soils from adjoining crop fields (S_4) and analyzed by the standard methods APHA (1995) and Trivedi and Goel (1984) some plant parts were also analyzed for the detection of metal contents.

Water samples (500 ml) were filtered using Whatman No. 41 (0.45 mm pore size) filter paper for estimation of dissolved metal content. Filtrate and as-collected water samples (500 ml each) were preserved with 2 ml nitric acid to prevent the precipitation of metals. Both the samples were concentrated to tenfold on a water bath and subjected to nitric acid digestion.

Soil samples were air-dried and ground into fine powder using pestle and mortar and passed through 1 mm sieve. Well-mixed samples of 2 g each were taken in 250 ml glass beakers and digested with 8 ml of aqua regia on a sand bath for 2 h. After evaporation to near dryness, the samples were dissolved with 10 ml of 2% nitric acid, filtered and then diluted to 50 ml with distilled water (Ming and Ma, 2001).

Path of heavy metals in various trophic levels may be different due to the nature of heavy metals and quality of host abiotic components. Transfer rate may be evaluated by the calculation of concentrations of heavy metals between two different trophic levels.

Transfer factor between plants and soil may be calculated for each metal according to the following formula-

TF = *Ps* (μg g–1 dry wt)/*St*(μg g–1 dry wt),

Where, *Ps* is the plant metal content originating from the soil and *St* is the total metal content in the soil (Lokeshwari and Chandrappa, 2006). Thus transfer factor (coefficient) may evaluate also between pond water and ground water, and from ground water to agricultural soil.

OBSERVATIONS

Effluent Drain Status

Colours of the waste water were found vary from pinkish red to brownish yellow. Hence, colour from the textile waste can cause significant aesthetic and health problem among the labours, which are engaged in dye houses. Odour is often associated with oil mists or solvent vapours and is removed by removal of the mist or by recovery of vapours. Sources of odour are Sulphur dyeing on cotton. Odour of the textile effluent was existed in the category No. 1 (Threshold) and 3 (Strong) of the odour table. Velocity of the effluents was totally dependent on the production output, amount of residual solids and amount of water used by the industry. Velocity was found nil at the pond site because ponds are itself the stagnant ecosystems (Malik *et al.*, 2006).

Table 8.1: Heavy metals in textile industrial effluents

Metals	EFF-1	EFF-2	EFF-3	Mean	SD
Cd	BDL	0.01	0.02	0.01	0.01
Cu	0.02	0.13	0.4	0.18	0.195
Fe	0.3	0.03	0.12	0.15	0.137
Mn	0.1	0.16	0.01	0.09	0.075
Ni	BDL	0.02	0.05	0.02	0.025
Pb	0.18	0.39	0.59	0.38	0.205
Zn	0.03	0.11	0.2	0.11	0.085

Status of Pond Water

Waste water of dye houses generally discharged openly into Binjhole pond water, thus polluted the surface water quality of the region (Malik *et al.*, 2006). After delaying for a long period of time the heavy metal contents may leach down in to ground water regime through soil profile very slowly. Because the ground water movement is very slow (CPCB, 2003), so metal contents remain in ground water for a long period even in toxic form. Thus metals reach in local ground water and deteriorated the ground water quality of neighborhood area.

Mainly ground water is use for irrigation purposes in most part of country and also in Haryana state. However, Yamuna is flowing in this region for irrigation utilization in agriculture sector of entire area but mostly agriculture farm holders have their own tube wells for facility. Nowadays, ground water is deteriorating continuously due to the heavy metal contents in wastewater of dye houses in textile industrial area. Heavy metals enter in to pond ecosystem and percolate down in to shallow ground water and may influence the drinking water quality, soil properties and agricultural crop health.

Metals in some samples of pond water were found very high concentration in comparison to other surface water of the area. All the seven metals were present in excess amount as comparing with textile effluents too. In pond water, average concentrations for Mn, Ni, Fe, Cu, Cd, Pb and Zn were observed 0.39, 0.08, 5.7, 0.36, 0.006, 0.91 and 0.13 mg l^{-1} respectively. Because all the textile effluents ends up in to a pond via a common drain, thus water quality of pond turns to vast condition due to the frequent discharge of industrial effluents without any adequate treatment (Malik *et al.*, 2006). Some local villagers guess that the same thing is responsible for the degradation of ground water quality of the area. The menace of dye house effluents is going an since a prolong time and will goes to a long period for surrounding.

Table 8.2: Heavy metals (mg l^{-1}) in pond water near textile industrial area

Metals	PW-Inlet	PW-Middle	PW-Outlet	Mean	SD
Cd	0.009	BDL	0.01	0.006	0.004
Cu	0.38	0.54	0.17	0.36	0.185
Fe	2.1	13.2	1.9	5.73	6.467
Mn	0.5	0.6	0.09	0.39	0.270
Ni	0.15	0.1	0.008	0.08	0.072
Pb	0.05	1.9	0.78	0.91	0.931
Zn	0.21	0.128	0.05	0.13	0.080

Metals in Pond Sediment

Due to the irrigation, agricultural soil is indirectly in touch of point source of metal pollution, but pond sediment is directly attached by heavy metal's source i.e. dyes (e.g. chrome and metal dyes) so, most of the metals having heavy nature, deposited on the bottom sediments ultimately on the pond bottom. In the present study, concentrations of heavy metals were found in high concentration in pond sediment, except Zn and Cd due to low adsorptive nature with soil (Lokeshwari and Chandrappa, 2006). The average concentrations of heavy metals like Mn, Ni, Fe, Cu, Cd, Pb and Zn in pond sediment were found as 0.11, 0.08, 0.48, 0.26, 0.02, 0.39, 0.14 mg g^{-1}, which can easily demonstrate the pollution potential on sediment medium.

Table 8.3: Heavy metals (mg l^{-1})in sediments of pond near textile industrial area

Metals	PSS-Inlet	PSS-Middle	PSS-Outlet	Mean	SD
Cd	0.05	0.002	0.008	0.02	0.026
Cu	0.29	0.39	0.12	0.26	0.136
Fe	0.89	0.19	0.38	0.48	0.361
Mn	0.05	0.17	0.11	0.11	0.06
Ni	0.13	0.06	0.05	0.08	0.043
Pb	0.79	0.23	0.15	0.39	0.348
Zn	0.038	0.27	0.1	0.14	0.120

Ground Water

The comparative average concentrations of heavy metals in textile effluents, pond water and ground water are given in tables 8.1, 8.2, 8.4 and 8.5. Results show that the concentrations of some metals like Pb and Fe are present in ground water in excess quantity (2.1 and 4.6 mg l^{-1}). In industrial area, metals from surface water may percolate down in to shallow aquifers via soil profile after delaying a long period (Kumar *et al.*, 2001). Leachate effect of heavy metals may results as the excess amount of these metals in the ground water of the region, which may cause health problems to human beings, cattle and plants also (De, 2000)

Table 8.4: Heavy metals (mg l^{-1}) in shallow ground waters (SGW) near textile industrial area

Metals	SGW-1	SGW-2	SGW-3	Mean	SD
Cd	0.009	0.007	BDL	0.005	0.004
Cu	0.57	0.42	0.13	0.37	0.224
Fe	4.6	1.3	0.46	2.12	2.188
Mn	0.43	0.58	0.61	0.54	0.096
Ni	0.16	0.009	0.13	0.09	0.079
Pb	0.84	2.1	0.55	1.16	0.824
Zn	0.25	0.14	0.06	0.15	0.095

Table 8.5: Heavy metals (mg l^{-1})in deep ground waters (DGW) near textile industrial area

Metals	DGW-1	DGW-2	DGW-3	Mean	SD
Cd	BDL	BDL	BDL	Nil	-
Cu	0.21	0.17	0.09	0.16	0.061
Fe	0.21	1.2	0.87	0.76	0.504
Mn	0.08	0.3	0.02	0.13	0.147
Ni	BDL	0.03	0.08	0.04	0.039
Pb	0.48	0.26	0.13	0.29	0.176
Zn	0.12	0.08	0.01	0.07	0.055

Soil Water

The main source of water on earth is rain and a large quantity of rain water goes to nearest water body by run-off method and rest amount percolate down in earth crust according to soil character. Lost rain water by run-off process is known as run away water, while rest water delay in soil and reach in water table. Generally, soil occupied four types of water, chemical bonded water (bounded with soil particles), hygroscopic water (remain on soil particle's surface), capillary water (between the soil particles and available for plants) and gravitational water (percolated down in to aquifers). All the four categories are shown in figure given below (Kaushik, 2006).

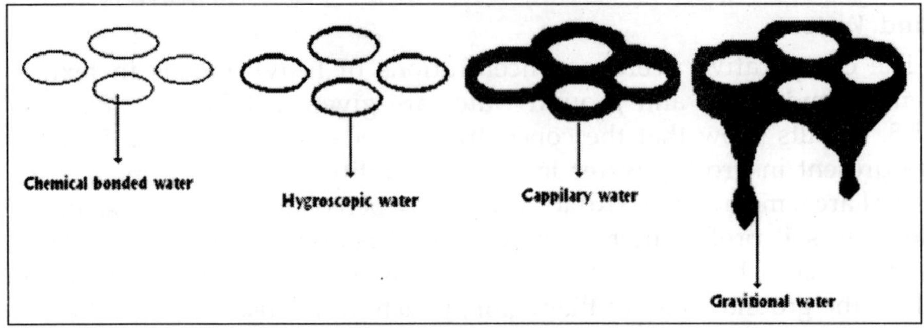

Fig. 8.3: Different types of soil water

Metals reach in agricultural soil through repeated irrigation by contaminated ground water. Some concentrations of metals again percolate in to ground water and some of them delay in soil water. Soil particles bound a huge amount of heavy metals due to adsorptive nature, which remain in capillary water and easily available for plants.

Metals in Agricultural Soil

Soil samples of irrigated land used for growing crops and vegetables showed the presence of all seven metals considered in the study. Concentration of Mn, Fe, Zn, Cu, Ni, Cr, Pb and Cd (mg g^{-1}) is depicted in table 8.6. The average total concentration of all metals in soil samples was lower than the pond sediment.

It was found that the average concentrations of heavy metals in surface soils, i.e. Mn, Ni, Fe, Cu, Cd, Pb and Zn were 0.08, 0.06, 0.48, 0.25, 0.016, 0.36 and 0.12 mg g^{-1} respectively, in which Fe, Pb, Cu were found in excess level due to their cumulative and adsorptive nature in soil after repeated irrigation by contaminated ground water. Cd and Zn were found minimum due to their weak adsorptive nature in soil (Mido and Satake, 2003currsci).

Table 8.6: Heavy metals (μg g^{-1}) in soils of agricultural fields (AGS) near textile industrial area

Metals	AGS-1	AGS -2	AGS-3	Mean	SD
Cd	0.04	0.001	0.007	0.016	0.021
Cu	0.28	0.42	0.05	0.25	0.186
Fe	0.92	0.14	0.39	0.48	0.398
Mn	0.02	0.15	0.08	0.08	0.065
Ni	0.11	0.05	0.04	0.06	0.037
Pb	0.73	0.21	0.16	0.36	0.315
Zn	0.04	0.23	0.09	0.12	0.098

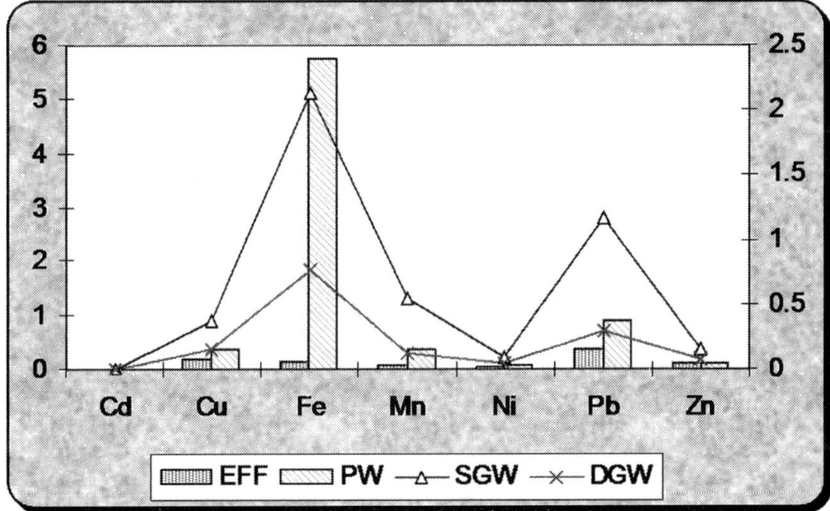

Fig. 8.4: Mean values of heavy metals concentration in mg l^{-1} in textile effluents, pond water, shallow and deep ground water (left scale for bar and right for line)

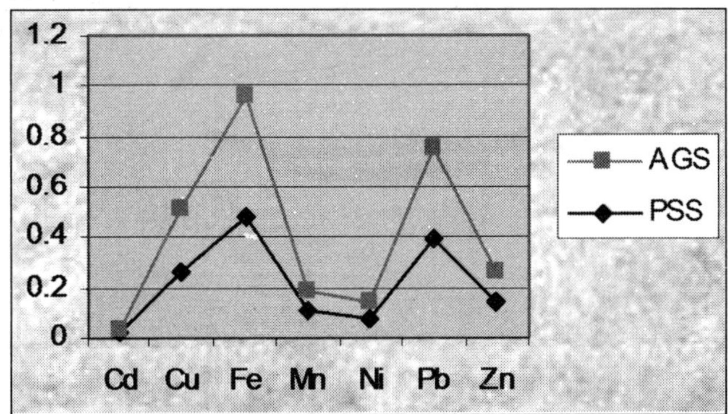

Fig. 8.5: Mean values of heavy metals concentration in μg g^{-1} in agricultural soil and pond sediment

Absorption by Plants

Plants absorb the sufficient amount of water for their different requirements. Metals present in this available water arrive in plant tissues with water and accumulate in various parts of plant bodies (Malik *et al.*, 2004). These metal contents may affect the plants activities and generate some physiological changes in plants sometimes (Garg and Kaushik, 2006). In other cases, accumulated amount of heavy metals may reach in livestock and human beings after continuous uptake of these crop parts.

Table 8.7: Transfer coefficient (TF) between various components of industrial environment (TF from effluent to pond water, from pond water to ground water and from ground water to irrigated agricultural soil)

	EFF Vs GW	EFF Vs PW	PW Vs GW	GW Vs AGS
Cd	1.66	1.49	1.11	0.37
Cu	0.60	0.50	1.19	1.21
Fe	0.05	0.02	2.07	5.72
Mn	0.34	0.22	1.52	3.12
Ni	0.32	0.27	1.19	1.07
Pb	0.52	0.42	1.23	2.01
Zn	1.12	0.88	1.28	0.84

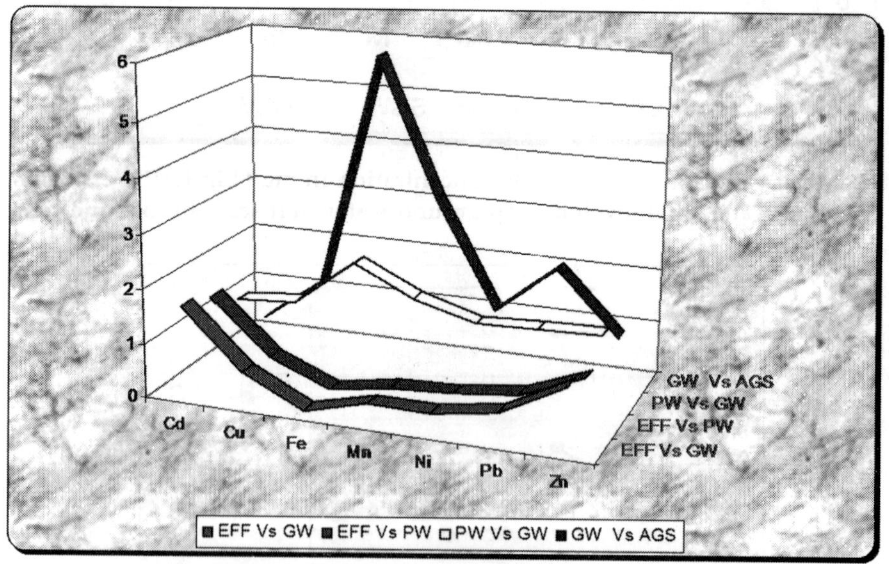

Fig. 8.6: Transfer factor (TF) of heavy metals from effluent to pond water, from effluent to ground water, from pond water to ground water and from ground water to irrigated agricultural soil

Fig. 8.7: Heavy metals in different agricultural soils in textile industrial area

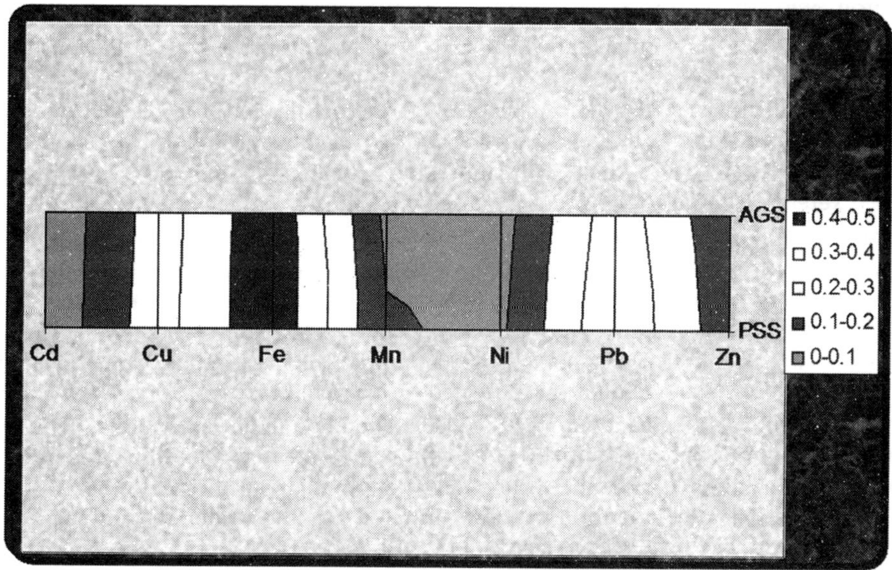

Fig. 8.8: Heavy metals in agricultural soils and pond sediment

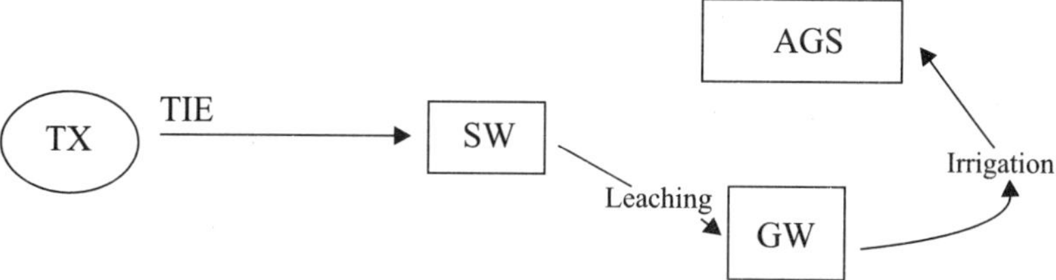

Fig. 8.9: A flow diagram of heavy metal route in Panipat industrial area

Transfer factor (coefficient) of heavy metals from ground water to agriculture soil was found for maximum for Mn and Zn. From pond water to ground water the transfer factor for Mn was also found maximum in relation to other metals. All the TF are given in table 8.7 for all the seven metals studied.

Keeping all above in the mind, all the facts, formula and functions related to water, soil, plants and heavy metals, it is concluded that heavy metals travel among all the abiotic environmental components and ultimately reach ground water and agricultural soil system. Available figure may also express the movement of heavy metals from textile industrial waste to surface water, from surface water to ground water, from ground water to agricultural soil, then in crop plants in the industrial environment, which may be harmful to all environmental living and non-living components of the region.

REFERENCES

APHA (1995): Standard methods for Examination of Water and Waste Water. *American Public Health Association,* 19th Edition. Inc, New York. pp: 1170.

CPCB (2003): Ground Water, *Parivesh, Central Pollution Control Board,* Delhi, pp: 40.

De, A.K. (2002): Environmental Chemistry, *New Age International (Ltd) Publishers, New Delhi*, pp: 392.

Garg, V.K. and Kaushik, P. (2006): Influence of Short-term Irrigation of Textile Mill Wastewater on the Growth of Chickpea Cultivars, *Chemistry and Ecology*, 22(3): 193-200.

Gopal, B. (1994): Conservation of Inland Water in India: An Overview. Verh. Internet. Verein. *Hydrobiologia*, 384: 267.

Kaushik, M.P. (2006): Vanaspati Vigyan, Prakash Prakashan, Muzaffarnagar, pp: 834.

Kumar, S.; Kushwaha, R.; Sapra, S; Gupta, A.B. and Bhargava, A. (2001): Impact of Textile Industry on Ground Water Quality of Sanagar, Jaipur, *J. Indian Water Works Association,* 33(4): 321-326.

Lokeshwari, H. and Chandrappa, G.T. (2006): Impact of Heavy Metal Contamination of Bellandur Lake on Soil and Cultivated Vegetation, *Current Science*, 91(9): 622-627.

Malik, D.S.; Bharti, P.K. and Grover, S. (2006): Alteration in Surface Water Quality Near Textile Industries at Panipat (Haryana), *Environment Conservation J.*, 7(2): 65-68.

Malik, D.S.; Yadav, R. and Bharti, P.K. (2004) Accumulation of Heavy Metals in Crop Plants through Irrigation of Contaminated Ground Water in Panipat Region, *Environmental Conservation Journal* 5 (3): 101-104.

Mido, Y. and Satake, M. (2003): Chemicals in the Environment. In *Toxic Metals* (eds. Sethi, M.S. and Iqbal, S.A.), Discovery Publishing House, New Delhi, pp: 45-68.

Ming Chen and Ma, Lena Q. (2001): Comparison of Three Aqua Regia Digestion methods for Twenty Florida Soils. *Soil Sci. Soc. Am. J.*, 65, 491-499.

Sharma, K.P.; Sharma, K.; Bharadwaj, S.M. and Chaturvedi, R.K. (1999): Environmental Impact Assessment of Textile Printing Industries in Sanagar, Jaipur: A Case Study. *J. Int. Bot. Soc.* 78: 71-74.

Trivedi, R.K. and Goel, P.K. (1984): Chemical and Biological methods for Water Pollution Studies, *Environmental Publication*, Karad, pp: 251.

Pages: 153-188

Metals Distribution in Environment
Edited by: **Dr. Deep Mala & Dr. Pawan Kumar 'Bharti'**
ISBN: 978-93-86841-91-9
***Edition:* 2019**
***Published by:* Discovery Publishing House Pvt. Ltd., New Delhi (India)**

9

Biocidal Analysis of New Ecofriendly Macro Cyclic Complexes of Long Chain Fatty Acid with Copper Metal

Neha Mathur[1]
Nisha Jain[2]
Arun Kumar Sharma[3]

ABSTRACT

Metals exhibit their own importance in organic synthesis. To understand molecular processes occurring in biochemistry and co-ordination chemistry, the role of complexes containing N donor ligands can -not be denied. Surfactants i.e. surface active agents show their interesting behaviour at surface and interface. Copper containing surfactants play significant role in specific phenomenon such as foaming, wetting, detergency emulsification etc. and also used as herbicides, pesticides, fungicides and insecticides etc. Micellization shown by surfactants is of immense theoretical, applied and biological interests. Copper soaps form complexes when combine with heterocyclic ligands containing donor atoms like N, O, S etc. In the present work nature of complexes of copper palmitate in different non-aqueous solvents is studied. This is quite important in explaining their characteristics under different conditions. It gives idea about micelle formation in mixed non-aqueous solvents. Of late, many notable physico-chemical properties of copper soaps have been reported. However, only scanty references are available regarding the physico-chemical properties of combined form of copper soap with nitrogen donor ligands in mixed

Department of Chemistry
1 **Pt. N.K.S. Govt. P.G. College, Dausa - 303 303, Rajasthan (India)**
2 **S.S. Jain Subhodh P.G. College Jaipur - 302 001, Rajasthan (India)**
3 **Govt. P.G. College, Jhalawar - 326 001, Rajasthan (India)**

solvents. Also, it is believed that biological activity is often enhanced on complexation. In the present study, we synthesize these complexes in the hope that they may possess potential biological activities.

The present work reveals:

1. Synthesis of copper palmitate derived from palmitic acid and their complexation with substituted benzothiazole and substituted phenylthiourea.
2. Spectral and analytical studies of these synthesized complexes to understand the structural insight (deeply).
3. Various physico-chemical properties i.e. density viscosity, fluidity, have been studied using propanol – benzene mixed solvent system.
4. Critical micelle concentration, various interactions like solute-solute and solute-solvent has been investigated. Antifungal and antibacterial activities have been carried out by disk diffusion method which shows its own importance in biochemistry.

INTRODUCTION

Basis and Scope of Present Work

The present research is an important effort to understand the characteristicnature and biocidal application of copper complexes of nitrogen donor ligands. The treatment with copper complexes produce remarkable pharmacological effects which are not observed when the parent ligands or inorganic forms of copper are used. The use of transition metal complexes as therapeutic compounds has become more and more pronounced. Owing to the aforesaid applications of copper and heterocyclic compounds, we have synthesized copper complexes containing heterocyclic ligands. Out of them, various copper complexes have been reported to inhibit bacterial, fungal, yeast, algal, mycoplasma and viral growth as well as is to cause the death of these microorganisms[1-4]. Copper complexes are also used as antitumor agents, anti-inflammatory, enzyme inhibitors or chemical nuclease[5-6]. The study and development of copper complexes could be helpful in the design and production of antiviral and antifungal materials. It is also able to deactivate HIV viruses and antibiotic resistant bacteria[7].

These copper complexes behave as good chelating agents. Their pathogenic activity and N-C-S linkage makes them to versatile biological interest and chemotherapeutic agents[8].

These copper complexes are biodegradable and eco-friendly. Copper complexes are also important in catalysis, material synthesis and photochemistry. They display diverse chemical, optical and magnetic properties. This thesis is aimed at having an insight on the modern applications of copper complexes in the production of drugs[9-10].

The solutions of copper surfactants in polar and non polar solvents have many applications in the field of pesticides, herbicides and preservatives. Thus it is worthwhile to construct some heterocycles fused azole series with transition metals on solid phase to find novel hit compounds towards multiple biological targets. Requirements of colloidal surfactants in day to day life can not be ignored because of its multifold significance in modern engineering and pharmacological fields. Copper soap with N & S ligands play a vital role in biological activities and interesting analytical, pharmaceutical and industrial applications. To access their comparative toxicity biocidal studies were conducted on synthesized copper complexes. Present work is quite efficient to investigate the nature and type of micelles formed by these surfactants. Various physical properties i.e. density, viscosity, fluidity of the complexes in non aqueous medium (Propanol + Benzene) have been investigated to determine critical micelle concentration. These physical parameters are used to understand molecular interactions between the component of the mixture. Information is also provided about solute–solute and solute–solvent interactions and structural insight of micelles. Present work generates new hopes in pharmacological field.

CHEMISTRY OF 2-AMINOBENZOTHIAZOLE AND PHENYL-THIOUREA

Nitrogen containing ligands have a tendency of complexation with the transition metal soaps and they are recognized as pharmacophores which have receive great attention in drug discovery and lead optimization.

The chemistry of nitrogen donor ligands is very interesting field. A heterocyclic compound is one, which possesses a cyclic structure containing one of more atoms of other element besides carbon atom in the ring. N, S and O are the most common heteroatoms. Heterocycles bearing N, S and thiazole moieties constitute the core structure of a number of biologically interesting compounds. The basic structure of benzothiazole consists of benzene ring fused with 4,5 position of thiazole. The two rings together constitutes the basic nucleus i.e. benzothiazole[11-15].

The benzothiazole ring is present in various marine and terrestrial natural compounds which have biological significance. Heterocycles containing thiazole moiety are present in many natural products such as epothiloneA, bleomycin, lyngbyabellin A and dolostatin. Being a heterocyclic compound benzothiazole finds use in research as a starting material for the synthesis of larger usually bioactive structures. Its aromaticity makes it relatively stable, although as heterocycle, it has reactive sites which allow for functionalization[16].

A large number of therapeutic agents are synthesized with the help of benzothiazole nucleus[17].

Thiazole antifungal are known as potent inhibitors of the cytochrome, monooxygenase in the process of fungal biosynthesis of ergosterol, which is an important constitution of fungal cell membrane[18].

The chemistry of substituted thiourea derivatives has attracted attention because of their potential use as reagents for the separation of metal ions and in medicinal chemistry.

Thioureas are versatile ligands, able to co-ordinate to metal centres either as neutral ligands, monoanions or dianions. O, N and S donor atoms of thiourea derivatives provide a multitude of bonding possibilities. Thiourea and its derivatives form a variety of complexes of varying symmetries with central metal ions.

The chelating thiourea ligands containing multiple donor atoms show remarkable biological activity. The role of benzoyl thiourea derivatives in co-ordination chemistry has been extensively studied and quite satisfactorily elucidated. New thiourea derivatives and their structures has received attention because of their wonderful complexation capacity.

Nitrogen containing ligands are found to be effective against many enzymes also. Among N-donor ligands phenylthiourea and 2-amino benzthiazole are very important and show N-C=S linkage which make them suitable for coloring paper, cellulose, nylon and wool.

These heterocyclic ligands are of interest because of these potential co-ordination sites i.e. S of CS group and N of NH group[19,20].

CHEMISTRY OF COPPER

Copper was the only metal known to man for nearly 5000 years. Today it is one of the most used and reused of our modern metals. It is earth's 25th most abundant element but one of the less common first row transition metals[21].

Copper's atomic symbol Cu, is derived from the Latin term 'Cuprim' meaning metal of Cyprus. Its atomic number is 29. There are 29 isotopes of copper. It occurs as a soft reddish metal that can be found native as large boulders weighing several hundred tons or as sulphide ores. The latter are complex copper, iron and sulphur mixtures in combination with other metals such as arsenic, zinc and silver. The copper concentration in such ores is typically between 0.5-2%. It is a ductile metal with very high thermal and electrical conductivity. Pure copper is soft and malleable. +1, +2, +3 oxidation states are shown normally by copper. Cu(0) and Cu(IV) are seen rarely. In two or three compounds copper exhibit +4 oxidation state i.e. with highly electronegative ligands F^- and O^{2-}. Cu(III) which is isoelectronic with Ni(II) occurs in several crystalline compounds but it is unstable in solution. Cu(II) compounds are expected to be diamagnetic in nature. Cu(I) ion is distorted square planar in solid compounds. Cu(II) ion is usually more stable in aqueous solution. Cu in +2 oxidation state often show distorted tetrahedral geometry[22-25].

Cu, Ag and Au are in group II of periodic table and they share certain attributes. They have one s orbital electron on top of a filled d electron shell and are characterized by high ductility, malleability and electrical conductivity. The filled d shell electrons in this do not contribute much to the inter atomic interactions which are dominated by the s electrons through metallic bonds. Unlike in metals with incomplete d shells metallic bonds in Cu are lacking a covalent character and are relatively weak. This explains low hardness and high ductility of single crystal of Cu. The softness of copper partly explain its high electrical conductivity and thus also high thermal conductivity[26].

The characteristic color of copper results from the electronic transitions between the filled 3d and empty 4s outer shell. Copper does not react with water but it slowly reacts with atmospheric oxygen to form a layer of brown black copper oxide which unlike the rust which is formed when iron is exposed to moist air, protects the underlying Cu from extensive corrosion. Copper tarnishes when exposed to sulphides, which react with it to form various copper sulphides[27,28].

The main areas where copper is found in humans are liver, muscles and bones. Copper compounds are used as bacteriostatic substances, fungicides and wood preservatives. Copper(II) complexes have shown noticeable results in the treatment of many diseases including cancer. It is a part of the prosthetic group of many proteins and enzymes and thus is essential for their proper function. Body does not synthesize copper, it must be taken from outside[29]. It is an integral part of numerous key metalloproteins and metalloenzymes which participate in many cellular and extracellular processes including production of ATP (adenosinetriphosphate), Cytochrome-c-oxidase, O_2 and maturation of extracellular matrix. Copper is very important for the functioning of immune system. Deficiency of copper can lead to adverse effects such as neutropenia, fragility in bones and anemia, shaggy skin, varicose veins and grayana of hair.

Copper oxide is used in agriculture as a fungicide to protect coffee, cocoa, tea, banana and other plants from major fungal leaf and fruit diseases. Copper oxide is also used as an active ingredient in various pesticides formulation. After the ban of TBT (Tributylate ion) in late 1980's, the use of oxide of copper in antifouling promotes the proper utilization of iron in the body. Main purpose of copper in an organism is serving as an enzyme co-factor. The ancients were aware of its antimicrobial property. Greeks used copper to cure ulcers and open wounds. Modern median applies copper bracelets to reduce arthritis and joint pain. This metallic element can help in enhancing the skin's elastic fibre[30].

SELECTION CRITERIA OF METAL AND LIGAND

Metal co-ordination complexes have been widely studied for their antifungal, antibacterial and anticancer properties. Many drugs possess pharmacological and toxicological properties when administered in the form of metallic complexes. This stimulates our interest to extend the studies to their cumulative form as complexes because biological activity is often enhanced by complexation. Copper in particular has attracted the researchers. Copper is an essential micronutrient required by all life forms. It is very significant element involved in a wide variety of life supporting biological processes. Most mammals have efficient transport system to prevent accumulation of excess Cu in cells and tissues[31].

Copper has been identified as a preemptory factor in amyloid and brain diseases. The potential antineoplastic properties of copper compounds have been under special interest during the recent years. This is not surprising because it has been suggested that as an essential co-factor in a number of enzymes and physiological processes copper may be less toxic than non-essential metals.

A prominent family of novel high energy density materials are azole based compounds since they are generally highly endothermic with high denesties and low sensitivities towards external stimuli[36-40].

The emergence of antibiotic resistant pathogens and the continuing emphasis on health care costs has provoked a renewed interest in the design and development of novel cost effective antimicrobial activity against the resistant strains.

Strategies currently being explored to tackle this problem include structural modification of existing antimicrobial drugs to which resistance has developed and the development of entirely new classes of antimicrobial agents that work on different target sites[41].

N containing heterocyclic compounds play an important role not only for life science industry but also in many other industrial fields related to special and fine chemistry[42].

Copper soaps show remarkable tendency of complexation with the compounds containing donor atom N, O and S. Benzothiazoles and phenylthiourea usually react with the metallic cation resulting in the complex formation in which ligand uses its donor atoms in bonding.

The choice of the co-ordinated ligand seems to be as important as the choice of the metal because besides being the integral part of biologically active complexes these organic molecules can exert a biological activity of their own.

Copper complexes containing heterocyclic compounds have been of considerable interest in terms of structural chemistry, catalysis and biological functions. This field has undergone spectacular growth due to the synthesis of multidentate ligands from heterocyclic compounds and the complexes of such ligands formed with metal ions[43-46].

In the development of antimicrobial drugs, copper complexes are playing increasing role and such metal chelates are known to possess antibacterial, antifungicidal, antiviral, antimalarial and anticancer activity. In several cases metal chelates are found to be more effective antimicrobials than the chelating agents themselves. Specially copper complexes of multidentate N donor ligand has received much attention due to enhanced list of interpretive data and has elevated antifungal susceptibility testing to a leaf of importance as a diagnostic test[47].

The biochemical activities, chemical and industrial versatility of copper complexes have been the subject of intensive study ever the long time. Copper complexes easily undergo redox reaction and N- donor ligand substitution allow them to participate in biological redox chemistry and interact with biological molecules. It is noticeable that investigation in this area are focused on the use of biologically active complexes formed by essential ion such as copper. Since any essential metal which escapes its normal metabolic pathways can be very toxic to the organism. Complexes of such metals may serve as cytotoxic agents. Copper complexes have been proven beneficial against several diseases such as tuberculosis, rheumatoid, gastric ulcers and cancer[48].

Metal complexes containing copper and N-donor ligands are found to be effective catalysts for oxidation of olefins. The co-ordination environment around copper plays the key role in stabilizing its different oxidation states and have dictated the redox properties of central atoms. Activity of biometal is very often altered through the formation of chelates with different bio ligands. These copper complexes are effective to prove them by killing the microbes or by inhibiting their activity[49,52].

SOLUBILITY AND SOLUBILIZATION

The investigation of solubilization of dichloromethane, chloroform and hydrocarbon in sodium soap was done by Demchenko. He studied the effect of electrolytes and non electrolytes on the solubilizing capacity of sodium and potassium soaps. Jain and Singh studied the solubilization of silver stearate by non ionic surfactants in organic solvents. Dimeric nature of copper soaps in chloroform and benzene was confirmed by Mehrotra and Rai *et al.* and Mehta *et al.*[53]

Colloidal aggregates are formed by surfactants with long hydrophobic chains, when a specific concentration is exceeded. Mc-Bain proposed the presence of molecular aggregation in soap solution because with changing soap concentration unusual changes in electrical conductivity was observed. The capacity to aggregate in solutions is the significant property of amphiphilic molecules. The nature of amphiphilic entity as well as the condition of the system, both affect aggregation process[54-58].

McBain suggested the coexistence of spherical ionic micelles and lamellar micelles. According to Hartley, micelles are spherical with the charged groups present at the micellar surface. Hartcing *et al.* through X-ray studies suggested the sandwich or lamellar model. Deby and Anacker reported that micelles are rod shaped instead of spherical or disc like[59,60].

To determine c.m.c. a number of methods have been given, with or without additives in the surfactant solution. According to William *et al.* the concentration of surfactant solute at which concentration of micelles would become zero is c.m.c. According to this definition, c.m.c. is the concentration at which two straight lines of solution properties below and above the c.m.c intersect each other[61].

To find out c.m.c or miceller features of Cu(II) soaps various physical properties like density, viscosity, apparent molar volume, surface tension parachore and electrical conductance have been used as a tool.

Mehrotra *et al.* investigated the colloid-chemical behaviour of copper(II) soap in non aqueous solvent mixture of varying composition using viscometric and allied parameters[62-65].

Differential thermal analysis of metal soaps was carried out by Hattiandi and other workers. Gilmour suggested a covalent chelate structure for copper laureate, based on magnetic measurements. Satake, Kishita and Martin simultaneously examined the structure of copper stearate, oleate and their complexes[66,67].

The molar susceptibility temperature variation of hydrated copper soaps were studied and it was concluded that curie and Weiss law was not obeyed by copper soaps. Dipole moment of copper oleate in benzene was studied by Banerjee and Patel[68].

Sharma *et al.* Sherwah and Sharma reported the viscometric studies at various temperature, apparent molar volume, surface tension, antifungal activities related with miceller features of copper soaps in various organic solvents[69-73].

STRUCTURAL FEATURES

Nuclear magnetic resonance spectra of copper stearate was studied by Grant. Matuura investigated the IR spectra and X-Ray diffraction patterns of copper oleate. Barday and Kennard studied the crystal structure of copper formate by X-ray technique. Grant studied the nuclear magnetic resonance spectra of copper stearate.

Matuura investigated the IR spectra and X-Ray diffraction patterns of copper oleate. Barclay and Kennard studied the crystal structure of copper formate by X-ray technique.

The IR spectra of copper soaps and Cu soaps with benzidine were also studied. Various other workers have studied different spectral techniques like IR, ESR, NMR and magnetic moment studies of various complexes containing copper so as to determine their geometrical and structural aspects[74].

Souva *et al.* explained thermal stability of various edible vegetable oils. Thermal stability of various edible vegetable oils were explained by Souza *et al.* It was established from TGA curves that the thermal decomposition of edible oils takes place in three steps corresponding to the thermal degradation of polyunsaturated, monounsaturated and saturated fatty acids respectively. The various kinetic parameters evaluated included energy of activation,orderof reaction and pre-exponential factor done by various other workers

Dervichan and Lachampt reviewed the various possible structures present in soap solution over the whole concentration range[81]. The various possible structures present in soap solution over the whole concentration range have been reviewed by Dervichain and LachamptLachampt suggested that the gelation involves the association of two layer systems in two directions but one is favoured over the other. This is in contrast to the growth of all lamellar micelles in all directions as postulated by Theissen and Spychalski. Schulman and Riely, with the help of X-Ray diffraction propounded the concept that the structure of copper(II) soaps consists of closely packed uniform water sphere in oil or oil in water.

It is pointed out by Anacker that the molecular weight obtained for soap solutions is incompatible with the assumption of a spherical micelle. According to Mc-Bain and Johnson, the spherical micellar concept is totally inadequate to account for the solubilization of hydrocarbons. In conformity with X-Ray diffraction data, Mc-Bain has postulated about the existence of lamellar micelles. Shinoda has also supported this on the basis of the results obtained from the effects of alcohols on c.m.c. Ooshika suggested that the change in c.m.c. on addition of alcohol is due to lamellar micellar structure[83,83].

Mattiello used copper soaps as driers for the preparation of paints, varnishes and other protective coating. It was observed that the addition of copper soaps to fuel oil reduced the smoke and fumes of burning oil and thus it helps in controlling pollution[84-93].

The use of copper linoleats as heavy duty wood preservative and many other biological activities of Cu metal containing surfactants have also been studied. Leyland, and Stanford, Gebhardt and Pedersen pointed out that the oxidation of natural rubber increases rapidly by the addition of Copper stearate. Copper stearate, Copper oleate and Copper abietate (from resins) are employed mainly for rot-proofing textiles, ropes etc[94-96].

The usefulness of copper soaps as fungicides, bacteriocides, herbicides and insecticides were studied by many workers. Several compounds incorporating benzothiazole moieties have been reported to possess useful antibacterial, antifungal and antitubercular activities[97-100]

EXPERIMENTAL

All the chemical used for the preparation of soap, ligands and complexes were of A-R grade. 4-nitroaniline and 4-methoxyaniline and copper sulphate used for the preparation of complexes were from Merck. Solvent was purified according to standard procedures. Analysis of various elements was done for soap as well as their complexes. All melting points were taken in open capillary tubes and are uncorrected.

We followed three stages for obtaining final complexes:

1. Preparation of copper(II) soap
2. Preparation of ligands
3. Preparation of complexes using soap and ligand

Preparation of Copper palmitate

Copper palmitate was prepared by mixing one gram of palmitic acid into 25 ml ethyl alcohol, shake the mixture in hot water bath at about 50° C and then add one drop of phenolphthalein. Prepare a saturated solution of KOH in another beaker and add it drop by drop into the first beaker until the light pink color appears. Meanwhile in another beaker prepare a saturated solution of $CuSO_4$ (approx 3-4 gms in 5 ml H_2O) and mix it into the above solution with constant stirring till the blue coloured soap is formed. Filtered it and washed with warm water and 10% ethyl alcohol, then dried and recrystallised with hot benzene.

Preparation of substituted benzothiazole

Thiocynogenation method was used for the preparation of substituted-2-amino benzothiazoles. In this method, 13.8g p-nitroaniline/12.3gm p-methoxy aniline (0.1 mole) was treated with a mixture of 7.6 gm ammonium thiocyanate and 80 ml glacial acetic acid in a 250 ml three necked round bottom flask, with stirrer dropping funnel and reflux condenser at room temperature for one and half an hour.

Aryl amine undergoes thiocynogenation in the presence of the thiocyanogen gas, which is generated in situ by the reaction of cupric chloride and ammonium thiocyanate. After cooling the reaction mixture, add 100 ml conc. HCl and heat it again for half an hour, then cool it and saturated solution of sodium carbonate (Na_2CO_3) is added to neutralize it, till the solid was formed. The solid separated out was filtered, washed with cold water, dried and recrystallized with ethanol.

Preparation of substituted phenylthiourea

In this method Aryl amine was treated with ammonium thiocyanate to prepare phenylthiourea. For this purpose 13.8 gm/12.3 gm (0.1 mole) p-nitroaniline/p-methoxy aniline was heated in a 250 ml three necked flask with stirrer, dropping funnel and reflux condenser with a mixture of 9 ml (6NHCl) and 25 ml water at a temperature of 32° C on water bath till the aniline hydrochloride was formed. The solution now obtained is allowed to cool at room temperature and then 7.6 gm (1 mole) ammonium thiocyanate was added to it. The reaction mixture was refluxed for about four hours on water bath. After cooling the solid separated out was filtered, washed with cold water, dried and then recrystallized with ethanol.

Preparation of complex using soap and ligand

Complexation of purified copper palmitate obtained from palmitic acid and substituted benzothiazole/substituted phenylthiourea was done by adding 0.001 mole copper palmitate with 0.002 mole benzothiazole/0.002 mole phenylthiourea in 25-30 ml ethyl alcohol and mixture was refluxed for about two hours with constant stirring.

After cooling the solid separated out was filtered, driedand recrystallized with hot benzene. IR, NMR techniques were used to confirm the formation of complexes. Thin layer chromatography was done to check the purity of the prepared complexes.

All the synthesized complexes were coloured and solid in nature. These are moderately soluble in organic solvents like methanol, ethanol, propanol, benzene and DMSO but insoluble in water. These complexes are highly soluble in binary solvent solvent mixture e.g. propanol + benzene mixture. Binuclear nature and 1:1 composition of metal ligand was revealed through elemental analysis. All the ligands and complexes are stable at room temperature.

The abbreviations used for copper soap and complexes are enlisted below:

Copper palmitate	: CP
Complex of copper palmitate with 2-amino-6-nitro benzothiazole	: CP[BTA]NA
Complex of copper palmitate with 2-amino-6-methoxy benzothiazole	: CP[BTA]A
Complex of copper palmitate with 4-nitro phenylthiourea	: CP[PTU]NA
Complex of copper palmitate with 4-methoxy phenylthiourea	: CP[PTU]A

Chromatography

TLC is probably most versatile technique for the analysis of complexes and their mixtures. TLC is quite efficient technique for separation and identification of synthesized soap, ligand and their complexes in sub microgram amounts using silica gel plates in various non-aqueous solvent systems. R_f of copper soap, ligands and the synthesized complexes in non-aqueous solvent systems has been determined. A thin layer chromatographic applicator was used for coating sorbent material on 20×3 cm glass plates to obtain absorbent layer of 0.25 mm thickness [7]. The coated plates were developed in glass jars of 24×6 cm. A glass sprayer was used to spray chromogenic reagent on the plate to detect the spot. Silica gel G acted as stationary phase whereas the following solvent systems were used as mobile phase.

1. Acetone : Carbon tetrachloride
2. Acetone : Petroleum ether
3. Benzene : Acetone : Petroleum ether

Silica gel G and double distilled water are mixed in 1:3 (w/v) ratio with constant mechanical shaking until homogenous slurry was obtained to prepare the plates. Approx. 10ml of the test solution was applied on thin layer plates by using micropipette. The solvent ascent was fixed to 10-12 cm in all cases. When the development was completed, the plates are withdrawn from the jar and dried at room temperature. The spots were visible in day light.

Spectroscopy

The spectral measurements (IR and NMR) and elemental analysis were carried out at the "Regional Sophisticated Instrumentation Centre", Central Drug Research Institute (RSIC, CDRI) Lucknow. The IR spectra of the complexes were obtained as KBr discs in the range 400-4000 cm^{-1} on Perkin Elmer spectrophotometer. ^{1}H NMR spectra were recorded at CDRI, Lucknow using $CDCl_3$ as reference. ESR spectra of the complexes were recorded at SAIF, IIT, Mumbai in the X-band region at microwave frequency 9.1 GHz and microwave power 5 mW under the magnetic field of strength

2000G at room temperature. Tetracynoethylene (TCNE) was used as the standard. Magnetic susceptibility measurements were conducted at S.P. University, VallabhVidhyanagar, Gujrat.

Biocidal

Step 1: Processing of the sample

The unknown compound is re-suspended in DMSO in mass concentration (w/v)

Step 2: Antimicrobial Susceptibility Testing (Kirby-Bauer and Stokes' methods.)

I. **Hinton susceptibility test agar**

(a) *Sabouraud* Dextrose Agar (antifungal screening) is the only susceptibility test medium that have been validated by NCCLS. Mueller-Hinton agar should always be used for disk diffusion susceptibility testing, according.

II. **McFarland turbidity standard**

(b) A McFarland 0.5 standard should be prepared and quality controlled prior to beginning susceptibility testing. If tightly sealed to prevent evaporation and stored in the dark, the standard can be stored for up to 6 months. The McFarland standard is used to adjust the turbidity of the inoculum for the susceptibility test.

III. **Preparation of inoculum**

(a) Each culture to be tested should be streaked onto a noninhibitory agar medium to obtain isolated colonies. After incubation at 35° C overnight, select 4 or 5 well-isolated colonies with an inoculating needle or loop, and transfer the growth to a tube of sterile saline or nonselective broth (Mueller-Hinton broth, Peptone water) and vortex thoroughly.

IV. **Inoculation procedure**

(a) Within 15 minutes after adjusting the turbidity of the inoculum suspension, dip a sterile cotton swab into the suspension. Pressing firmly against the inside wall of the tube just above the fluid level, rotate the swab to remove excess liquid. Streak the swab over the entire surface of the medium three times, rotating the plate approximately 60 degrees after each application to ensure an even distribution of the inoculum. Finally, swab all around the edge of the agar surface.

(b) The Mueller-Hinton plate should be swabbed over the entire surface of the medium three times, rotating the plate 60 degrees after each application.

V. Loading the plate with Positive, negative control and sample

(a) The working supply of antibiotic (streptomycin, positive control) should be stored in the refrigerator (4° C). 50 µl of the antibiotic suspension was dispensed in the well labeled with C (control) to the plates as soon as possible, but no longer than 15 minutes after inoculation. Diffusion of the drug in the well begins immediately.

(b) 50 µl of the sample (S) and 50 µl of the reference (R, negative control) was dispensed in the well labeled with C (control) to the plates as soon as possible, but no longer than 15 minutes after inoculation.

VI. Recording and interpreting results

(a) After the Loading of C, S, R on the plate, invert the plate and incubate at 35° C for 16 to 18 hours. After incubation, measure the diameter of the zones of complete inhibition (including the diameter of the well) and record it in millimeters. The measurements can be made with a ruler on the undersurface of the plate without opening the lid. The zones of growth inhibition should be compared and recorded as susceptible, intermediate, or resistant to each drug tested. Colonies growing within the clear zone of inhibition may represent resistant variants or a mixed inoculum. The distance from the colony(ies) closest to the well to the center of the well should be measured and then doubled to obtain a diameter. The diameter of the outer clear zone should be recorded as well and an interpretation recorded for each diameter. The colony(ies) inside the zone should be picked, re-isolated, re-identified, and retested in the well diffusion test to confirm the previous results. The presence of colonies within a zone of inhibition may predict eventual resistance to that agent.

Note:

- Di methyl sulfoxide (negative control) does not show any activity against test organism.
- **Antifungal Sensitivity** (Itraconozole 5 mg/well) serves as a positive control.
- Sample (unknown chemical compound) (5mg/well (w/v))

CHARACTERIZATION

Chromatography

The results were reproducible with in ±0.02 R_f unit values for various substituted compounds using procedure for three solvent systems – the main part of the chromatographic studies was as attempt to obtain the standard conditions for their resolution and identification. The best shaped spots given by the solvents were considered to be suitable, and are A = Acetone = carbon tetrachloride, B = Acetone = Petroleum ether, C = Benzene = Acetone = Petroleum ether. In pure acetone spots run along with the solvent front hence could not be used. Single spot was given by all compounds, uniform in shape in present investigation, so all of them are chromatographically pure.

Acetone = Carbon tetrachloride, Acetone, Petroleum ether and Benzene, Acetone = Petroleum ether and Benzene, Acetone = Petroleum ether were selected as best solvent systems for synthesized compounds. In benzene, with or without nitrobenzene, the spots were diffused and comet likes having tail against the flow of solvent. We have observed that R_f values for the series of compounds under investigation increased as the amount of benzene was increased in the solvent system. It is observed from the tables that for all the ligands as well as complexes; nitro derivatives gave higher R_f values as compared to methoxy derivatives [10].

Spectroscopy

1. IR Spectral studies

The IR spectra provide valuable information regarding coordination site of the ligand attached to the metal ion.

(A) Copper Palmitate

The IR spectrum of copper palmitate asymmetric stretching vibration of methyl and methylene group is observed at 2910 cm^{-1} whereas, the symmetric stretching vibration of the group occurred at lower frequency i.e. at 2840 cm^{-1}. The disappearance of the characteristic bands of esters and appearance of the bands of carboxylate ion indicate the formation of copper palmitate soap. The absence of C=O band in the spectra of soap indicate that there is a resonance in the two C=O bonds of carboxylate group. On comparing the IR spectra of palmitic acid and copper palmitate, it is found that the acid (palmitic acid) exist with dimeric structure through hydrogen bonding between carboxyl group of the two acid molecules whereas, copper palmitate soap is ionic in nature and the metal to oxygen bond has ionic character. The band in the region 485 cm^{-1} is due to copper to oxygen bond stretching vibration. This is called characteristic absorption of metal constituent of soap molecule.

(B) CP[PTU]A: Complex of Copper palmitate with 4-methoxy phenylthiourea

The detailed infrared spectral investigation reveals that there are marked differences between the spectra of copper palmitate (soap) and free ligands than those of corresponding complexes.

The absorption bands observed in the region 2920 cm^{-1} and 2848 cm^{-1} correspond to C-H symmetric and asymmetric stretching of methyl ($-CH_3$) and methylene ($-CH_2$) groups of the soap segment present in the complex.

The band resulting from the methylene rocking vibrations, in which all of the methylene groups rocks in phase, appears near 725 cm^{-1} whereas absorption, due to methyl rocking vibrations is observed in the 1110 cm^{-1} region. Absorption due to $-CH_2$ twisting and wagging vibration is observed at 1360 cm^{-1}. The carboxylate ion give raise to two bands i.e. a weak asymmetrical stretching band near 1510.1 cm^{-1} and another symmetrical stretching band at 1470 cm^{-1}. The band in the region 505.6 cm^{-1} is due to $\upsilon_{M\text{-}O}$ symmetric stretching. This is called characteristic absorption of metal constituent of soap molecule.

The thiocarbonyl moiety of the ligand shows absorption in the 1170 cm^{-1} region. Complex contains C=S group which is attached to a nitrogen atom, shows an absorption band in the general C=S stretching region. In addition, several other bands in the broad region of 1510 cm^{-1} can be attributed to vibrations involving interactions between C=S stretching and C-N stretching. Complex have N-C=S group which is an essential structural feature responsible for various biocidal properties. N-C=S structure band occur near 1310 cm^{-1}.

The most prominent bands in the spectra of aromatic compounds occur in the low frequency range between 900 cm^{-1} and 670 cm^{-1}. These strong absorption bands results from the out of plane (OOP) bending of the ring C-H bonds, which is found in this complex at 825 cm^{-1}. The N-H stretching vibration was appeared near 3410 cm^{-1}. The spectra of phenylthiourea complex contain Ar-O-CH_3 group, which display an 'asymmetrical stretching vibration at 1240 cm^{-1} and symmetrical stretching vibration near 1025 cm^{-1}.

The strong band at 1615 cm^{-1} is characteristic feature of the N-H bending vibration of the NH_2 group in the free ligand (4-methoxy phenylthiourea) but in this complex it is shifted to lower frequency at 1595 indicating that the primary nitrogen is the coordinating site in this complex. The conclusive evidence of bonding of metal to ligand is indicated the appearance of band ($\upsilon_{M\text{-}N}$) at 555.8 cm^{-1}. These values are comparable with other reported complexes.

(C) CP[PTU]NA: Complex of Copper palmitate with 4-nitro phenylthiourea

The asymmetric stretching vibration of methyl and methylene group is observed at 2915 cm^{-1} whereas the symmetric stretching vibration of the above group is observed at lower frequency 2845 cm^{-1}. Two bands resulting from the methyl and methylene rocking vibrations appeared at 1110.8 cm^{-1} and 720.7 cm^{-1} region. The band appearing at 1395 cm^{-1} is due to methylene twisting and wagging vibrations. The spectrum shows two bands at 1508.9cm^{-1} and 1475.8 cm^{-1} attributed respectively to $\upsilon_{(C\text{-}O)}$ antisymmetric and $\upsilon_{(C\text{-}O)}$ symmetric vibrations of carboxylate group. The bond in the region 495.0 cm^{-1} is due to $\upsilon_{(Cu\text{-}O)}$.

Apart from these bands the following bands were also found corresponding to ligand moiety. In case of CP[PTU]NA a clear peak is observed at 1440 cm^{-1} corresponding to Ar-C-NO_2 vibrations. The N-H stretching vibration region occurs at 3475 cm^{-1}. The band near 1315 cm^{-1} may be due to the N-C=S symmetric vibration. The band appearing at 1177 cm^{-1} is due to $v_{(C=S)}$ stretching while other band at 835 is due to the $v_{(C-H)}$ deformation.

The strong band at 1602 cm^{-1} is characteristic feature of the N-H bending vibration of the -NH_2 group in the free ligand (4-nitro Phenylthiourea) but in this complex it is shifted to lower frequency at 1595 cm^{-1} indicating that the primary nitrogen is the coordinating site in this complex. The new band appeared in the region 570 cm^{-1}which was absent in ligand may be due to formation of Cu-N bond. The above arguments indicate that the ligand behaves as monodentate and is coordinating with copper metal through a primary nitrogen atom of NH_2 group.

NMR Spectral Studies

The ^{1}H NMR spectra of free ligands and corresponding complexes have been compared and determine the bonding. The signals were assigned on the basis of chemical shifts, spin-spin interaction and their effect on substitution.

(A) **CP[PTU]A : Complex of Copper palmitate with 4-methoxy phenylthiourea**

The ligand to metal bonding is further supported by ^{1}H NMR spectra. The complex showed broadened peak at d 3.70-3.78 ranges due to the protons. This peak indicates the co-ordination through the –NH_2group of phenylthiourea segment to the metal (copper) atom of the soap segment. In addition to the above signal, resonances corresponding to CH_3 and CH_2 protons attached to -CH_2-R groups are also observed in δ 0.88 and δ 1.20 region.

(B) CP[PTU]NA: Complex of Copper palmitate with 4-nitro phenylthiourea

The ligand to metal bonding is further supported by ^{1}H NMR spectra. The complex snowed broadened peak at δ 3.65-3.70 ranges due to the protons. This peak indicates the co-ordination through the –NH_2 group of phenylthiourea to the metal (copper) atom of the soap segment. In addition to the above signal, resonance corresponding to CH_3 and CH_2 protons attached to –CH_2-R groups is also observed in δ 0.90 and δ 1.22 region.

ESR Spectral Studies

ESR spectrum is characterized by the position, intensity and shape of the component lines. The position of ESR is referred to as g-values and is directly determined by the energy levels. The variation in g-value is interpreted in terms of first and second order spin orbit interaction. The g-value for ESR signal is calculated by the formula.

$$v = \frac{hv}{BH}$$

Where

v = Frequency of band in KHz

B = Bohr Magneton

H = Magnetic field

h = Plank's constant

On the basis of $g_{||}$ and $g_{|}$ the values of g_{av} and G were calculated using the following relations.

$g_{av}\ (g_{||} + 2\ g\perp)/3$

$G = g_{||} - 2/g\perp - 2$

(A) CP[PTU]A : Complex of Copper palmitate with 4-methoxy phenylthiourea

The ESR spectrum of Cu(II) complex is recorded at room temperature. The g-tensor value of the copper complex can be used to derive the ground state. In octahedral complexes, the unpaired electron may lie in the$d_{x2\text{-}y2}$or $d_z{}^2$ orbital. The Spin Hamiltonian parameters for the copper complex are calculated from the spectra are 2.35, 2.05, 2.15 etc. g-tensor values are $g_{||}> g\perp> g_0$ suggest that complex has distorted octahedral geometry with unpaired electron lying in $d_{x2\text{-}y2}$ orbital.

The ESR parameters of the complex coincide well with the related systems, which suggest that the complex has octahedral geometry and the systems are axially symmetric. In the axial spectra, the g-values are related with exchange interaction coupling constant (G) by the expression:

$G = g_{||}-2/g\perp - 2$

According to Hathaway, if the value is larger than four, the exchange interaction is negligible because the local tetragonal axes are aligned paralled or slightly misaligned. If the value is less than four, the exchange interaction is considerable and the local tetragonal axes are misaligned. For the present copper complex, it is higher than 4, which misaligned suggests that the local tetragonal axes are aligned parallel or slightly misaligned and consistent with a $d_{x2\text{-}y2}$ ground state.

(B) CP[PTU]NA : Complex of Copper palmitate with 4-nitro phenylthiourea

The value of $g_{||}$, $g\perp$ and g_{av} calculated are 2.37, 2.08, 2.012and 4.122. The g tensor values are $g_{||}> g\perp> g_0$. The order of g values obtained from ESR spectra indicated the presence of an octahedral environment around the copper (II) ions and a distortion from regular octahedron has taken place in the shape of the complex. It suggests that the unpaired electron lies predominantly in the $d_{x2\text{-}y2}$ orbital of Cu (II) giving $^2B_{1g}$ as the ground state. Since the value of G is greater than four for complex of copper palmitate with 4-nitro phenylthiourea; it is suggestive of negligible exchange coupling interaction between the two copper centers in complexes.

Magnetic Moment Studies

As is reported earlier, the presence of copper ion leads to a magnetic moment of 1.73 BM. Various scientist have reported subnormal values for the magnetic moment of copper soap and fatty acid, inferring that the soap exists as a binuclear molecule. This has been attributed to the formation of δ-bonds arising from inter-molecular exchange demagnetization through lateral overlapping of $3d_{x2-y2}$ orbital on each copper ion. The studies also reveal that these values of magnetic moments in the range 1.92-2.08 BM is due to the sub-dispersion unit of soap/complex which retains its binuclear configuration even in solution. It may be suggested that sub-dispersion units are bound together by weak polar forces resulting from the interaction between $3d_{xy}$ and $3d_{xz}$ orbital of two copper atoms. The lower values of magnetic moments of copper ions in copper complex in benzene, as compared to those in solid state, reflect the terminals of binuclear molecules as $[Cu_2(RCOO)_4L_2]$ Where L represents the solvent molecule in solution, but is replaced by the ligand on complexation.

Conductivity Studies

The nature of the complexes is found to be non-electrolytic as the molar conductance values in benzene, lies in the range of 3.9-6.14 mhos cm^2 mol^{-1}

Biocidal Studies

The study aims to evaluate the bioactivity of synthesized complexes against test organisms. Antimicrobial sensitivity was performed for synthesized complexes (Compound S_1, S_2) on Muller Hinton Agar against *Candida abicans, Trichodermaharzianum*by Kirby-Bauer Stokes' method. Results obtained using Itraconazole (5 mg (w/v))as antifungal agent control (C) and for negative reference Ethanol/Methanol (R) are mentioned in table 9.1 and figure 9.1-9.2.

Activity index = zone of inhibition of sample[S]/zone of inhibition of reference [R] And the activity can be found out by

Activity = activity index × 10

If the Zone of Inhibition is:

< 13 = it means that the extract is inactive,

13 – 18 = it means that the extract is bioactive,

> 18 = it means that the extract is highly active

Table 9.1: Antibacterial activity of the synthesized complexes against test bacteria

S. No.	Microorganism	Sample	Zone of Inhibition (mm)					Reference	Activity Index
			Positive Control	Sample			Mean Zone of Inhibition		
Antibacterial sensitivity (Streptomycin 5 mg/well)									
1.	*Staphylococcus aureus* (ATCC 29213)	S1CP[PTU]NA	30	20	20	20.5	20.17	8	2.52
2.	*Escherichia coli* (ATCC 25922)		34	17	16.5	17	16.83	9	1.87
3.	*Staphylococcus aureus* (ATCC 29213)	S2CP[PTU]A	30	14	13	13	13.33	8	1.67
4.	*Escherichia coli* (ATCC 25922)		34	nil	nil	Nil	0	9	0
5.	*Staphylococcus aureus* (ATCC 29213)	S3CP[BTA] A	30	17	16.5	17	16.83	8	2.104
6.	*Escherichia coli* (ATCC 25922)		34	12	11.5	12	11.83	9	1.31
7.	*Staphylococcus aureus* (ATCC 29213)	S 4CP[BTA]NA	30	12	11	11.5	11.5	8	1.43
8.	*Escherichia coli* (ATCC 25922)		34	nil	nil	nil	0	9	0

Table 9.2: Antifungal activity of the synthesized complexes against test fungi

S. No.	Microorganism	Sample	Zone of Inhibition (mm)				Mean Zone of Inhibition	Reference	Activity
			Positive Control	Sample					
	Antifungal Sensitivity (Itraconozole5 mg/well)								
1.	*Candida albicans*	S1CP[PTU]NA	19	33	32	31	32	10	3.2
2.	*Trichodermaharzianum*		23.5	37	36	36	36.33	9	4.04
3.	*Candida albicans*	S2CP[PTU]A	19	10	10.5	10	10.17	10	1.02
4.	*Trichodermaharzianum*		23.5	14	15	14	14.33	9	1.59
5.	*Candida albicans*	S3CP[BTA] A	19	10.5	11	11	10.83	10	1.08
6.	*Trichodermaharzianum*		23.5	15	14.5	15	14.83	9	1.65
7.	*Candida albicans*	S4CP[BTA]NA	19	11	10	11	10.67	10	1.07
8.	*Trichodermaharzianum*		23.5	13	12	12.5	12.5	9	1.39

Note:

Sample I : Sample (5 mg/well (w/v))

Diameter of the zone of inhibition is given.

Diameter of the well was 8mm.

Dimethyl Sulphoxide (negative control)

RESULT AND DISCUSSION

Chromatography

The results were reproducible with in ±0.02 R_f unit values for various substituted compounds using procedure for three solvent systems – the main part of the chromatographic studies was as attempt to obtain the standard conditions for their resolution and identification. The best shaped spots given by the solvents were considered to be suitable, and are A = Acetone = carbon tetrachloride, B = Acetone = Petroleum ether, C = Benzene = Acetone = Petroleum ether. In pure acetone spots run along with the solvent front hence could not be used [9]. Single spot was given by all compounds, uniform in shape in present investigation, so all of them are chromatographically pure.

Acetone = Carbontetrachloride, Acetone, Petroleum ether and Benzene, Acetone = Petroleum ether and Benzene, Acetone = Petroleum ether were selected as best solvent systems for synthesized compounds. In benzene, with or without nitrobenzene, the spots were diffused and comet likes having tail against the flow of solvent.We have observed that R_f values for the series of compounds under investigation increased as the amount of benzene was increased in the solvent system. It is observed from the tables that for all the ligands as well as complexes; nitro derivatives gave higher R_f values as compared to methoxy derivatives [10].

Spectroscopy

1. IR Spectral studies

The IR spectra provide valuable information regarding coordination site of the ligand attached to the metal ion. The selected bands of diagnostic importance of the complexes with relative intensities/peaks are given[11-12]

(A) Copper Palmitate

The IR spectrum of copper palmitate asymmetric stretching vibration of methyl and methylene group is observed at 2910 cm^{-1} whereas, the symmetric stretching vibration of the group occurred at lower frequency i.e. at 2840 cm^{-1}. The disappearance of the characteristic bands of esters and appearance of the bands of carboxylate ion indicate the formation of copper palmitate soap. The absence of C=O band in the spectra of soap indicate that there is a resonance in the two C=O bonds of carboxylate group.On comparing the IR spectra of palmitic acid and copper palmitate, it is found that the acid (palmitic acid) exist with dimeric structure through hydrogen bonding between carboxyl group of the two acid molecules whereas, copper palmitate soap is ionic in nature and the metal to oxygen bond has ionic character. The band in the region 485 cm^{-1} is due to copper to oxygen bond stretching vibration. This is called characteristic absorption of metal constituent of soap molecule[13].

(B) CP[PTU]A: Complex of Copper palmitate with 4-methoxy phenylthiourea

The detailed infrared spectral investigation reveals that there are marked differences between the spectra of copper palmitate (soap) and free ligands than those of corresponding complexes [14].

The absorption bands observed in the region 2920 cm^{-1} and 2848 cm^{-1} correspond to C-H symmetric and asymmetric stretching of methyl ($-CH_3$) and methylene ($-CH_2$) groups of the soap segment present in the complex. The band resulting from the methylene rocking vibrations, in which all of the methylene groups rocks in phase, appears near 725 cm^{-1} whereas absorption, due to methyl rocking vibrations is observed in the 1110 cm^{-1} region. Absorption due to $-CH_2$ twisting and wagging vibration is observed at 1360 cm^{-1}. The carboxylate ion give raise to two bands i.e. a weak asymmetrical stretching band near 1510.1 cm^{-1} and another symmetrical stretching band at 1470 cm^{-1}. The band in the region 505.6 cm^{-1} is due to $\upsilon_{M\text{-}O}$ symmetric stretching. This is called characteristic absorption of metal constituent of soap molecule [15].

The thiocarbonyl moiety of the ligand shows absorption in the 1170 cm^{-1} region. Complex contains C=S group which is attached to a nitrogen atom, shows an absorption band in the general C=S stretching region. In addition, several other bands in the broad region of 1510 cm^{-1} can be attributed to vibrations involving interactions between C=S stretching and C-N stretching. Complex have N-C=S group which is an essential structural feature responsible for various biocidal properties. N-C=S structure band occur near 1310 cm^{-1}. (Fig. 9.2)

The most prominent bands in the spectra of aromatic compounds occur in the low frequency range between 900 cm^{-1} and 670 cm^{-1}. These strong absorption bands results from the out of plane (OOP) bending of the ring C-H bonds, which is found in this complex at 825 cm^{-1}. The N-H stretching vibration was appeared near 3410 cm^{-1}. The spectra of phenylthiourea complex contain $Ar\text{-}O\text{-}CH_3$ group, which display an 'asymmetrical stretching vibration at 1240 cm^{-1} and symmetrical stretching vibration near 1025 cm^{-1}.

The strong band at 1615 cm^{-1} is characteristic feature of the N-H bending vibration of the NH_2 group in the free ligand (4-methoxy phenylthiourea) but in this complex it is shifted to lower frequency at 1595 indicating that the primary nitrogen is the coordinating site in this complex. The conclusive evidence of bonding of metal to ligand is indicated the appearance of band ($\upsilon_{M\text{-}N}$) at 555.8 cm^{-1}. These values are comparable with other reported complexes [16].

(C) CP[PTU]NA : Complex of Copper palmitate with 4-nitro phenylthiourea

The asymmetric stretching vibration of methyl and methylene group is observed at 2915 cm^{-1} whereas the symmetric stretching vibration of the above group is observed at lower frequency 2845 cm^{-1}. Two bands resulting from the methyl and methylene rocking vibrations appeared at 1110.8 cm^{-1} and 720.7 cm^{-1} region. The band appearing at 1395 cm^{-1} is due to methylene twisting and wagging vibrations. The spectrum shows two bands at 1508.9cm^{-1} and 1475.8 cm^{-1} attributed respectively to $\upsilon_{(C\text{-}O)}$ antisymmetric and $\upsilon_{(C\text{-}O)}$ symmetric vibrations of carboxylate group. The bond in the region 495.0 cm^{-1} is due to $\upsilon_{(Cu\text{-}O)}$.

Apart from these bands the following bands were also found corresponding to ligand moiety. In case of CP[PTU]NA a clear peak is observed at 1440 cm^{-1} corresponding to Ar-C-NO_2 vibrations. The N-H stretching vibration region occurs at 3475 cm^{-1}. The band near 1315 cm^{-1} may be due to the N-C=S symmetric vibration. The band appearing at 1177 cm^{-1} is due to $\upsilon_{(C=S)}$ stretching while other band at 835 is due to the $\upsilon_{(C\text{-}H)}$ deformation [17].

The strong band at 1602 cm^{-1} is characteristic feature of the N-H bending vibration of the -NH_2 group in the free ligand (4-nitro Phenylthiourea) but in this complex it is shifted to lower frequency at 1595 cm^{-1} indicating that the primary nitrogen is the coordinating site in this complex. The new band appeared in the region 570 cm^{-1}which was absent in ligand may be due to formation of Cu-N bond. The above arguments indicate that the ligand behaves as monodentate and is coordinating with copper metal through a primary nitrogen atom of NH_2 group. (Fig. 9.3)

(2) NMR Spectral studies

The ^{1}H NMR spectra of free ligands and corresponding complexes have been compared and determine the bonding. The signals were assigned on the basis of chemical shifts, spin-spin interaction and their effect on substitution [18].

(A) CP[PTU]A : Complex of Copper palmitate with 4-methoxy phenylthiourea

The ligand to metal bonding is further supported by ^{1}H NMR spectra. The complex showed broadened peak at δ 3.70-3.78 ranges due to the protons. This peak indicates the co-ordination through the –NH_2group of phenylthiourea segment to the metal (copper) atom of the soap segment. In addition to the above signal, resonances corresponding to CH_3 and CH_2 protons attached to -CH_2-R groups are also observed in δ 0.88 and δ 1.20region.

(B) CP[PTU]NA: Complex of Copper palmitate with 4-nitro phenylthiourea

The ligand to metal bonding is further supported by ^{1}H NMR spectra. The complex snowed broadened peak at δ 3.65-3.70 ranges due to the protons. This peak indicates the co-ordination through the –NH_2 group of phenylthiourea to the metal (copper) atom of the soap segment. In addition to the above signal, resonance corresponding to CH_3 and CH_2 protons attached to $-CH_2$-R groups is also observed in δ 0.90 and δ 1.22 region.

(3) ESR Spectral studies

ESR spectrum is characterized by the position, intensity and shape of the component lines. The position of ESR is referred to as g-values and is directly determined by the energy levels. The variation in g-value is interpreted in terms of first and second order spin orbit interaction. The g-value for ESR signal is calculated by the formula [19].

$$g = \frac{hv}{BH}$$

Where

v = Frequency of band in KHz

B = Bohr Magneton

H = Magnetic field

h = Plank's constant

On the basis of $g_{||}$ and $g_{|}$ the values of g_{av} and G were calculated using the following relations [20].

g_{av} $(g_{||} + 2\, g\perp)/3$

$G = g_{||} - 2/g\perp - 2$

(A) CP[PTU]A : Complex of Copper palmitate with 4-methoxy phenylthiourea

The ESR.spectrum of Cu(II) complex is recorded at room temperature. The g-tensor value of the copper complex can be used to derive the ground state. In octahedral complexes, the unpaired electron may lie in thed$_{x2-y2}$or $d_z{}^2$ orbital. The Spin Hamiltonian parameters for the copper complex are calculated from the spectra are 2.35, 2.05, 2.15 etc. g-tensor values are $g_{||} > g\perp > g_0$ suggest that complex has distorted octahedral geometry with unpaired electron lying in d_{x2-y2} orbital.

The ESR parameters of the complex coincide well with the related systems, which suggest that the complex has octahedral geometry and the systems are axially symmetric. In the axial spectra, the g-values are related with exchange interaction coupling constant (G) by the expression:

$G = g_{||} - 2/g\perp - 2$

According to Hathaway, if the value is larger than four, the exchange interaction is negligible because the local tetragonal axes are aligned paralled or slightly misaligned. If the value is less than four, the exchange interaction is considerable and the local tetragonal axes are misaligned. For the present copper complex, it is higher than 4, which misaligned suggests that the local tetragonal axes are aligned parallel or slightly misaligned and consistent with a d_{x2-y2} ground state.

(B) CP[PTU]NA : Complex of Copper palmitate with 4-nitro phenylthiourea

The value of $g_{||}$, g⊥ and g_{av} calculated are 2.37, 2.08, 2.012and 4.122. The g tensor values are $g_{||}$> g⊥> g_0. The order of g values obtained from ESR spectra indicated the presence of an octahedral environment around the copper (II) ions and a distortion from regular octahedron has taken place in the shape of the complex. It suggests that the unpaired electron lies predominantly in the d_{x2-y2} orbital of Cu (II) giving $^2B_{1g}$ as the ground state. Since the value of G is greater than four for complex of copper palmitate with 4-nitro phenylthiourea; it is suggestive of negligible exchange coupling interaction between the two copper centers in complexes.

Magnetic Moment Studies

As is reported earlier, the presence of copper ion leads to a magnetic moment of 1.73 BM. Various scientist have reported subnormal values for the magnetic moment of copper soap and fatty acid, inferring that the soap exists as a binuclear molecule. This has been attributed to the formation of d-bonds arising from inter-molecular exchange demagnetization through lateral overlapping of $3d_{x2-y2}$ orbital on each copper ion. The studies also reveal that these values of magnetic moments in the range 1.92-2.08 BM is due to the sub-dispersion unit of soap/complex which retains its binuclear configuration even in solution. It may be suggested that sub-dispersion units are bound together by weak polar forces resulting from the interaction between $3d_{xy}$ and $3d_{xz}$ orbital of two copper atoms. The lower values of magnetic moments of copper ions in copper complex in benzene, as compared to those in solid state, reflect the terminals of binuclear molecules as $[Cu_2(RCOO)_4L_2]$ Where L represents the solvent molecule in solution, but is replaced by the ligand on complexation[21].

Conductivity Studies

The nature of the complexes is found to be non-electrolytic as the molar conductance values in benzene, lies in the range of 3.9-6.14 mhos cm^2 mol^{-1} [22]

Biocidal Studies

The study aims to evaluate the bioactivity of synthesized complexes against test organisms.Antimicrobial sensitivity was performed for synthesized complexes (Compound S_1, S_2) on Muller Hinton Agar against *Candida abicans, Trichodermaharzianum*by Kirby-Bauer Stokes' method [23-24].Results obtained using Itraconazole (5 mg (w/v))as antifungal agent control (C) and for negative reference Ethanol/Methanol (R) are mentioned in tables 9.1-9.2 and figures 9.1-9.5.

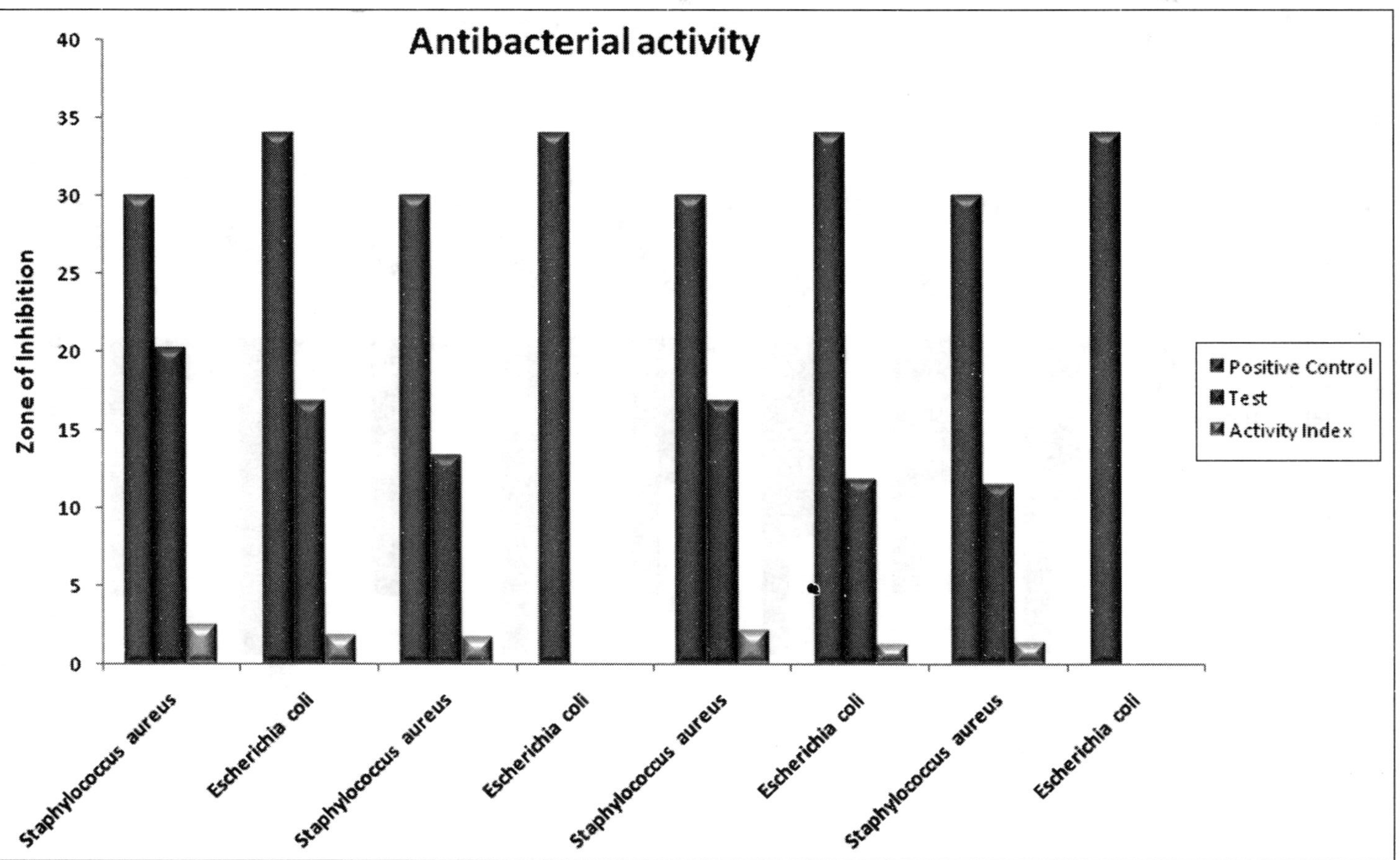

Fig. 9.1: Plots presenting the comparative study of complex sensitivity against different bacteria under study

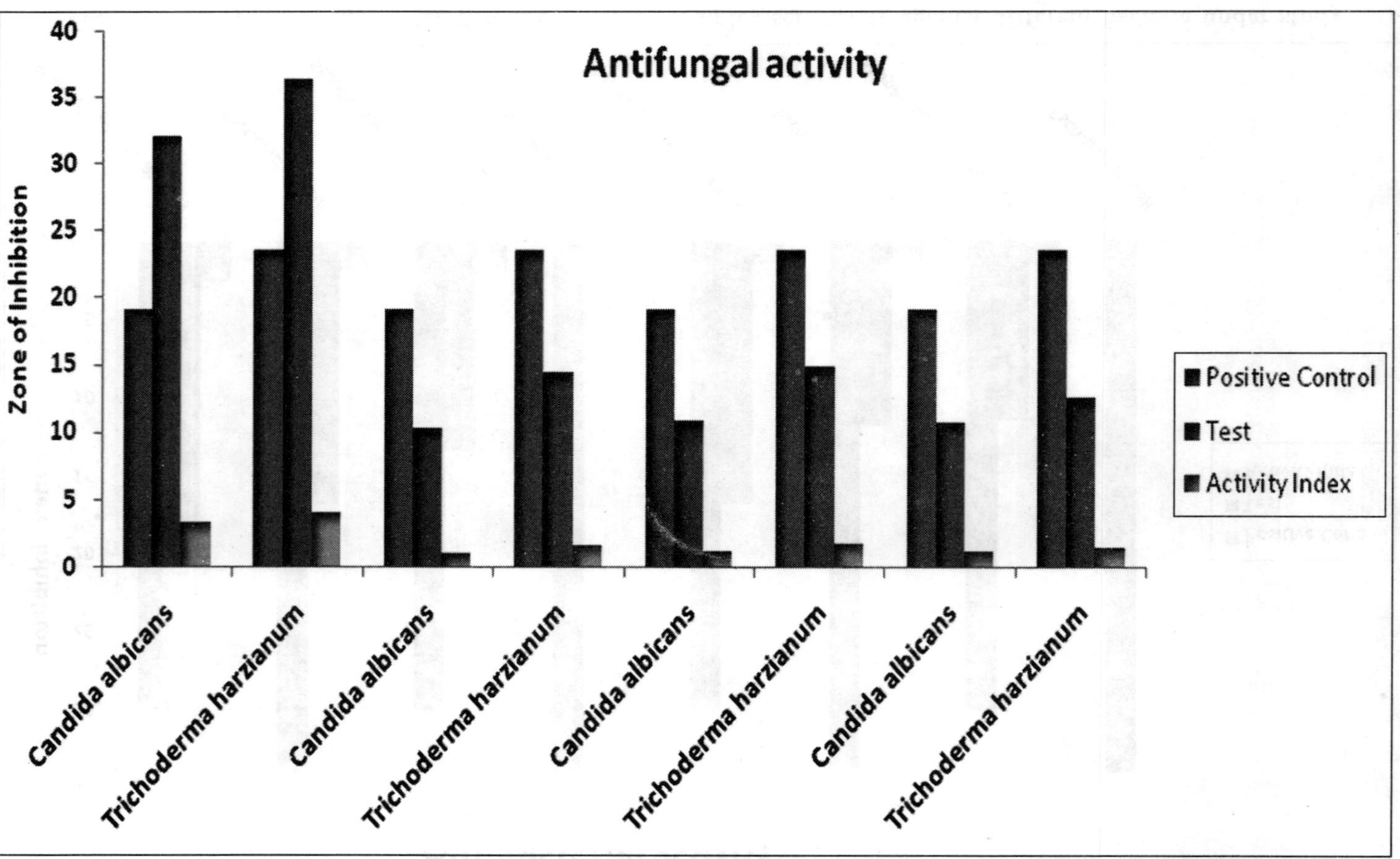

Fig. 9.2: Plots presenting the comparative study of complex sensitivity against different fungi under study

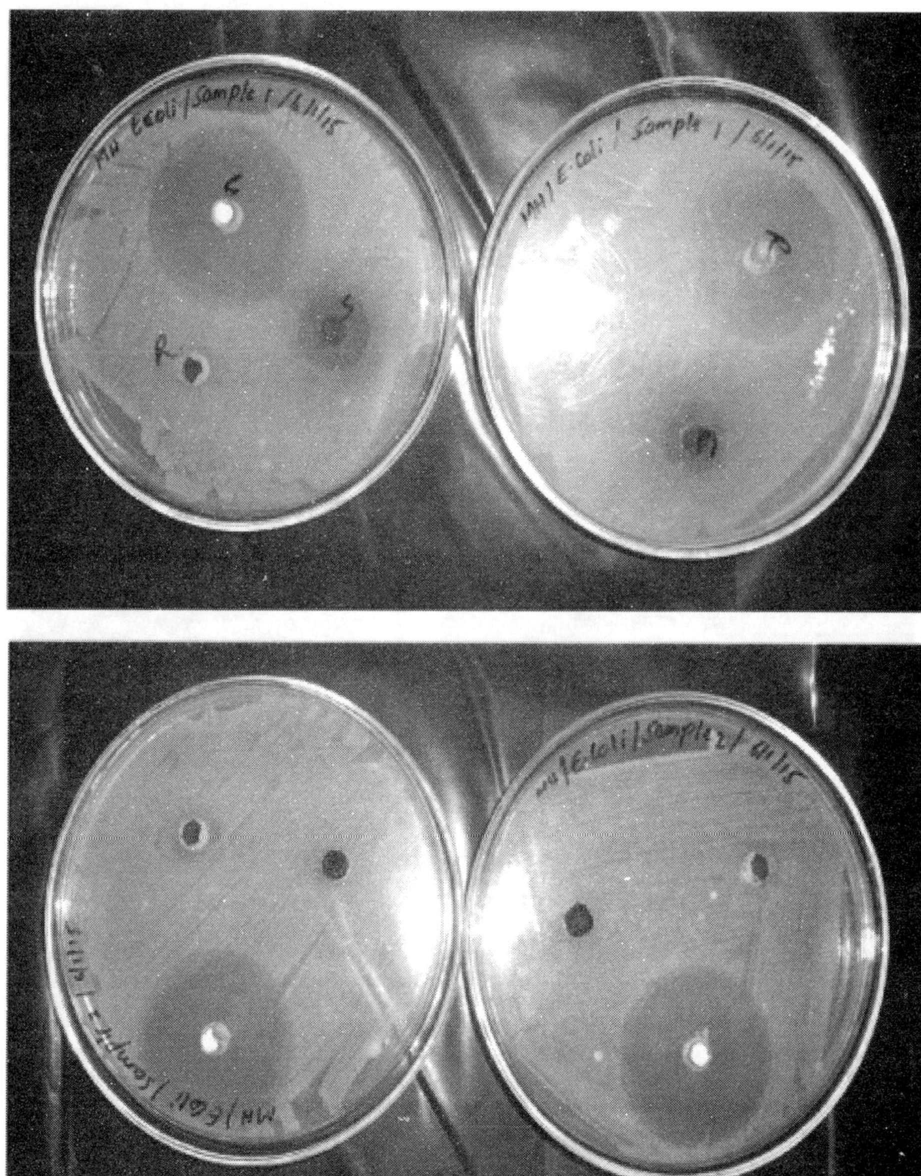

Fig. 9.3: Test disks presenting sensitivity of complexes against *Eschericha coli*

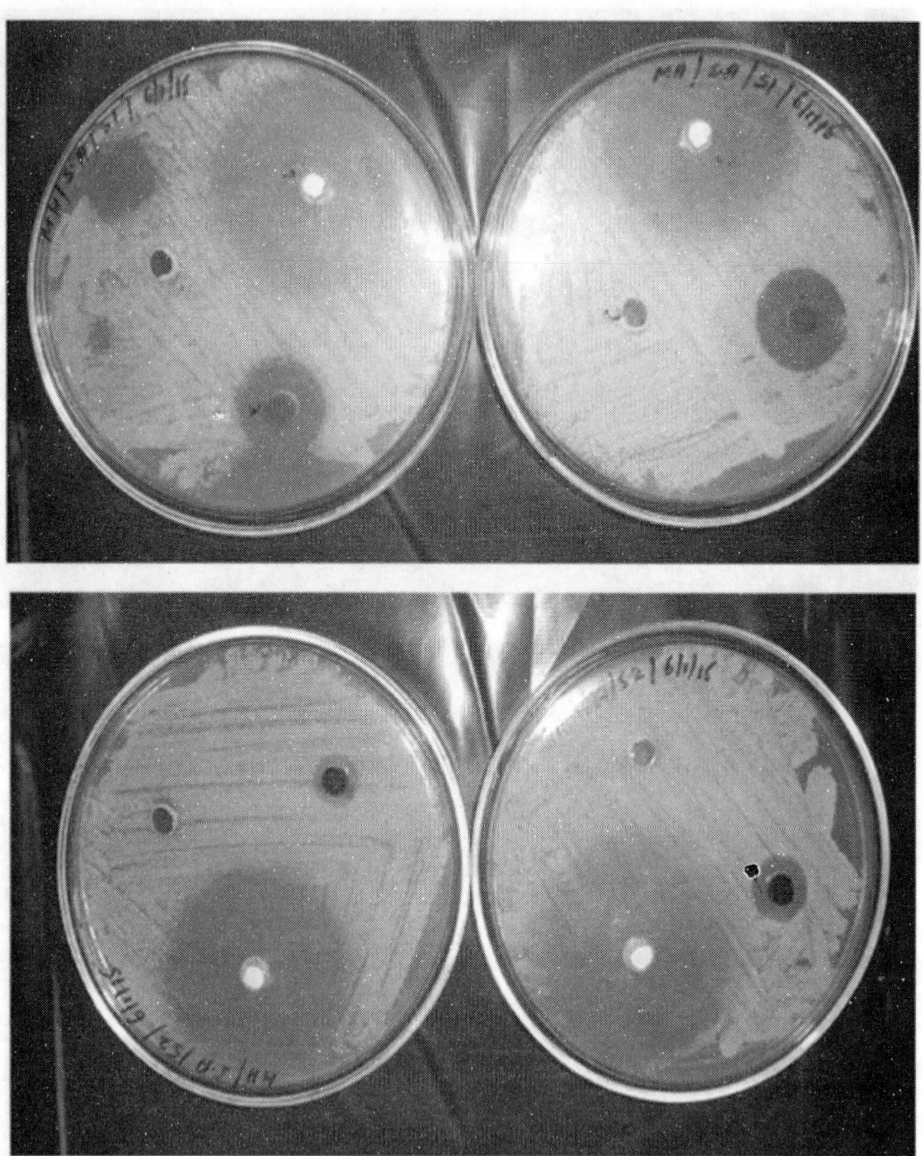

Fig. 9.4: Test disks presenting sensitivity of complexes against *Staphylococcus aureus*

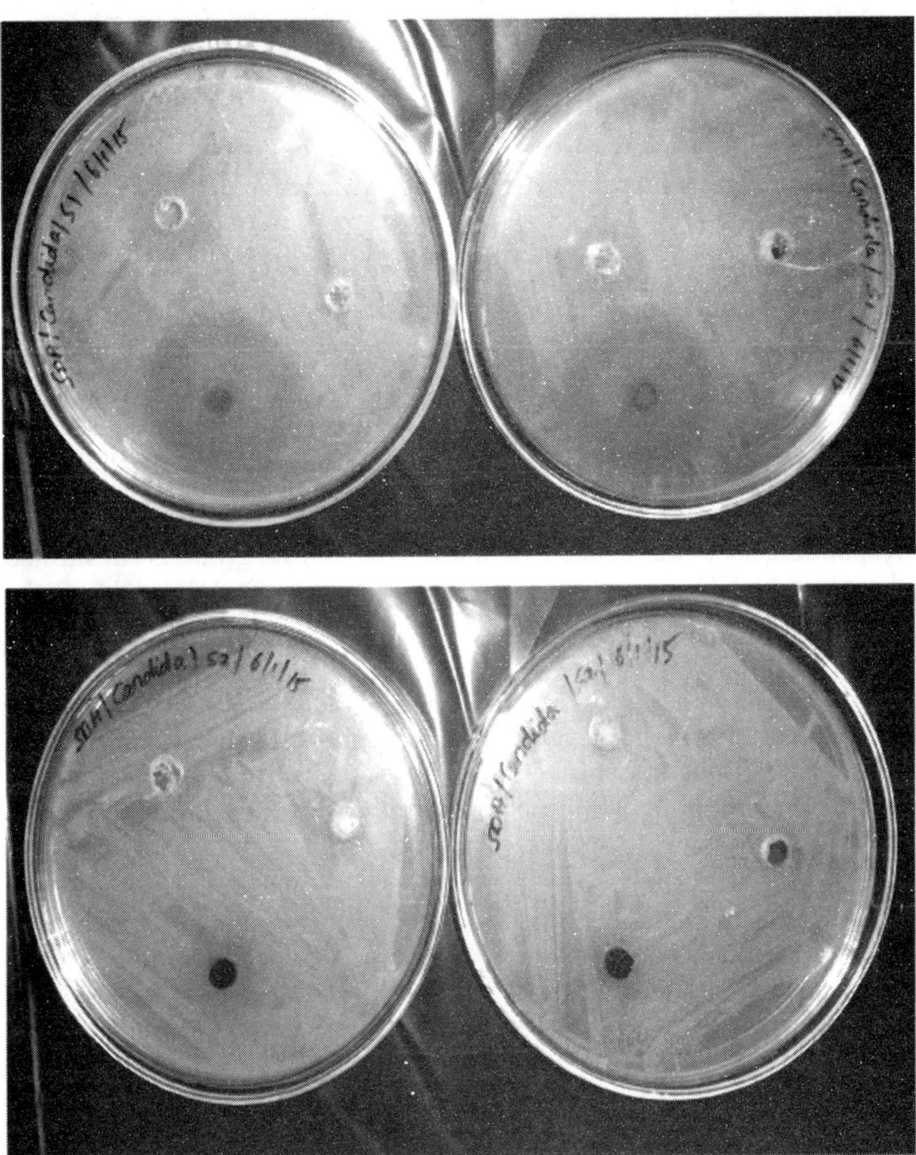

Fig. 9.5: Test disks presenting sensitivity of complexes against *Candida albicans*

Activity index = zone of inhibition of sample[S]/zone of inhibition of reference [R] And the activity can be found out by

Activity = activity index × 10

If the Zone of Inhibition is[25]

< 13 = it means that the extract is inactive,

13 – 18 = it means that the extract is bioactive,

> 18 = it means that the extract is highly active

CONCLUSION

Chromatography

All the compounds gave single spot, uniform in shape in our present investigation so all of them are chromatographically pure. We found that results were reproducible with in ±0.02 R_f unit.

For various compounds under investigation we found R_f values were increased as the amount of acetone in various systems is increased. Concerning the general R_f value of synthesized compounds, it was particularly noticeable that complexes have higher R_f values than corresponding soap and ligands. Similarly when OCH_3 group is substituted at the place of NO_2 group, increase in R_f values were noticed in all the solvent systems.

Spectral Studies

From the forgoing discussion it is concluded that the ligands react with Cu(II) palmitate to form complexes. Based upon analytical and spectral studies the co-ordination number six for copper ion in dimeric complexes of the type $Cu_2(C_{15}H_{31}COO)_4L_2$ have been reported.

Biocidal Studies

The studies clearly shows that activity of complex of copper palmitate with 4-nitro phenylthiourea (S_1) against *Staphylococcus aureus*and *Escherichia coli* is greater than the activity of complex of copper palmitate with 2-amino-6-nitro benzothiazole (S_4) against these test bacteria. In the same way studies were done for the complexes of methoxy substituted benzothiazole and phenylthiourea against the above mentioned bacteria. We observed that activity of complex of copper palmitate with 2-amino-6-methoxy Benzothiazole (S_3) against *Staphylococcus aureus* as well as *Escherichia coli* is greater than activity of complex of copper palmitate with 4-methoxy phenylthiourea (S_2). Further studies elaborated that the activity of complex of copper palmitate with 4-nitro phenylthiourea (S_1) against *Candida albicans* and *Trichodermaharzinum* is greater than the activity of complex of copper palmitate with 2-amino-6-nitro benzothiazole (S_4) against these test fungi. Activity of complex of copper palmitate with 2-amino-6-methoxy benzothiazole (S_3) against these test fungi is slightly higher than the activity of complex of copper palmitate with 4-methoxy phenylthiourea. We can conclude that antifungal and antibacterial activity of various complexes of copper palmitate varies according to the nature of the groups attached to the copper soap.

RECOMMONDATION

Copper is very important metal because all forms of life require copper metalas an essential micronutrient. Various biological processes, directly or indirectly are dependent on copper metal. Copper soaps are used as fungicides, bacteriosides, herbicides and insecticides. Heterocycles having nitrogen play significant role in life science industry and industrial field related to special and fine chemistry.

Copper complexes including heterocyclic compounds have attracted our attention in a magnificent way because of its utility in catalysis and biological functions. Copper compounds incorporating benzothiazole moieties have been observed to show useful antibacterial, antifungal, antiviral, antimalarial, anticancer and antitubercular activities. Copper complexes are recommended as therapeutic compounds. In the present study the synthesized complexes are checked to inhibit the growth of various fungi and bacteria. The complexes explored have wide array of applications. Such complexes are useful in paint industry to avoid any fungal growth, in textile industry to avoid infections and in many touch surfaces to reduce the spread of infectious microorganisms. These complexes can be used in polymer industries efficiently.

REFERENCES

1. Mathur N. and Bargotya S., Res. J. Chem. Sci., 8(4), 30-34 (2018).
2. Walaa H. Mahmood, Omar M.M. and Sayed I.N., J. Thermal Anal. Calorimet, 124(2), 1071 (2016).
3. Vamsikrishna N., Kumar P.K., Gali R., Ganj N., Daravath S. and Shivaraj, J. Chem. Sci., 29(5), 609 (2017).
4. Elham G.G., Niaz M. and Mojtoba M., J. Appl. Chem., 11(41), 119 (2017).
5. Mathur N., Bargotya S., Int. J. Pharma. Sci., 6(6), 2538 (2015).
6. Sakarya H.C., Gorgon K., Ogretir C., Arabian J. Chem., 9, 1314 (2016).
7. Mathur N. and Bargotya S., Chem. Sci. Trans., 5(1), 117 (2016).
8. Bargotya S. and Mathur N., J. Appl. Chem., 10, 18 (2017).
9. Vincent M., Hartemann P., Engles-Deutsch M., Elsevier, Ind. J. Hygiene and Environ. Health, 219, 585 (2016).
10. Malik S., Jain B., Mirza A.S., Singh A., The Pharma and Chem. J., 3(4), 119 (2016)
11. Ugale V.G., Patel H.M., Wadodkar S.G., Bari S.B., Shrikhedkar A.A. and Surana S.J., Europ. J. Med. Chem., 53, 107 (2012).
12. Patil V.S., Nandre K.P. and Ghosh S., Europ. J. Med. Chem., 59, 304 (2013).
13. Telvekar V.N., Bairwa V.K., Satardekar K. and Bellubi A., 22(1), 649(2012).

14. Bolelli K., Yalcin I., Ertan-Bolelli T., Med. Chem. Res., 21(11), 3818(2012).
15. Navale A., Pawar S., Deodhar M. and Kale A., Med. Chem. Res.,22(9), 4316(2013).
16. Jevtovic V., Ivkovic S., Kaisarevic S. and Kovacevic R., Anticanc. Act. New Cooper (II) Com. Incor. Contem. Mat., 1(2), 137 (2010).
17. Devkurari V.P. and Ghodasara T.J., Archives of Appl. Sci. Res., 2(1), 198(2010).
18. Bansod N.H., Kale P.D. and Mawande S.D., J.Chem. Pharm. Res., 4(5), 2429 (2012).
19. Thavuduraj K., Antonysamy K. and ThillaiarasuP.Chem. Sci. Trans., 2278(2013).
20. Mathur N.,J. Curr. Chem. Pharm. Sci., 1(1), 37(2011).
21. Hoda A., Bayoumi, Abdel-Nasser M.A. Alaghaz and Mutlaksh A.A., Int. J. Electron. Sci., 8, 93 (2013).
22. Xiao P., Dumur F., Zhang J., Fouassier J.P., Gigmes D. and Lalevee J. (2014). Macromol., 47(12), 3837.
23. Irena K. and Luciano S., Curr. Med. Chem., 20, 4609(2013).
24. Weaver L., Michels H.T. and Heevil C.W., Lett. Appl. Microbiol., 50(1), 18.
25. Sartaj T., Samira A., Farukh A., Clavdio P., Fabio M., Norberto M., Giullio, L. and Riccardo, P.Eur. J. Med. Chem., 60, 216(2013).
26. Magdy S. and Elsevier, SpectrochimicaActa Part A. Mol. and Bimol. Spect., 117, 127 (2014).
27. Raman N., Sobha S. and Mitu L., J. Saudi Chem. Soc., 17(2), 151 (2013).
28. Chatyala V.K., Kumar K.S., Subhashini N.J.P. and Shivaraj P.R., J. Coord. Chem., 66(2) (2013).
29. Selvarani V., Annaraj B., Neelakantan M.A., Sundaramoorthy S. and Velmurugan D., Polyhedron, 54, 74(2013).
30. Harinath Y., Harikishore D. Reddy K., Kumar B.N. Ch., Apparao, SeshaiahK.,Elsevier Spectromica Acta Part A. Mol. Biomol. Spect., 101, 264 (2013).
31. Kumar N. and Kachroo Plant P.L., J. Indian Chem. Soc., VII, 98, 1 (1980).
32. Mukherjee G.N. and Das A., J. Indian Chem. Soc., 78 (2001).
33. Singh N., Sangwan N.K. and Dhindsu K.S., Pest Manag. Sci., 56, 284 (2004).
34. Mehrotra K.N., Mehta V.P. and Nagar T.N., Cellulose Chem. Technol., 1, 38 (1978).
35. Fisel S., Acad. Rep. Popular Romaine Filialalaji Studic Careetaxi Stiint, 7(2), 13 (1956).
36. Fisel S., Zhur. Neorg. Khim., 5, 1090 (1955).
37. Kaufman H.P. and Lissling F., UND. Seifen, 55, 90 (1953).
38. Mahapatra B.B. and Ray P., J. Indian Chem. Soc., 79, 536 (2002).
39. Mahapatra B.B. and Mishra R.R., J. Indian Chem. Soc., 78, 395 (2001).
40. Patel R.N., Kumar and Pandeya K.B. Indian J. Chem., 39A, 1124 (2001).
41. Chandra S. and Sharma S.D., J. Indian Chem. Soc., 79, 495(2002).
42. Hussain Reddy K. and Radhakrishna Reddy M., J. Indian Chem. Soc.,79, 219 (2012).
43. Kumar Devendra and Sharma R.C., J. Indian Chem. Soc., 79, 284 (2002).
44. Singh Bihari, Singh G.P., Kumar M., Kumar B. and Kumari P., J. Indican Chem. Soc., 79, 278 (2002).
45. Ojha K.G., Jaisinghani N. and Tahiliani H., J. Indian Chem. Soc., 79, 191 (2002).
46. Gupta A., Sharma R. and Prakash L., J. Indian Chem. Soc.,74, 635 (1994).
47. Schacht E., Dejardin S. and Lemmouchi Y., Bioact. and Comp. Poly., 13, 4 (1998).
48. Mc Bain J.W. and Morrill R.C. Jr., J. Am. Chem. Soc., 63, 670 (1941).

49. Mc Bain J.W. and Green A.A., J. Am. Chem. Soc.,68, 1731 (1946).
50. Mc Bain J.W. and Laing M.F., J. Am. Chem. Soc., 58, 2610 (1936).
51. Carino L. and Nagy G., Pest. Sci., 181, 23 (1978).
52. Von Hann F.V., Kollid, 2, 62, 202 (1932).
53. Preston W.C., J. Phys. Chem., 52, 84 (1948).
54. Kreschek G.C., Plenum press, New York, 96 (1975).
55. Heckmann K., Gotz K.G.*et al*. Discussion Faraday Soc., 25, 71 (1958).
56. Luzzati, V. and Hussan F., J. Cell Biol., 12, 207 (1962).
57. Stockenius W., J. Cell Biol., 12, 221 (1962).
58. Kolthoff I.M. and Strieks W., J. Phys. Colloid Chem., 52, 915 (1949).
59. McBain J.W., Trans Faraday Soc., 9, 99 (1913).
60. Hartle G.S., Hermann, Paris (1936).
61. McBain J.W., Colloid Chemistry, Theoretical and Applied (J. Alexander, ed.) Reinhold New York (1944).
62. Mattoon R.H., Stearns R.S. and Harpins W.D., J. Phys. Chem., 15, 209 (1947).
63. Debye P. and Anacker E.W., J. Phys. Colloid Chem., 5, 644 (1951).
64. Shinoda K., Colloidal Surfactants, Chapter 1 Academic Press, New York (1963).
65. Williams R.J., Phillips J.N. and Mysels K.J., Trans. Faraday Soc., 51, 728 (1955).
66. Corrin M.L., J. Colloid Sci., 3, 333 (1948).
67. Mehrotra K.N., Mehta V.P. and Nagar T.N., J. Prakt. Chem., 312 (1970).
68. Gilmour A. and Pink R.C., J. Indian Chem. Soc., 2198 (1953).
69. Satake I. and Matuura R., Chem. Fac. Sci. Kyushu Univ. Ser. C5 1, 13 (1962).
70. Kishita M., Inoue M. and Kubo M., Nippon Kagaku Kaishi, 84, 758 (1963).
71. Martin R.L. and Waterman H., J. Indian Chem. Soc., 2545 (1957).
72. Kokot R. and Martin R.L., Inorg. Chem., 3(9), 1306 (1964).
73. Martin R.L. and Whitelay A., J. Indian Chem. Soc., 1394 (1952).
74. Theissen P.A. and Spychaliski R., Z. Phys. Chem., 156A, 435 (1931).
75. Schulman J.H. and Riley D.P., J. Colloid Sci., 3, 383 (1948).
76. Anacker, E.W., J. Colloid Sci., 8, 402 (1953).
77. Mc Bain, J.W. and Johnson, K.E., J. Am. Chem. Soc., 66, 9 (1944).
78. Shinoda K., Bull. Chem. Soc. Jpn., 26, 101 (1953).
79. Ooshika V., J. Colloid Sci., 9, 254 (1954).
80. Matuura R., Nippon Kagaku Kaishi, 82, 1624 (1961).
81 Barclay G.A. and Kennard C.H.L., J. Indian Chem. Soc., 3289 (1962).
82. Kurodo Y. and Kaishi N.K., 86, 560 (1965).
83. Manhas B.S., Kalia S.B. and Sardana A.K., Indian J. Chem., 45A, 377 (2006).
84. Reddy R.K., Reddy K.M. and Mahendra K.N., Indian J. Chem., 45A, 377 (2006).
85. Mijanuddin M., Gangopadhyay S., Mondal S., Mukharjee M. and Ali M., Indian J. Chem., 45A, 858 (2006).
86. Erden L., Demirhan N. and Avciata U., Indian J. Chem., 45A, 1395 (2006).
87. Sharma V.K. and Shrivastava S., Indian J. Chem., 45A, 1368 (2006).
88. Souza A.G., Santos J.C.O., Conceicao M.M., Dantas Silva M.C. and Prasad S., Brazilian J. Chem. Engg., 21(2), 265 (2004).

89. Souza A.G., Conceicao M.M. and Macedo R.O., An. Assoc. Bras. Quim, 47, 361 (1998).
90. Santos J.C.O., Santoas A.V., Souza A.G., Prasad S. and Santos I.M.G., J. Food Sci., 67(4), 1393 (2002).
91. Santos J.C.O., Santos A.V.andSouzaA.G., Europ J. Pharm. Sci.,13, 523 (2001).
92. Santos J.C.O., Santos M.G. and Conecicao M.M. *et al*., J. Thermal Anal. Color., 75(2), 419 (2004).
93. Tank P. Ph.D. Thesis M.D.S. University, Ajmer, India (2007).
94. Rasheed A. and Bhobe R.A., J. Indian Chem. Soc.,53, 442 (1976).
95. Adeoson S.O., J. Therm. Anal., 14(3), 235 (1978).
96. Marsh B.P., Ind. Eng. Chem., 36, 176 (1944).
97. Samsonova O.A., TekStil Prom., (1/2), 15 (1943).
98. Mattiello J.J., Vol. 1, Wiley, New York (1941).
99. ESSO Research and Engg. Co.Fr. 1 381, 305 (CI.C. 109) (1964).
100. Reddy K.H., Reddy P.S. and Bahu P.R., Trans. Met. Chem., 25, 154 (2004).

Pages: 189-197

Metals Distribution in Environment

Edited by: **Dr. Deep Mala & Dr. Pawan Kumar 'Bharti'**

ISBN: 978-93-86841-91-9

Edition: **2019**

Published by: **Discovery Publishing House Pvt. Ltd., New Delhi (India)**

Toxic Metal Removal Efficiency of *Lemna minor* and *Pistia stratiotes* in Laboratory Scale Experiments

Rashmi Yadav

Pawan K Bharti

ABSTRACT

In modern era of industrialization, the water pollution is always a big problem among human beings. Polluted water may harms to animals, soil productivity, agriculture crop, aquatic biota, material and properties in different way. It may cause some severe health problems also, so it is essential to keep water clean and adopt some strategies against polluted water for remedial process. Chemical or other advance techniques are very expensive, so phytoremediation is the only way to protect and purify the polluted water without any more expense. Phytoremediation using *Lemna minor* and *Pistia stratiotes* aquatic plants may absorb a huge concentration of metals from the conducted laboratory experiment. Plants decrease the concentrations of metals from 52.4% to 75% within 10 days, 15 days and 20 days experiments.

Keywords: *Heavy metals, aquatic macrophytes, phytoremediation, Lemna minor, Pistia stratiotes*

INTRODUCTION

As the water, the most abundant and vital natural resource is extremely essential for survival of all living organisms, but today clean water has become a precious commodity and its quality is threatened by numerous sources of pollution. Water pollution creates physical, chemical and biological changes in the water, and further affects the water quality for a long time of period. As the heavy metals enter in the food chains of aquatic

Department of Zoology & Environmental Science, Gurukula Kangri University, Haridwar (Uttarakhand) – 249 404

ecosystem, ultimately affect the health of higher animals of that particular ecosystem. Different heavy metals like Mercury, Lead, Chromium, and Nickel, Cadmium etc. release from various sources like agriculture, urban and industrial uses, and these factors degrade the water quality.

The aquatic macrophytes are of considerable ecological and economic importance (Goudet, 1974) and contribute significantly to enhancing the biological productivity of water bodies, mobilize mineral element from the bottom sediment and provide shelter and food to aquatic fauna. They also respond to the changes in water quality and have been used as an indicator of pollution in several cases. (Nasu and Kugimoto, 1981; Westlake, 1981; Best, 1981; Varshney, 1982; Gopal and Chamanlal, 1991). The aquatic plants are commonly found in shoreline of lakes, rivers and water logged areas (Gopal 1990; Chamanlal and Malvika Sah, 1990; Pathak, 1993).

In recent past, there has been great emphasis on the importance of macrophytes in removing nutrient from the polluted water and their use in upgrading waste water quality (Denny, 1972). Aquatic plants posses tremendous potential to reduce the level of toxic metals, nutrients, BOD and to improve other physico-chemical characteristics of waste water. However, use of these plants in designing a low cost treatment system is still at the experimental stage and is considered to be a potentially important area of environmental management.

Keep this in view; phytoremediation technique is adopted in which two macrophytes *Lemna* and *Pistia* were used for waste water treatment as a clean and cheap technology for special reference to Indian sub-continent.

MATERIALS AND METHODS

Two aquatic macrophytic plants *Lemna minor* and *Pistia stratiotes* were selected and plants were collected from natural ponds for experimental work. Plants were grown in the 150 L capacity glass aquarium in the laboratory. All the parts of the plants were thoroughly cleaned up by distilled water before used and after that all the plants placed in aquarium filled with 100 L water.

Plants were selected with almost of same biomass (100 mg). These plants were kept in 10% Hoagland's solution (Hoagland and Arnon, 1938) for 30 days for acclimatization. After clean up, the plants placed in the aquariums which were filled with different heavy metals ion solutions, and observations recorded in 10 days, 15 days and 20 days respectively. Firstly prepared the two different metals concentration solution 50 ppm and 100 ppm respectively by the stock solutions for phytoremediation process. For control set one aquarium filled with only water without macrophytes.

Lemna

Lemna minor is submerged or floating herb 1/4 inches long aquatic plant. The plant body looks like thallus. The tail about 1/2 inch long, translucent, thin flat, elliptic lanceolate or oblanceolate, connate, serrate near the apex. The young fronds hastate at length tailed and attenuated in to a stalk by which they remain attached to the parent frond. Each frond giving rise to a single root-fiber; root cap acute, Ovary solitary, Seed horizontal testa rough, grooved. The characteristic of this plant is that the young fronds rise at right angles from one or both sides of the parent frond and remain connected with it crosswise.

Pistia

Pistia stratiotes is a monotypic genus of small free floating, perennial aquatic herb of gregarious nature. The plant is found in ponds. It grows by means of offsets. The leaves are sessile. They arise in close spirals and form cup shaped rosettes in the region of nodes. A cluster of adventitious roots arise from each node for providing stability. The roots bear root pockets. The plant is able to remain afloat on the surface of water by means of spongy offsets, minute arenchymatous floats and the horizontally spreading of outer leaves. The leaves are spatulate or obsordate in outline. They possess cuticle and stomata. Mesophyll is differentiated into palisade and spongy parenchyma.

Metals Estimation

Approximately 100 mg fresh weight of treated and control macrophytic plants were taken for metal estimation. The plants were washed and kept in an oven at 105°C for 48 h. The dried plants samples were digested in concentrated HNO3: HClO4 (v/v 3:1) at 80°C temperature on hot plate. The solution was filtered through Whatman filter paper No. 44 in a volumetric flask, by adding double distilled water in volumetric flasks and final volume made up to 50 ml. Digested solutions were analyzed by AAS (Atomic Absorption Spectrophotometer Model No.4129) for different metals concentration (Zn, Pb, Cd, Cr, Ni) and metal concentrations were calculated by formula.

Metal concentration (μg^{-1} DW) = X*V/W

Where,

X = reading in ppm on AAS

V = Final volume (ml)

W = Dry weight of the plant material (g).

RESULTS AND DISCUSSION

The plants remove metals by surface/root zone adsorption/absorption and incorporate them into their own system or them in a bound form. Effluent ameliorated by these plants thus cause less damage to the aquatic environment (Lavoic and De La Noue, 1983; Beveridge, 1989).

Several aquatic macrophytes including free floating submerged and emergent plants are very much effective for the removal of toxic metal substances (Chandra *et al.*, 1997; Vajpayee *et al.*, 1995).

The uptake of metals by the plants of *Pistia stratiotes* and *Lemna minor* were observed with increasing metals concentration (50 ppm and 100 ppm respectively) and exposure periods (10 days, 15 days, 20 days). The bioaccumulation patterns of metals in the different plants (*Pistia stratiotes* and *Lemna minor*) are presented in tables 10.1 & 10.2, and Fig. 10.1, 10.2 & 10.3(A-B).

Table 10.1: Absorption rate (%) of heavy metals by *Lemna minor*

Metals	Conc. (ppm)	10 Days	15 Days	20 Days	Mean
Zn	50	70.2	73.2	75.0	72.80
	100	65.2	68.3	71.2	68.23
Pb	50	60.2	62.2	64.2	62.20
	100	58.0	61.4	63.2	60.88
Cd	50	58.2	61.1	64.2	61.17
	100	56.1	58.3	62.8	59.07
Cr	50	56.0	58.6	64.3	59.63
	100	54.1	57.1	62.6	57.93
Ni	50	58.2	62.5	64.2	61.63
	100	56.8	61.7	63.8	60.77

Table 10.2: Absorption rate (%) of heavy metals by *Pistia stratiotes*

Metals	Conc, (ppm)	10 Days	15 Days	20 Days	Mean
Zn	50	65.3	71.4	73.2	69.97
	100	63.0	69.0	71.5	67.83
Pb	50	60.0	62.2	64.3	62.17
	100	58.2	60.0	61.1	59.77
Cd	50	55.6	58.0	61.2	58.27
	100	52.4	56.2	60.1	56.23
Cr	50	60.0	63.4	67.0	63.47
	100	58.0	61.2	64.0	61.07
Ni	50	56.2	58.3	61.0	58.50
	100	52.4	55.2	58.1	55.23

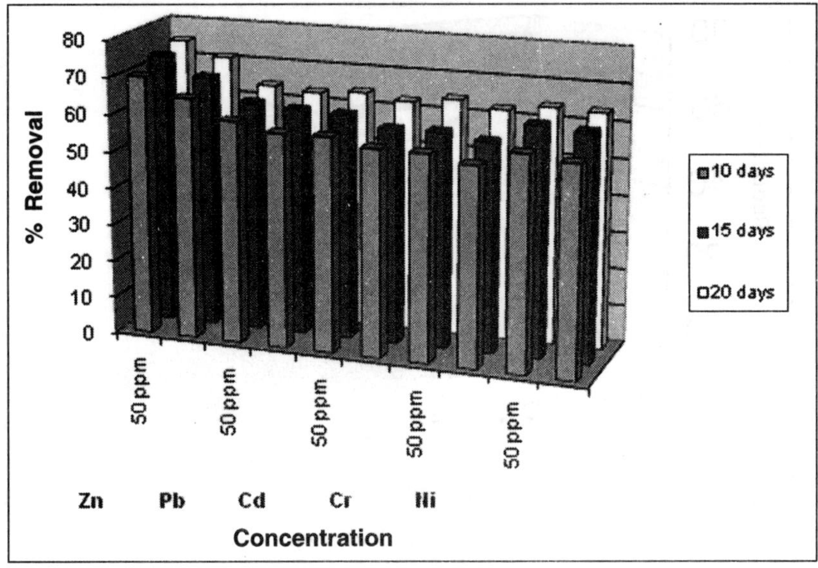

Fig. 10.1: Heavy metals removal by *Lemna minor* from water at various test concentration

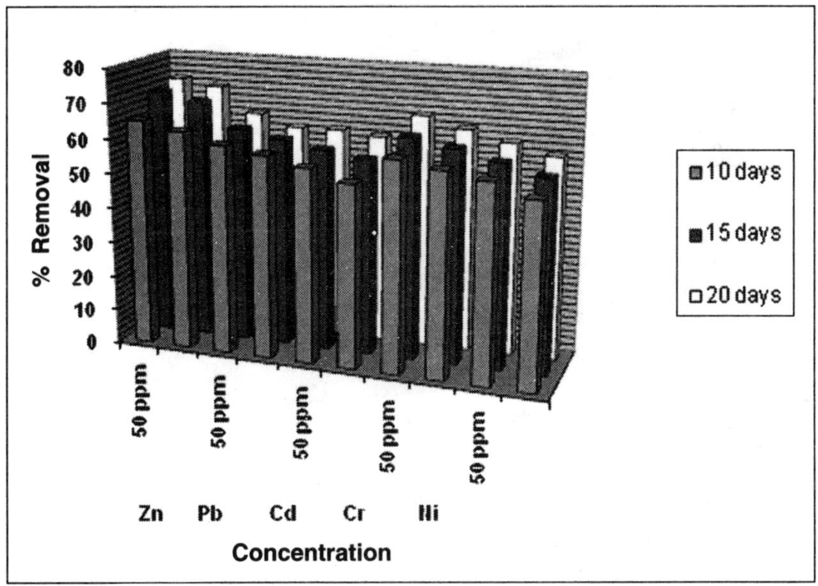

Fig. 10.2: Heavy metals removal by *Pistia stratiotes* from water at various test concentration

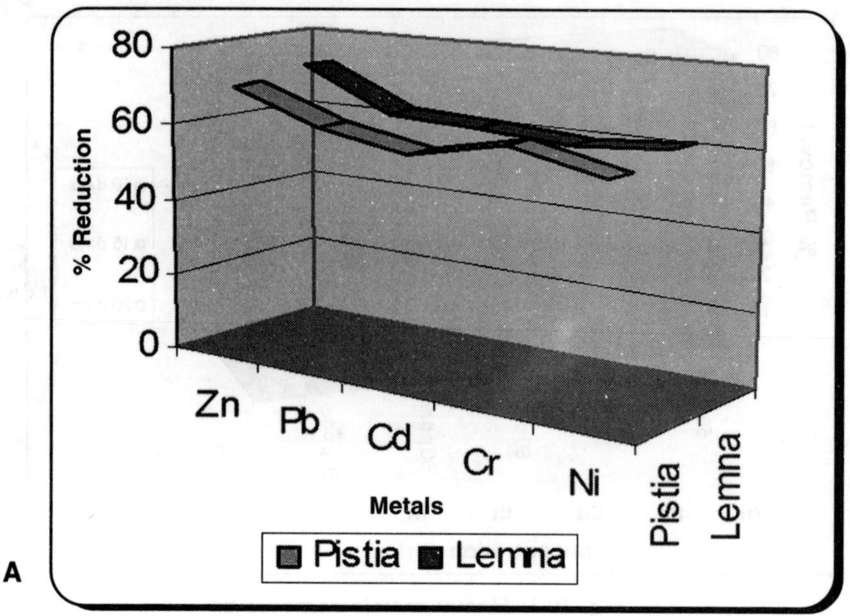

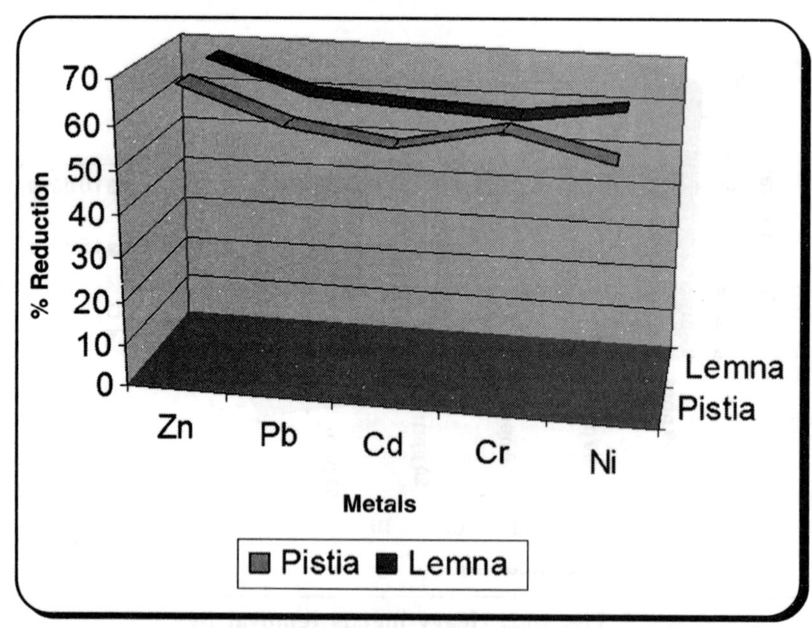

Fig. 10.3 (A-B): Heavy metals removal by *Pistia stratiotes* and *Lemna minor* from water at 50 ppm and 100 ppm concentration respectively

Both macrophytes showed same pattern of absorption of metals from water in different concentrations. Floating aquatic plants are a viable option for treating of secondary effluent of diluted effluent with heavy metals at marginal land in subtropical and tropical climate condition (Olguin and Hernandez, 1998).

Lemna minor could remove maximum quantity of Zn at 50 ppm concentration on 10th day (70.2%), 15th day (73.2%), 20th day (75.0%) and at 100 ppm concentration on 10th day (65.2%), 15th day (68.3%), 20th day (71.2%) and Cr, Ni were removed in least quantity. Cr at 50 ppm concentration on 10th day (56.0%), 15th day (58.6%), 20th day (64.3%) and at 100 ppm concentration on 10th day (54.1%), 15th day (57.1%), 20th day (62.6%) and Ni at 50 ppm concentration on 10th day (58.2%), 15th day (62.5%), 20th day (64.2%) and at 100 ppm concentration on 10th day (56.8%), 15th day (61.7%), 20th day (63.8%). Staves and Knaus, (1985) worked on metal removal by using different species of duckweeds (*Lemna minor*) and observed it highly significant for aquatic environment clearance. Tripathi *et al.* (1991) also stated the removal efficiency of aquatic plants that during the summer and rainy seasons, the Eichhornia, followed by the Pistia, Lemna and Salvinia, during the winter month the Lemna had a higher removal rate than the Pistia. Rest of all metals was removed in almost same quantity.

Pistia stratiotes also removed Zn (at 50 ppm concentration on 10th day 65.3%, 15th day 71.4%, 20th day 73.2% and at 100 ppm concentration on 10th day 63.0%, 15th day 69.0%, 20th day 71.5%) in maximum quantity and Cadmium and nickel in least quantity (Cd at 50 ppm concentration on 10th day 55.6%, 15th day 58.0%, 20th day 61.2% and at 100 ppm concentration on 10th day 52.4%, 15th day 56.2%, 20th day 60.1% and Ni at 50 ppm concentration on 10th day 56.2%, 15th day 58.3%, 20th day 61.0% and at 100 ppm concentration on 10th day 52.4%, 15th day 55.2%, 20th day 58.1%) rest of all the metals show same pattern of removal.

Pistia Stratiotes accumulate metals ions for the metabolism and enzyme activities of macrophyte during the experiment conducted for removal of hazardous ions from waste water (Satyakala and Jamil Kaiser, 1997). Not only do the aquatic macrophytes take up metals from water and sediments and release them subsequently on aging and decomposition (Mayes *et al.*, 1977, McIntosh *et al.*, 1978), they also serve as food for animals in which metals are concentrated (Newman and McIntosh, 1983). Guilizzoni *et al.*, (1989) worked on ecology and heavy metal concentration in aquatic macrophytes. They demonstrated the accumulation of heavy metals in plants tissues and their storing capacity of metal concentrations. Aquatic macrophytes like *Pistia stratiotes* and *Eichhornia crassipes* have great potential as biological filter for absorbing pollutants, including heavy metals from water (Jamil *et al.*, 1987).

Aquatic plants play an important role in the trace elements removal process. The potential of duckweed (*Lemna minor* L.) to accumulate Cd, Cr, Cu, Ni, Pb, and Se, when supplied individually in a nutrient solution at a series of concentration ranging from 0.1-10 mg l^{-1}, was investigated. Under experimental condition duckweed proved to be an accumulator of Cd, Se and Cu, a moderate accumulator of Cr and poor accumulator of Ni and Pb (Zayed *et al.*, 1998).

Although some chemical and advance technological processes are being use widely for the treatment of waste water in the modern era of technology but for an eco-friendly approach without any negative impact on environment, phytoremediation may be used for pollutants removal from wastewater. *Lemna minor* and *Pistia stratiotes* are the good accumulator of Zn in small scale experiment, similarly, various species of aquatic plants may be used for the removal of different metals. However, chromium may be harmful for some aquatic plants and may cause some physiological changes. Corradi *et al.* (1987) working on *Lemna minor* and *Pistia statiotes* observed some morphological alteration due to Cr (VI). The main changes were inhibition of growth and appearance of chlorotic bands in the plants.

Small macrophytes combat fast against the heavy metal with a low concentration in comparison to high concentration in a lab scale experiment. So, on the similar theme, some another large macrophytes may also be used as metal accumulator in water environment even with a high concentration.

REFERENCES

1. Best, E.P.H. Effect of Water Pollution on Fresh Water Submerged Macrophytes. In: Water Pollution and Management Reviews Edited by C.K. Varshney, SAP, India. 1981; pp: 27-56.
2. Beveridge, T.J. Role of Cellular Design in Bacterial Metal Accumulation and Mineralization. *Ann. Rev. Microbial.* (43): 147-171.
3. Chamanlal and Malvika Sah. Range Extension of Three Aquatic Macrophytes in North India. *J. Bombay Nat. His. Soc.*1990; 87(3): 469.
4. Chandra, P.; Sinha, S. and Rai, U.N. Bioremediation of Chromium from Water and Soil by Vascular Aquatic Plants. American Chemical Society Symp. 1997; 664: 274-282.
5. Corradi, M.; Realini, M. and Bassi, M. Morphological Alteration Induced by Cr (VI) in Fresh Water Plants, *14th Int. Bot. Congr. Berlin*, 1987; pp: 407.
6. Denny, P. Sites of Nutrients Absorption in Aquatic Macrophytes, *J. Ecol.* (U.K.). 1972; 60 (4): 819-826.
7. Gopal, B. Nutrient Dynamics of Aquatic Plant Communities, In: Ecology and Management of Aquatic Vegetation in the Indian Subcontinent Edited by B. Gopal: 1990; 177-197.
8. Gopal, B. and Chamanlal. Distribution of Aquatic Macrophytes in Polluted Water Bodies & their Bioindicator Value, *Verh. Internatl. Verei. Limnol.* 1991; 24: 2125-2129.

9. Goudet, J.J. Mineral Concentration in *Papyrus* in Various African Swamps, *J. Ecol.* 1974; 63: 483-491.
10. Guilizzoni, Maggiorizzoni, P.G., Galanti and H. Muntau. The Aquatic Macrophytes of Lake Hyke Species Composition, Spatial Distribution and Heavy Metal Concentration in Tissue. *Mem.1st Ital. Idrobiol.* 1989; (46): 23 5-260.
11. Hoagland, D. and Arnon, D.L. The Water Culture method for Growing Plants with out Soil. *Bull. Calif. Agric. Stat.* 1938; 346.
12. Jamil, K. Madhavendra, S.S.; Jamil, M.Z. and Rao, P.V.R. Studies on Water Hyacinth as a Biological Filter for Treating Contaminants from Agriculture Waste and Industrial Effluent, *J. Environ. Sci. Hlth.* 1987; 2(1): 103-112.
13. Lavoic, A. and DeLa Noue, J. Harvesting Microalgae with Chitosan. J. *World Maricul. Soc.* 1983; (14): 685-694.
14. Mayes, R.A., McIntosh, A.W and Anderson, V.L. Uptake of Cadmium and Lead by a Rooted Aquatic Macrophyte (Elodea Canadensis), *Ecology*. 1977; (58): 1176-1180.
15. McIntosh, A.W., Shephard, B.K. Mayer, R.A. Atchison, G.J. and Nelson, D.W. Some Aspects of Sediment Distribution and Macrophyte Cycling of Heavy Metals in a Contaminated Lake. *J. Environ Qual.* 1978; (7): 301-305.
16. Nasu, Y. and Kugimoto, M. Lemna (Duckweed) as an Indicator of Water Pollution (I), The Sensitivity of *Lemna paucicostata* to Heavy Metals. *Arch. Env. Contam. Toxicol.*1981; 10: 159-169.
17. Newman, M.C. and McIntosh, A.W. Slow Accumulation of Lead from Contaminated Food Sources by Fresh Water Gastropods. *Physa integra* and Campeloma *decisum. Arch. Environ. Contain. Toxical.* 1983; (12): 685-692.
18. Olguin, E.J. and Hernandez, E. Use of Aquatic Plants for Recovery of Nutrients and Heavy Metals from Waste Water, Roundtable on Municipal Water, *Vancouver*, Canada, 1998; March 15.
19. Pathak, S.K. Hydrophytes of Jalutbari and its Vicinity, In: Higher Plants of Indian Subcontinent. 1993; (4): 169-185.
20. Satyakala, G. and Jamil Kaiser. Studies on the Effect of Heavy Metal Pollution on *Pistia statiotes L.* (Water Lettuce). *Indian J. Env. Health.* 1997; 39: 1-7.
21. Staves, R.P. and Knaus, R.M. Chromium Removal by Three Species of Duckweeds. *Aquat. Bot.* 1985; (23): 261-263.
22. Tripathi, B. D., Srivastava, Jaya, Misra, Kiron. Nitrogen and Phosphorus Removal-Capacity of Four Chosen Aquatic Macrophytes in Tropical Freshwater Ponds, *Journal Environmental Conservation.* 1991; 18: 143-147.
23. Vajpayee, P.; Rai, U.N.; Sinha, S.; Tripathi, R.D. and Chandra, P. Bioaccumulation of Tannery Effluent by Aquatic Macrophytes, *Bull. Environ. Contam. Toxicol.* 1995; 55: 546-553.
24. Varshney, C.K. Macrophytes as Indicators of Water Quality, Paper Presented at WHO Workshop on Biological Indicators and Indices of Environmental Pollution, 1982; *CPCB, OSM Univ.* Hyderabad.
25. Westlake, D.F. The Primary Productivity of Water Plants. In: Studies on Aquatic Vascular Plants Edited by Symoens, J.J., Hopper, S.S and Compers, P., *Bot. Soc. Belgium*, Brussels, 1981: 165-180.
26. Zayed, A.; Gowthaman, S. and Terry, N. Phytoaccumulation of Trace Elements by Wetland Plants, *J. Environ. Qual.* 1998; 27(3): 715-721.

Index

T

W

Y

Z